S0-AUE-762

DON'T MOVE—

IMPROVE!

# DON'T MOVE—IMPROVE!

## Hundreds of Ways to Make a Good House Better

Cle Kinney and Barry Roberts

A Funk & Wagnalls, Martin Dale book.

Thomas Y. Crowell, Publishers
Established 1834
New York

 For information address Thomas Y. Crowell, Publishers, 10 East 53rd Street, New York, N.Y. 10022. Published simultaneously in Canada by Fitzhenry & Whiteside Limited, Toronto.

FIRST EDITION

Library of Congress Cataloging in Publication Data

Kinney, Cle.
Don't move—improve!

"A Funk & Wagnalls, Martin Dale book."
Includes index.
1. Dwellings—Remodeling—Amateurs' manuals.
2. Interior decoration—Amateurs' manuals. I. Roberts, Barry, joint author. II. Title.
TH4816.K555 1978 643'.7 78-3305
ISBN 0-308-10315-7

78 79 80 81 82 83 10 9 8 7 6 5 4 3 2 1

# CONTENTS

*I like to see a man*
*proud of the place*
*in which he lives.*

*I like to see a man*
*live so that his place*
*is proud of him.*

*Abraham Lincoln*

# Introduction
# The Practical Approach to an Improved Quality of Life

How you live is inseparable from where you live. Your lifestyle is molded by your home just as your home is fashioned by your lifestyle. The word "home" has many meanings. It's where you hang your hat, your place of origin, or your destination. For the poet Frost, it's "the place where, when you have to go there, they have to take you in." For a child, home is the place where school isn't.

In every case, home is where you are most fully at ease to be yourself.

When you chose to live where you do, you did so because of how you lived and wanted to live. Unless a job transfer or other circumstance dictated where you moved, you probably liked everything about your locale from its climate to the neighborhood. Above all, you liked your house, both the building and the grounds, especially if you built your house. "This is the place for us!" meant the place you wanted to be to do the things you wanted to do.

Ideally, your new home fit your lifestyle like a tailor-made suit. There was just enough of the right kind of space, and the parts of the house worked well as a whole.

Realistically, though, the fit of a house to lifestyle is often less than perfect. The Smiths are party givers who don't have the room to give the parties they'd like to. The Joneses have teenagers who lack a place of their own to socialize with their friends. Mr. Brown loves woodworking but doesn't have a workshop. Mrs. Green wants to sew but has to do it at the dining room table, setting up each time she uses the machine. The Whites have an unmarried daughter who deserves a bathroom of her own.

Regardless of the original fit of home to living, the fact is that how you live changes as your family grows, so that where you live may no longer fit. Just as pants have to be let out, lifestyle changes result in needs or desires or both for home changes. A new child may call for a nursery; with a raise you might want to build a swimming pool; at retirement you may need a room in which to pursue a hobby.

Put another way: when you're ready to live better, you're ready for a better home.

Where is this better home to be found?

You can always decide to move, and there may be good reasons to do so. Obviously, if you've been promoted in your job and transferred to another town, a move is all but mandated. But there are other reasons for moving. A physical deterioration of your street or neighborhood could be the cause.

Perhaps as your children approach school age, you decide that the local schools will not give them the quality education you desire, or property simply have risen prohibitively high.

But let's suppose instead that you have no real reason to pull up stakes other than unsuitable living arrangements. In fact, everything else is urging you to stay put: you love your street and your neighbors, your family's best friends are nearby, your schools are fine, you're content in your place of worship, your town is safe, and taxes are no higher than anyplace else you know of. Then, too, there are the established relationships with the butcher, the garage mechanic, the hairdresser, and the pediatrician. In so many words, you've put down roots.

You have something else going for you, the most important thing: your home itself It stopped being a house, or someone else's home, the day you moved into it. From that time on, with your decorating and furnishing, it has increasingly become as much a part of you as you've become a part of it.

So, don't decide to move until you've given thought, deliberate thought, to the alternative of home improvement. Assess your lifestyle and your home, analyzing each in terms of the other. Determine your present needs and desires, and try to anticipate how they'll change. And remember that your home belongs to your whole family. Everyone must be considered in this analysis.

The good news is that your carefully planned home improvement can be, in a very real sense, your new home. New house space can be added, and old house space can be rearranged for new use. A whole house can be reoriented with remodeling. With expertise, imagination, and a sound investment of time and money, you can enjoy an improved quality of living right where you are.

## The Cost of Relocating vs. the Cost of Improving/Enlarging

The homeowner wondering whether to move or improve looks hard indeed before he leaps. A decision to uproot and replant elsewhere is a challenging one to reach. The homeowner knows that there's more cost involved than that computed in dollars. Relocation means dislocation, and dislocation means at least discomfort, if not pain. Separation from your house, neighborhood, school, church or synagogue, and friends is anything but pleasant.

In addition, the homeowner must look hard at the dollar cost of moving, as against that of improving. It's a fact that the cost of moving to a new house can be as much as a couple of thousand dollars beyond the cost of the house itself.

This added expense is worth breaking down. It includes the following expenses: broker's fee; lawyer's fees (closing on both the old house and the new one); moving expenses (possibly the cost of disposing of unwanted possessions); decorating costs; new furniture and new appliance costs; possible increase in insurance; even the cost for telephone installation. When selling your old house, you could well have paid for repair work and redecorating to spruce it up. The previous owner of your new house might not have done so, leaving you with that expense.

When building a new house, the costs multiply. There's the cost of the lot, with the closing fee. The property may need to be surveyed. House plans cost, especially if they're prepared by an architect. A building permit is needed. The general contractor, or the subcontractors if you serve as the general contractor, must be paid. There are insurance costs for a house under construction. Inevitably, there are "extras" when building that add to the planned cost. Grading and landscaping need to be done. A driveway costs a lot. You might require one or more utility poles if the house is far from the road. There may be water and sewer assessments, or the need for a well and a septic system.

Even a brand-new house soon needs repair. With the settling of the structure, cracks can appear in the foundation and in walls and ceilings, and floor boards and trim pieces can separate. Doors and windows can stick and leak. The heating plant could need adjustment for efficiency, and there could be wiring and plumbing problems to solve. A newly constructed house, like a newly launched ship, undergoes its shakedown cruise. It's been estimated that new house maintenance costs are twice those for an old house in the first two years of ownership.

Whether the house is old or new, there are further costs to consider. First, new mortgage interest rates are almost certain to be higher than the old ones. There's the real possibility, if you buy before you sell, of being saddled with two mortgages for some time. Second, new taxes may be higher than the old ones, along with water and sewer assessments. Third, a move could easily result in a more expensive new lifestyle.

All of the above might seem as if we're trying to discourage the homeowner from moving. We're not. Our intent is to point out and to stress that the purchase price or construction cost of a new house is bound to be considerably less than the total expense of actually moving.

With improving as with moving, some costs are nonmonetary. Remodeling brings a sense of dislocation, with disorder and disruption of the normal lifestyle. The homeowner who improves has to be prepared to live around all the necessary intrusions of men, machines, tools, and materials.

As would be expected, the dollar cost of improving is easier to break down than that of moving. To begin with, there may be planning costs involving an architect's services, especially with a major improvement. There could be a home improvement loan, with finance charges. Probably, a building permit will be required. The cost of the job itself could run over the builder's estimate, due to unforeseen plan changes. If the improvement is an addition, there are the matters of grading and landscaping. With a large addition, the job might necessitate increasing the capacity of the heating plant. As with a brand-new house, a new addition will be subject to shakedown problems. Then, too, taxes will certainly increase.

An important aspect of home improvement cost must be considered: what are the returns on the investment?

The question can be answered in two ways. First, if the improvement meets the wants and needs of the homeowner and his lifestyle, the returns can only be seen as good. After all, he has his "new" home in his familiar setting. He has his cake and is eating it, too. In short, if he and his family are happy with their investment, their happiness is return enough.

The second answer is less easily determined. In terms of dollars, the homeowner may or may not come out ahead if and when he sells his improved house. Two main factors are at play.

One factor is the average worth of the other houses in the neighborhood compared to the new worth of his improved house. In a neighborhood of, say, $50,000 homes, a $7,500 investment to improve a $40,000 home will likely be a good one. Selling his improved home, the homeowner could get his money back, probably more.

The same investment in the same home in an area of $35,000 homes will probably not pay off. The house will be overbuilt and overpriced for the area. In the same way, any considerable home improvement investment in a neighborhood going downhill may be good money thrown after money gone bad.

The other main factor at play in being able to make back an investment in home remodeling is the kind of change made. There are home improvements that, while they satisfy the homeowner himself, just don't appeal to prospective buyers. Imagine a three-bedroom house belonging to a couple whose children are no longer living at home. With perfectly good reason, the couple might combine two of the bedrooms to form a master bedroom with bath. But this floor plan would hardly appeal to young couples with two or more children. It's a rule of thumb that houses with three small bedrooms are more salable than those with two large ones. For that matter, an extra bedroom is a better selling point than a family or recreation room. Similarly, an extra bath sells. Conversely, a swimming pool has been known to actually frighten away would-be buyers.

Remodeling for dollar gain is a speculative business at best and had best be left to the true speculators. The homeowner who improves instead of moves would be wise to settle for lifestyle returns on his investment and not be overly concerned about possible monetary returns.

## Count the Headaches in Your House

In an analysis of your home, a positive approach is to take a negative one. Instead of asking what's right about your house, ask what's wrong about it that you'd like to correct.

For practical purposes, what's wrong is what you don't like about your home, what you wish to get rid of, and what you'd like to add.

There are the obvious headaches: a door that opens the wrong way into a room; a lack of closet space; a seldom used front door; a room with insufficient natural light.

There are also headaches that aren't so apparent, in each case that "something" that's there but that you can't quite put your finger on. With realization, these can turn out to be anything from a living room picture window too near the street and passersby, to a dining room too seldom used to merit its size.

To help you identify faults you may want to correct in your home, listed below are the headaches commonly found in each of the main living areas.

### Entrance Approach

- As the invitation to your home, it's simply not attractive enough.
- It doesn't lead from the driveway.
- It is neither easily accessible nor clearly defined.
- It isn't wide enough for two, preferably three, persons to walk side by side.
- It's not surfaced for both safety and comfort.
- It isn't covered for protection against the weather.
- It lacks adequate lighting.

### Entrance Hall

- It doesn't exist—guests come through the front door and step right into the living room.
- It doesn't have closets, space for a telephone table, or wall space for a mirror.
- It isn't surfaced to withstand wet footwear.
- It's not sufficiently raised above the entrance to prevent drafts, nor sufficiently insulated.
- It's unlighted or lighted too brightly for desired transition into the main house.
- It allows undesirable viewing of the bathroom door, the bedroom hallway, the kitchen, or the dining room.
- A stairway intrudes into its space.

### Living Room

- It's been abandoned for the family room.
- It's neither defined as an all-day family area nor as an evening entertaining area and is unsuccessfully used for both.
- It's too small, or too large, for its use.
- It's too formal.
- It's used as a passageway.
- It faces the wrong direction for desired natural light.
- It lacks sufficient windows for natural light.
- It has so many windows, doors, or radiators that it can't be furnished or decorated as desired.
- Windows are too high for viewing outside from a sitting position.
- It has a picture window that intrudes on privacy.
- It is inadequately ventilated to remove smoke and odors.
- Electrical outlets are too few or inconveniently located.
- It lacks a fireplace.
- Its fireplace is so located that it attracts people away from the usable room space.

### Kitchen

- It's too small.
- The work area is poorly organized for work traffic.
- It has insufficient counter space.
- It has insufficient storage space.
- The appliances are inefficient.
- Electrical outlets are too few or inconveniently placed.
- It has inadequate lighting, both overall and for specific areas.
- It has poor ventilation.
- It lacks windows for natural light and for viewing outside, especially a window over the sink.
- Its work area is used as a walk-through to

other rooms.
- It lacks a closet.
- It isn't easily accessible from the driveway or garage for grocery delivery.
- It lacks easy access to the dining room or dining area.
- It isn't cheerful.
- It lacks an outside entrance to a porch or a patio.

### Dining Room

- It just isn't used for dining.
- It's depressing or too formal.
- It's too small, or too large, for its use.
- It faces the wrong direction for desired morning light.
- The lighting is inappropriate for dining, either too bright or too cool.

### Family Room

- It doesn't exist.
- It isn't used as a family room—the living room is.
- It's located too far from the kitchen, the "command post" for motherly supervision.
- It's too small for a table and chairs for informal dining, and for other furniture for family activity.
- It faces the wrong direction for desired natural light.
- It lacks storage space.
- It isn't durable enough for the hard use it gets.
- It doesn't have easy access to a bathroom.
- It lacks an outside entrance.

### Recreation Room

- It doesn't exist.
- It's not needed as a distinct play or game room.
- It lacks natural light.
- It isn't directly accessible from the out-of-doors.
- It's not sufficiently removed from the main house areas.
- It lacks storage space.
- It doesn't relate to outdoor space.
- It doesn't have easy access to a bathroom.
- It's drab.

### Bedroom

- It lacks privacy.
- It's too small to accommodate anything other than bedroom furniture.
- Windows and radiators dictate bed placement.
- Electrical outlets are inconveniently located.
- Closet space is inadequate.
- It has poor cross ventilation, if any.
- It lacks its own bathroom or dressing room.

### Bathroom

- It's too small for the use it gets.
- Its fixtures are poorly arranged for traffic flow.
- It lacks adequate storage space.
- It lacks natural light.
- It isn't easily accessible to all the rooms around it.
- It can be directly looked into from other rooms.
- Its toilet is directly opposite the door.
- Access to it requires passing through a bedroom.
- It lacks a vanity.

The lists above are in no way intended to be complete. Home area headaches come in great variety and great number, often in combinations. For that matter, lists could be made as well for such other home areas as the study, shop, patio, and deck. Our intention is to help you get started counting the headaches in your home.

## Assets and Potential in Your House

Home improvement is an American tradition dating back to the 1600s. The colonial "saltbox" is a classic case of remodeling.

While the saltbox (actually shaped like the box salt was kept in) was built as such in the colonies, it was often instead the result of an addition. The basic house, consisting of two rooms over two rooms with a central fireplace, was expanded in back with a lean-to whose roof was an extension of the existing roof. The first floor, containing a "hall" or living room and a kitchen room, now contained a rear kitchen, a pantry, and a borning room, as well as a parlor or sitting room.

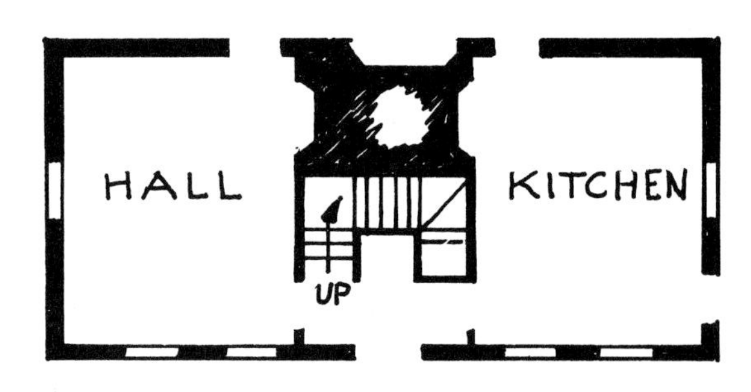


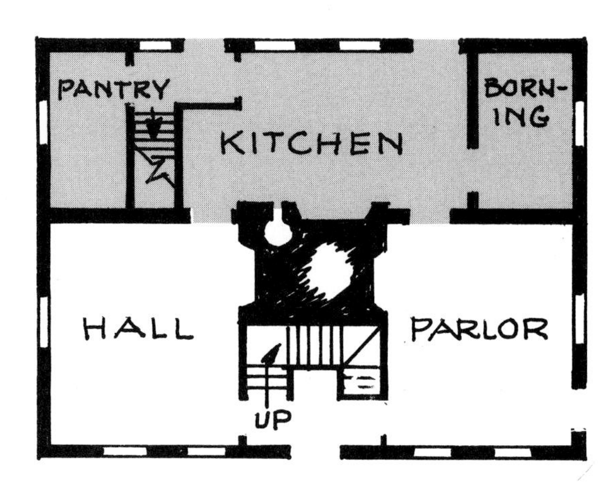


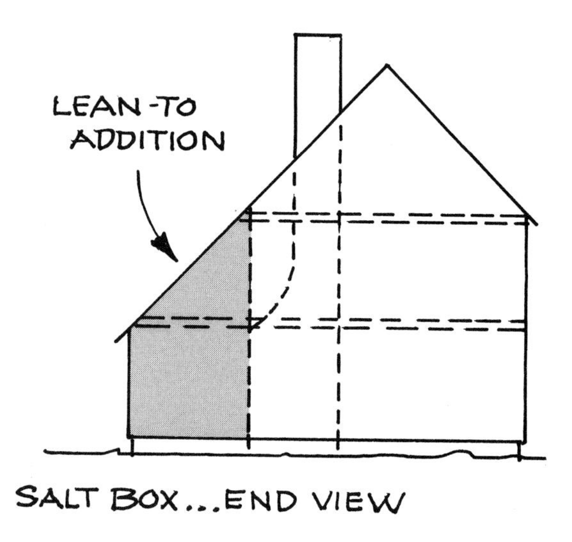


SALT BOX...END VIEW

For the colonist, the lean-to addition constituted improvement in an already good house. Now, as then, any addition or other remodeling should be extensions of original assets. What is good in a house should be the basis for what can be better in it.

There's little point in considering a house's assets if its liabilities—the "headaches" discussed in the previous section—are collectively so enormous as to be practically incurable. Its assets aren't worth much consideration either, if for other good reasons—an irredeemably deteriorating neighborhood, say—you're bound and determined to pull up stakes. The good in your home, like the bad, does merit appreciation, though, when improvement is a real alternative to moving.

In a way, it's the old story of letting our blessings go uncounted, so that we feel worse off than we actually are. Home blessings, like any other kind, are too often taken for granted—when they are noticed, the drawbacks are seen in a new, more favorable light.

What, then, is good about your house? What are the assets that provide improvement potential?

One way to analyze your home is to mentally step back from it. Try to determine what there is about it that you miss when you are away and are glad to come back to. "It's good to be home!" is a powerful statement. Children, after school, rush to their rooms. Fathers, the workday over, settle in the easy chair in the living room or family room. Mothers cherish their special corners for relaxing with a book.

Analyzing your home in terms of your various satisfactions, you'll pinpoint its specific assets.

To begin with, the house is probably structurally sound. The wood is free from rot and termites. The foundation has no major cracks. There's no alarming sagging of the structure due to settling. The roof is in good condition, as are the gutters. The wiring is adequate and safe, and the plumbing is in good repair. There's sufficient insulation. The heating system works well.

Presumably, you're satisfied, too, that

your house is architecturally sound. Put simply, you like the way it looks and the way it works. It's attractively placed on a landscaped site. The rooms are so arranged as to make living in them both convenient and pleasant. The house relates well to its lot for indoor-outdoor living.

As mentioned earlier, there may be further assets in your location. Your house may be part of a sound neighborhood zoned "residential," and the other residences are as solid and as good-looking as your own. The well-maintained streets might be lined with trees. The basic utilities are provided, and services like garbage collection are either provided or made available. Furthermore, good schools and houses of worship are nearby, shopping is convenient, and there's public transportation.

Your house has value not only because of what it is but also because of where it is. You can be satisfied that your house is a sound investment. As you pay off your mortgage and pay your taxes, as you pay for the upkeep of your house, you watch its value grow.

A final asset is that your house has the potential to be improved.

Potential for remodeling involves having interior space that can be put to better or to new use, and exterior space for an addition or an auxiliary building.

Improvement potential can be realized through alteration in many areas: a basement or an attic to finish; a no longer needed bedroom converted into a study; a kitchen and little used formal dining room combined into a "country" kitchen with dining area; a living room opened up to include a dining area; an entrance hall redesigned to contain a powder room; two small bedrooms becoming a master bedroom with bath (when the loss of one bedroom is not a sacrifice of resale potential).

Realizing improvement potential with an addition covers such possibilities as a bedroom wing, a covered patio, a protected entrance approach, a dormer. Auxiliary buildings could be a garage, gazebo, garden shed, barn, or guest house.

Given a house full of assets, including the asset of potential, all it takes is planning and investment to fulfill your desires and needs.

Every home has exciting remodeling possibilities. Improvement can be within, and it can be without—forward, backward, to the side, upward, even downward (see the extraordinary remodeling on p. 128), or separate from the house on the lot.

In the pages that follow, you will see case histories of home improvement involving every major room of the house, and others involving the whole house. Each homeowner's story stands as proof that your good house too can be made better.

The challenge to improve is there.

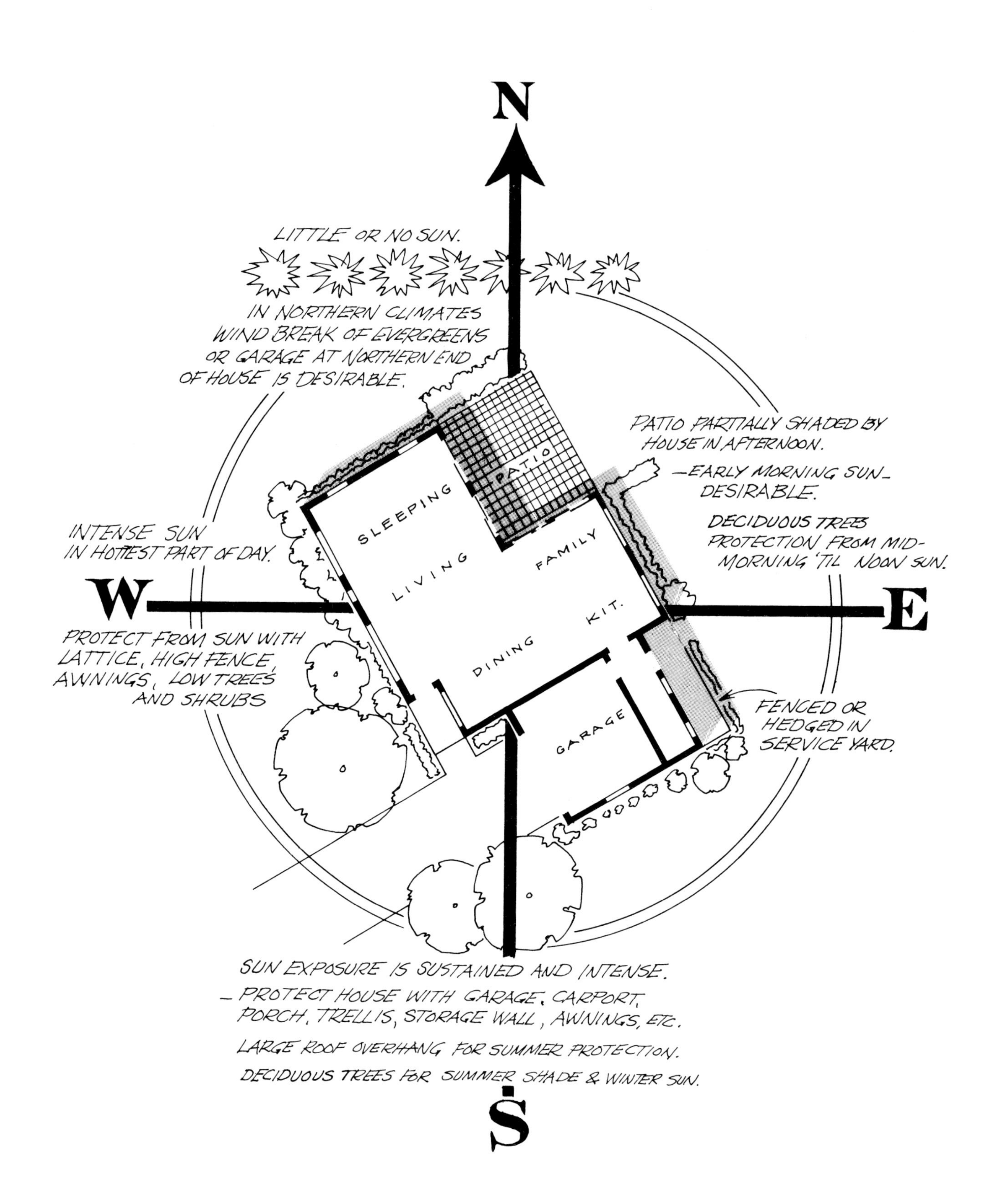


Desire for sun, or lack of it, determines orientation of house. Orientation is direction faced by side of house having large window areas. Landscaping features, natural and constructed, protect from sun, as well as from prevailing winds.

PART ONE

# HUNDREDS OF CREATIVE IDEAS TO HELP YOU IMPROVE YOUR HOME

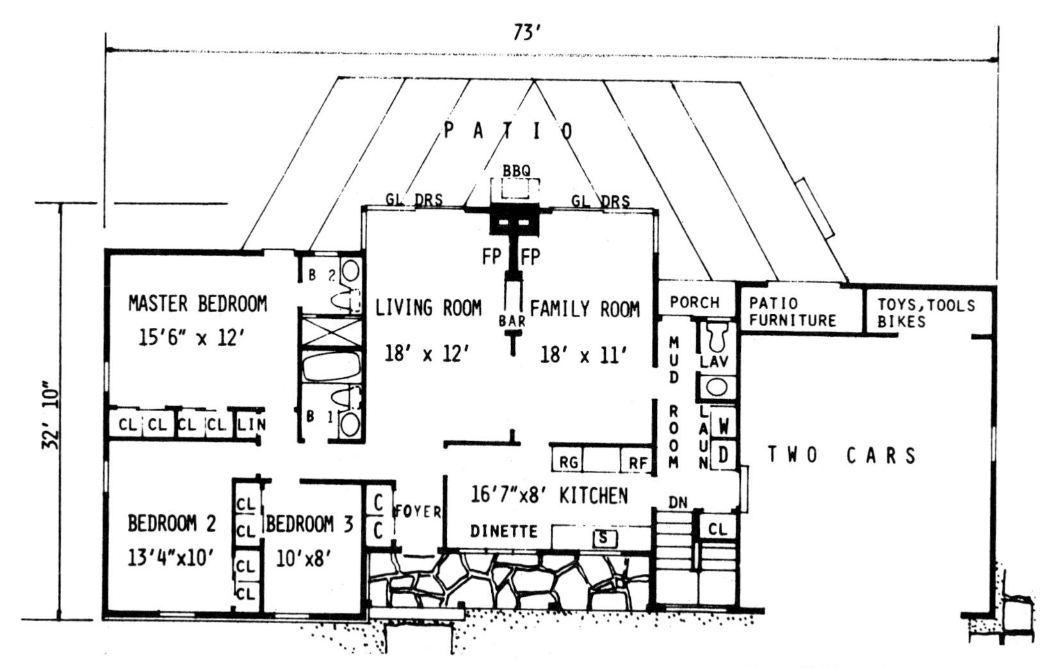


Overall Dimensions: 73' x 32'10".
Square Feet: 1,200; 145 service corridor.
Architect: Lester Cohen.

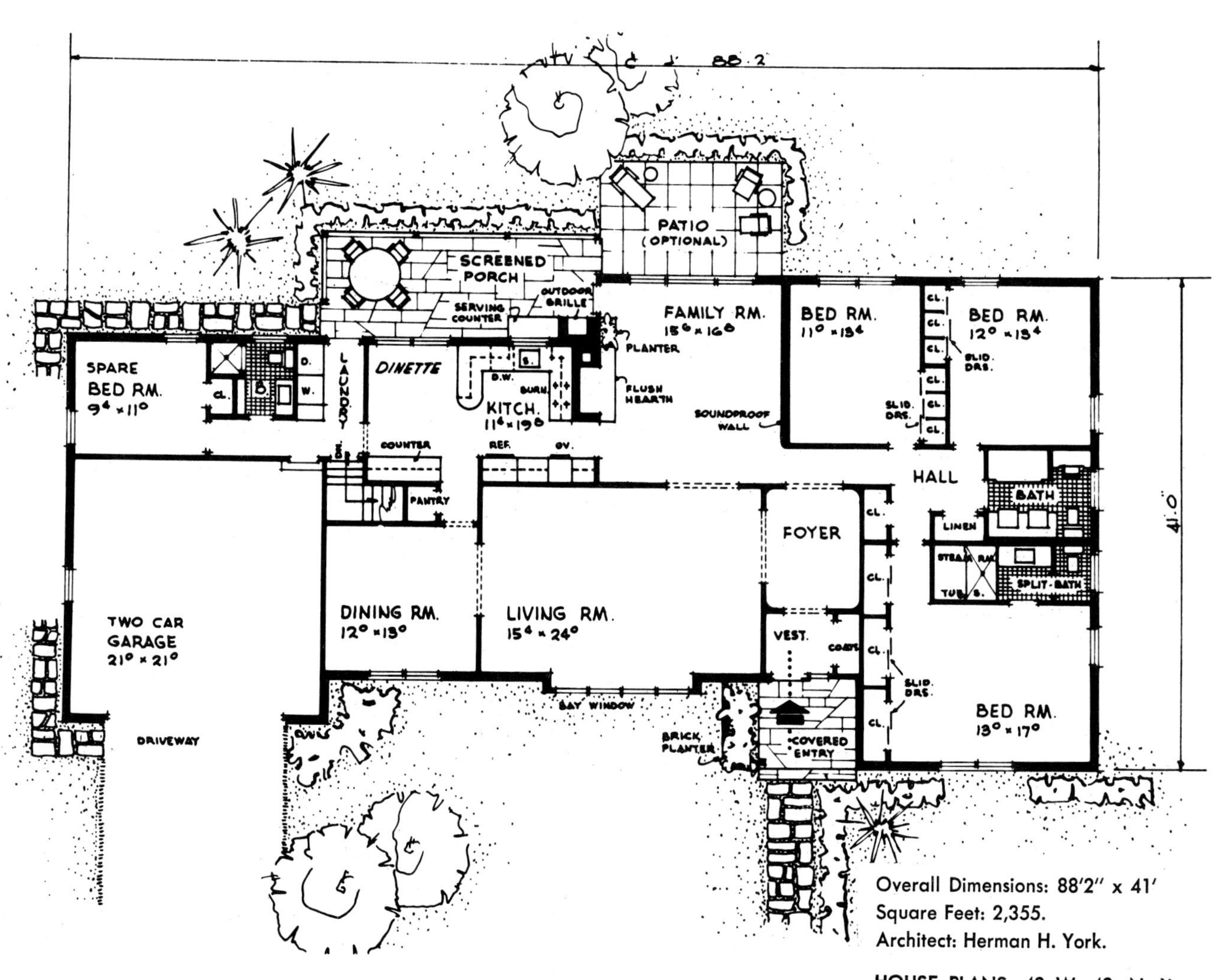


Overall Dimensions: 88'2" x 41'
Square Feet: 2,355.
Architect: Herman H. York.

HOUSE PLANS, 48 W. 48, N. Y.

# 1. Basic Principles of Good House Design

Before undertaking a large or small home remodeling project, the homeowner needs to understand the basic principles of good house design. Just as sound house design is the best prevention for home headaches, remodeling with these principles in mind is the best cure for existing problems. The principles apply, before or after the fact.

While we make an effort here to consider the basic ideas separately, it will readily be seen that the individual ideas are interwoven. A floor plan involves "zoning," "circulation," "orientation," and "house-site relationship." Privacy and convenience are also basic considerations.

The floor plan of a house divides the floor space into rooms with adjacent halls, closets, and stairs. In making this division, "zones" come into play.

Two plans on facing page illustrate zoning and good circulation. House is divided into living, working, and sleeping zones reflecting three basic living activities. While separate, zones are related to each other. (Note in each plan how bedrooms are grouped for privacy and are removed from noisy kitchen area.) Circulation involves arrangement of rooms for convenient movement from room to room and zone to zone. (Note that each plan incorporates direct access from kitchen to family room for informal dining and same accessibility from garage to kitchen for grocery delivery. Note, too, direct access from living room to bathroom.) These plans also show principle of house-site relationship, relating indoor living areas to corresponding outdoor areas. (Note proximity of family room to patio.)

## Zoning

The three zones of a house reflect the three main living activities in the home. The zones are variously labeled, from "living, sleeping, and working" to "public, private, and utility." Whatever the labeling, the point is that these areas should be separated from one another while remaining correctly related.

Generally, the living or public area includes the entrance hall, the living room, and the dining room; the sleeping or private area the bedrooms; and the working or utility area the kitchen, laundry, shop, and studio. Depending on who uses the space most—family or family with guests—a room may be considered private or public. A den, for example, would probably be labeled private, a powder room public.

Such a grouping of rooms into zones is simply to effect cushions between distinct living activities for their comfortable co-existence within the same four exterior walls. Kitchens can be noisy, while bedrooms require quiet. Parents entertaining in the living room like to be separated from children playing in the recreation room, and no doubt vice versa.

The traditional two-story house, with a central hall and stairs, illustrates zoning, with the sleeping area upstairs and the living and working areas downstairs. In any house, halls, closets, even bathrooms, can serve to separate the zones.

## Circulation

Rooms are arranged within zones and between them to achieve convenient movement from room to room. This movement is known as circulation.

Certain rules apply to good house circulation. One is that you should be able to go from the front entrance to the living room without going through another room (excluding an entrance hall, which is highly desirable). Another rule is that you should be able to pass from any room into another without having to pass through a third room, the dining room excepted. The living room especially should not be a highway for home traffic. Still another rule is that there should be direct access from any room to a bathroom.

The idea of circulation takes in the exterior as well as the interior of the house. The main entrance should be directly accessible from the driveway and the street, and the kitchen entrance as easily accessible from the driveway and the garage. There should be direct access from the outside living area to indoor living areas and, for outdoor eating, direct access to the kitchen.

Finally, circulation within rooms should be considered. The kitchen suffers most from poor circulation because of the need for a work traffic area free of other traffic. Other rooms can suffer, too, when door, window, closet, and wall placement are not planned with furniture in mind. It's as irritating, in a bedroom, to walk around a bed to get to a dresser as it is maddening, in a living room, to talk to the back of someone sitting in front of a fire. In any room, the poor placement of an electrical outlet can lead to poor circulation and discomfort.

## Orientation

Orientation refers to the direction faced by that side of a house having large window areas for natural light. In the Northern Hemisphere a house should face the south.

In our part of the world, the sun is in the south all day in winter and most of the day in summer. In winter, it rises in the southeast and sets in the southwest; in summer, it rises in the northeast to set in the northwest. It has been calculated that the south side of a house receives five times as much sun heat in winter as in summer, the east and west sides six times as much in summer as in winter. The north side receives no heat from the sun in winter and little in summer.

To make best use of the sun, not only for light all year long but for heat in the winter months, a house should be oriented to it.

For daytime living, then, rooms such as the kitchen, the dining room, and the family room should have a southern exposure. So should the living room, if it is used as a living area during the day. For year-round morning light, a bedroom should have an eastern exposure. A bedroom facing west, if unshielded from the sun, might be uncomfortably warm at bedtime in the summer. Similarly, an uncovered patio on the west side of a house would be hot in the summer and would be better located on the east side, or if not possible, on the south or north side. And so on.

Orientation involves not only the sun but prevailing winds as well. Windows directed to the south and not the north both welcome the sun and refuse entry to the north wind in winter. In summer, especially for patio and other outdoor living, prevailing breezes can be invited with correct orientation.

It should be noted that orientation of a house to the sun, as well as to winds and breezes, is subject both to geographical location and climatic conditions, of course.

## House-Site Relationship

Just as a house is zoned into interior living areas, a house and its site can be zoned into exterior living areas. As inside, the labels "public, private, and utility" can apply.

The public zone of a house includes the driveway, the entrance approach, and the front yard, in short the overall area open to the world. The private zone includes the patio or terrace, the garden and the backyard play space. The utility zone includes the trash storage area and the storage space for lawn-care and gardening machines and tools—that area best shielded from public or private view.

The most desirable relationship of house to site is one that uses as small an amount of space as possible to meet public and utility needs in order to take as much as possible for private use for recreation and outdoor living. To this aim, a house is usually located forward on its site or, if the lot is wide rather than deep, to one side.

House-site relationship involves more than location. It is the marriage of indoor with outdoor living.

A classic example of a bad house-site marriage is the picture window that offers a view of the street to the family and a view of the family to the street. No wonder that marriage has gone on the rocks! It makes sense, these days, to turn a house around in remodeling, to put the living room at the back, with glass to enjoy a private zone view, to put the bedrooms or utility rooms in the front, where no view is needed or wanted.

Good house-site relationship weds kitchen to outdoor eating area, pool to bathroom, clothesline to laundry room, recreation room to croquet lawn area, garden to potting room, fireplace to woodpile.

The principles of zoning, circulation, orientation, and house-site relationship are inseparable when planning any home improvement. In house design there has to be a give and take among these different components, perhaps sacrificing ideal orientation to gain a better house-site relationship or settling on good but not great circulation between rooms to provide a desired division between zones. An appreciation of each of the design principles is necessary if the homeowner is to come out ahead.

1920s Tiffany penthouse atop Manhattan office building. New York City has 20,000 acres of unused rooftop area.

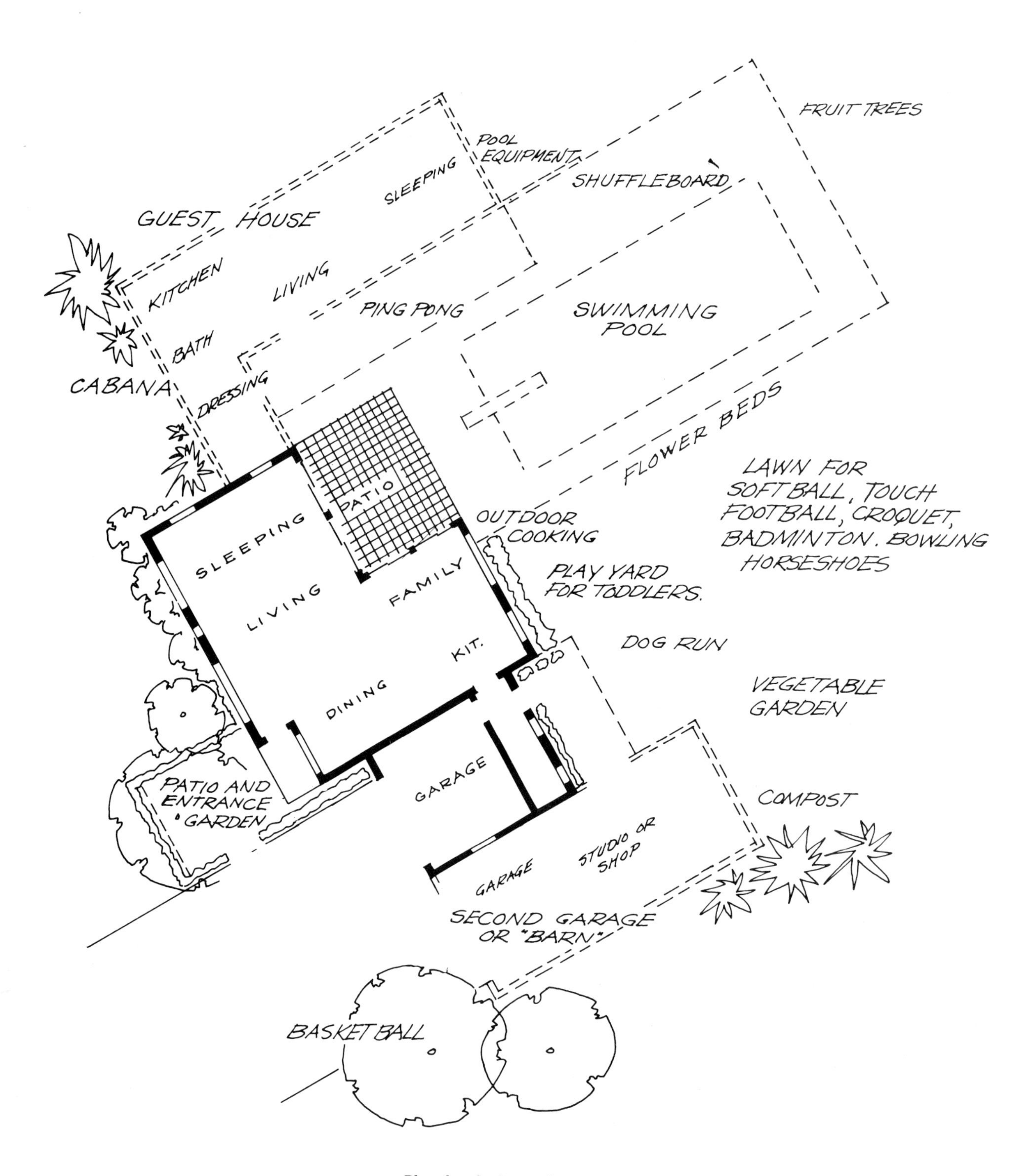


Plot plan for better living accommodates future additions such as guest house, pool, or barn, as well as areas for present family activities.

# 2. The Plot Plan... Good Living on Your Land

In a successful home, both indoor and outdoor space is used to best advantage for play, work, relaxation, convenience, and privacy. To achieve this, the house becomes an integral part of the site. As living well in your house requires a plan, so does living well on your land.

## Plot Plan

A plot plan is no more than a study of your land in terms of your house and your lifestyle.

Like a house plan, a plot plan is based on your wants and needs as a family, so an assessment of these is a first step.

Your requirements could include such activity areas as a play area for the children, with swing set and sandbox; a garden; a family game area for croquet, badminton, or horseshoes; a large open lawn for touch football or soccer; a barbecue and eating terrace; a swimming pool and deck; a quiet spot just for sitting; a dog run; and so on.

Your plot plan would arrange your land into these areas, taking several factors into account.

## Location, Orientation, and Zoning

A major factor is the location of your house on its lot. Whether the house is set forward, or back, or to one side on the lot will have a great bearing on the arrangement of the areas.

Another important factor is the orientation of your house to the sun and prevailing winds, making consideration of shade and windbreaks necessary.

Remember, too, that the land around your house, like the house itself, can be divided into public, private, and utility zones. As much as possible, interior zones should be related to their exterior counterparts. A liv-

Generous patio has dining and cooking area near kitchen. Covered section offers protection from summer showers.

Play area away from street and near family room lets children entertain friends without disturbing adults.

ing room might open onto a patio. A kitchen should have direct access to a garbage storage area.

## Convenience and Privacy

Convenience is essential to a good plot plan. A parking area needs to be large enough to accommodate guests and close to the entrance approach. A tool shed needs to be near the garden. A backyard entertaining/cooking area ought to be accessible from the front without having to go through the house. A walkway from the driveway to the kitchen entrance should be covered.

No doubt the prime factor to be considered in a plot plan is the demand for overall privacy. Family activity is personal activity, even when it includes guests. While children might not care about playing in sight of the neighbors, their parents undoubtedly would care about entertaining in the same plain view.

Privacy, it should be pointed out, is a two-way concern. Just as we don't want to be on display for our neighbors, we don't want them to be on display for us.

A plot plan, then, is a consideration of your home as house and land with no functional distinction between indoor and outdoor living. It's a consideration grounded on your wants and needs for a lifestyle that flows from house to land and back to house.

## Landscaping

Landscaping is planning for the best use of outdoor space, taking full advantage of positive natural features, eliminating negative ones, and adding plantings and man-made features such as fences, walls, walks, and patios for desired effects. Landscaping provides, too, the sheer pleasure of being among growing things, whether trees, shrubs, flowers, or grass. We landscape to enjoy the land as land itself.

Ideally, landscaping should go hand in hand with house planning. Unfortunately, landscaping is too often scheduled as a last step in the building process. Made dependent on the house as an accomplished fact, it is often robbed of its original potential. On moving in, most homeowners therefore find themselves with ready-made problems. But isn't this what home improvement is all about?

## Evaluating Your Plot

When you've established your plot wants and needs—from activity areas to convenience, privacy, and pleasure—the next step is to analyze your plot as it presently appears.

This "sand-box set" has fenced-in play yard which mother can oversee from kitchen window.

Pool at far corner of lot makes land look larger and keeps noise from house.

It's worth noting here that in analyzing your plot, and later in designing to meet your wants and needs, you might consider the services of a landscape architect. This professional, like the building architect (discussed at length in Part Two, Chapter 1), can see your landscaping project through from start to finish. He can plan with you, prepare working drawings and specifications for the nurseryman or contractor who will do your job, and supervise the work as it is done.

In any case, your evaluation should be put on paper, sketched roughly or, preferably, drawn to scale (graph paper is most helpful). Indicate your plot dimensions and locate your house. Then show the existing landscape features—trees, shrubs, hedges, lawn expanses, outcroppings, garden areas, walks, fences, walls, patio area, whatever—that will influence your planning.

On the same drawing, or using an overlay, note sun and shade patterns and the direction of prevailing winds. Note as well patterns followed by rain or melted snow runoff.

Again, using the same sketch or another overlay, indicate views, both those into your lot and house and those out from them. Here, it's especially important that windows and doors be accurately positioned in the drawing of your house. You'll want to know which views to screen, which to leave open, and which to open up.

In your house drawing, it's advantageous to include its floor plan to more easily relate indoor living to outdoor space.

With your evaluation of your plot on paper and the overall picture it affords, you're ready to construct your plot plan for the future.

## Your Design

When designing, be sure to allow for changes in the existing landscape—even great changes. The master key to better outdoor living could be extensive grading of your lot that would necessitate the removal of otherwise attractive features, either natural or man-made. Moving a walk, even a driveway, could well be worthwhile. And beware of sentimental attachments to such features as trees—often some trees should come down. In all, your goal should dictate the kinds of plantings and structures, and their locations.

It's advisable to think of your lot as a solid, three-dimensional shape, like a room, with the ground the floor, the boundaries the walls, and trees, structures, and the sky the ceiling. So thinking of your lot, you should look at it again from the outside, from all sides, as seen from the street and by your

Active sports are far from house. Hard-top section used for paddle tennis and basketball.

Hideaway across brook has barbecue grill, shed for storage, table, and reclining seating.

neighbors. Heights, widths, and depths are going to matter in your planning.

## Landscape Features to Consider

The following comments on landscaping features may be helpful to you in planning.

Trees are essential to landscaping. To begin with, they highlight your house: in front, they frame the house; behind, they provide a background. Caution should be taken to choose trees that will be in scale with the house. Large trees make a house look smaller, while small ones make it seem larger. It must be kept in mind that trees grow, some of them quite rapidly. Trees also serve practical functions. Deciduous trees shade a house or outdoor living area in summer and allow sun and warmth to reach it in winter. Evergreens screen unwanted views year-round whether of a parking area or a neighbor's yard. Trees add interest to other plantings, such as shrubs and hedges. At the bottom of an abrupt change in grade, they soften the angle.

Shrubs enhance entrance approaches and soften otherwise harsh architectural lines of a house. They break up dull wall expanses and mark the boundaries of your lot, where they also serve as background for flower plantings. They can be used to divide outdoor living areas. Specimen shrubs have a particular attraction when set off from other plantings and serve to draw attention to open areas. For variety, they can be combined, by type, shape, and size.

Flowers, in beds or along boundaries, contrast colorfully with lawn, shrubs, and trees. When located for viewing from the house, they provide special pleasure.

Man-made structures, like plantings, offer privacy, organize space, protect from sun and wind, and even hold slopes in the land. Fences enclose and protect garden areas, keep children and pets on your lot, serve as planting backgrounds, and screen views. Walls enclose areas, raise beds for plantings, and serve as seats. Retaining walls provide reinforcement for a raised area in your yard. Steps, permitting movement from one area to another, can follow a curved or straight course. Ramps are useful when moving wheelbarrows and other pieces of equipment.

Structures can be made from a wide variety of durable, attractive surface materials, from brick to crushed stone to wood chips.

Trees, shrubs, flowers, and structures are the landscaping tools with which you can extend your living areas from the house to the land.

Neat shrubs in scale with small house echo roof shape for interesting harmony.

Large shrubs help "anchor" tall house to setting and camouflage addition at right.

## Plantings and Design

Plantings need to be considered in design terms. Trees and shrubs do have form, texture, and color. In landscape design, the goal is unity and harmony.

Plant forms vary greatly. Deciduous trees can be round, oval, columnar, triangular; evergreens can be columnar, narrow or broad triangular. Shrubs are found to be round, oval, triangular, rectangular. Shapes abound. Plants should be selected for the form that they will have when mature, and in forms that relate naturally to the landscape. While form variety is desirable, one form should dominate with others accenting the one.

Texture is a plant's roughness or smoothness, denseness or sparseness, heaviness or lightness. Texture is also the size relationship between a plant's foliage and the plant itself. Textures should be varied for contrast.

In landscape gardening, the most important color to consider is foliage color—the shades of green, the grays and blues, the warmer colors. A plant's flowers are short-lived, and so less important. Still, when plants flower together they should be harmonized. Any brightly colored plants should be used for dashes of accent.

Contemporary architecture adapted to difficult site with dramatic bridge entrance approach.

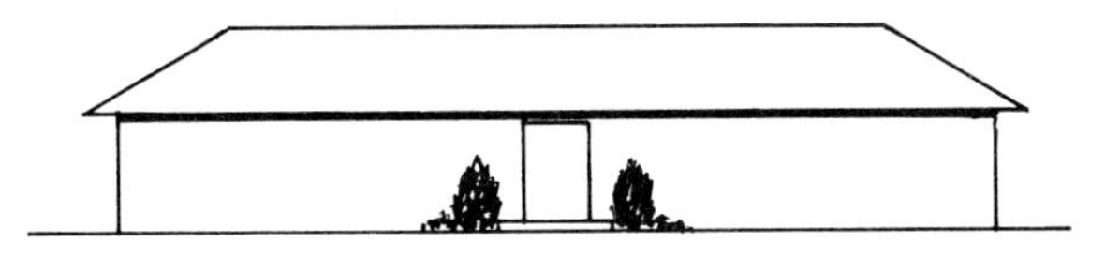

Doorway plantings for house with formal balance should carry out theme—shrubs at either side.

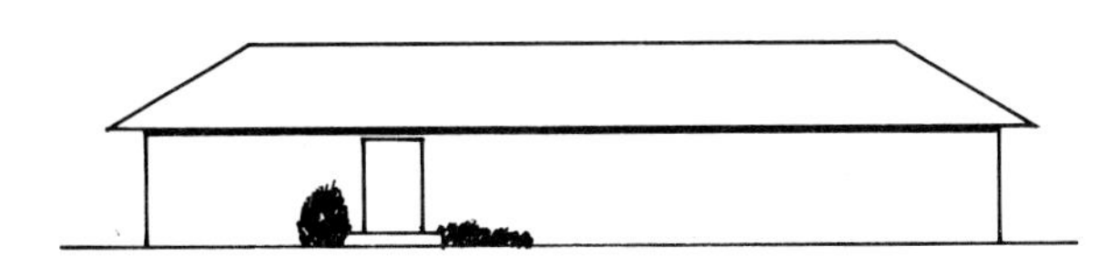

Asymmetrical balance calls for taller shrubs on narrow side, low evergreens on longer side.

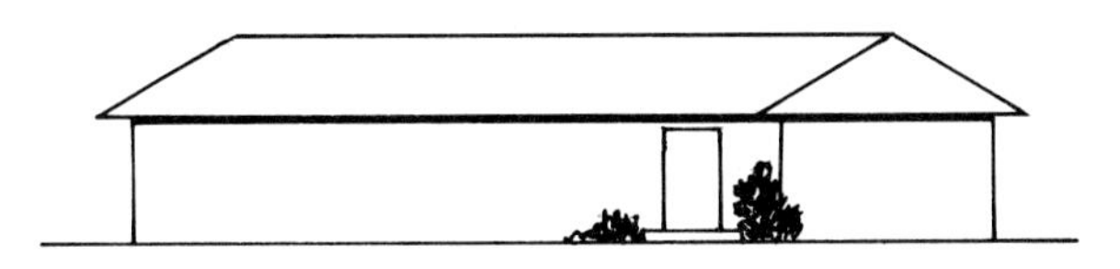

Same principle of higher plantings on short side applies when door is near projecting wing.

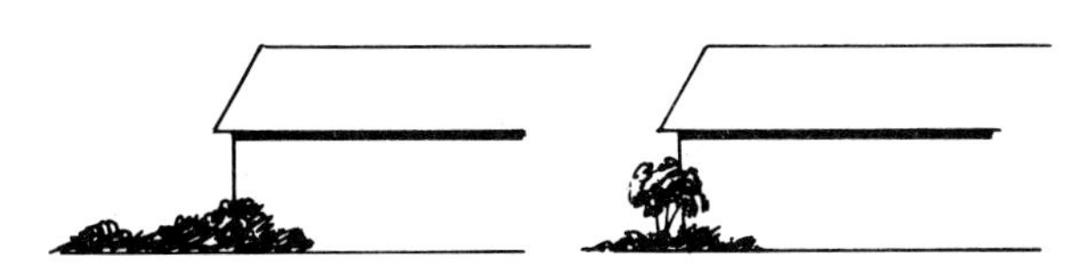

Corner plantings for small, low house should be one-third height to eaves. Larger house will take tall shrubs with low-spreading evergreens.

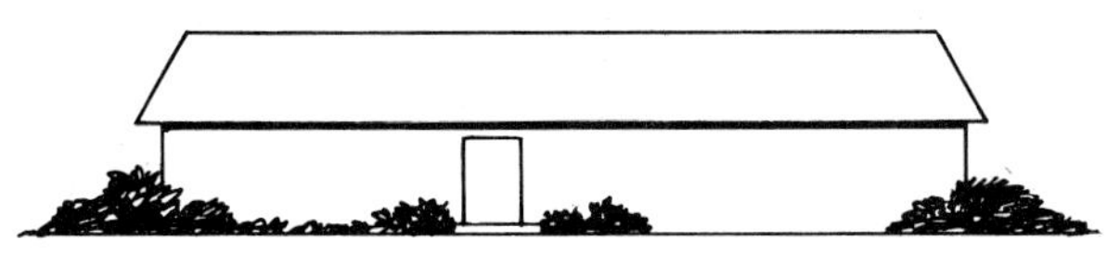

Ground cover ties corner and entrance plantings together. Low foundation permits uninterrupted panel of grass to extend to house on longer wall.

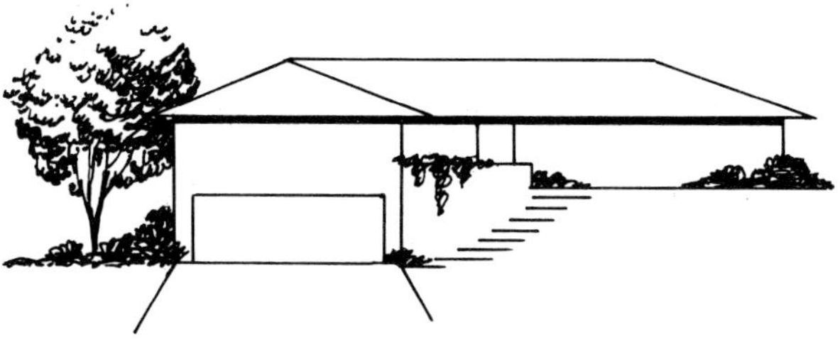

Tall trees and shrubs for tall house, low-spreading shrubs for low house combine for split-level.

## Fences and Outdoor Living

As mentioned earlier, fences have many functions: defining space outdoors as the walls of a room define it indoors; screening views; acting as a barrier to keep children and animals in or out; helping to control sun and wind; delineating boundaries; enhancing plantings—or adding decorative interest themselves. You will want to be as fully informed as you can on the use of these tools in order to do the best job.

Its purpose will, of course, determine the kind of fence you'll use. For example, to keep out the dog, a wire mesh fence would be effective and inexpensive, if less than attractive. Here, plantings would improve its appearance.

The most common function of fencing is to afford privacy, either to the whole outdoor living area or to a part of it. In either case, fencing doesn't have to be continuous. In the first case, a series of baffles within the property line might do the trick; in the second case a fence section or panel.

The type of fence used determines the degree of privacy. A solid board fence offers a maximum. Horizontal louvers give more than vertical louvers. A post and rail fence affords a minimum. Various types of fences are illustrated at the right, and the amount of privacy they provide can readily be seen. Of course, considerations other than privacy come into play when choosing a fence—cost, upkeep, ease of installation, attractiveness, and so on.

Wood is by no means the only suitable material for fencing. To lumber in its many forms—split, rough-sawn, finished—can be added masonry, from poured concrete and concrete block (including pierced and decorative block) to brick, tile, and stone. Sheets of asbestos, plastic, fiberglass, aluminum, and other materials can be used in combination with wood and/or masonry for stunning effects.

The role of fencing in outdoor living is a dramatic one.

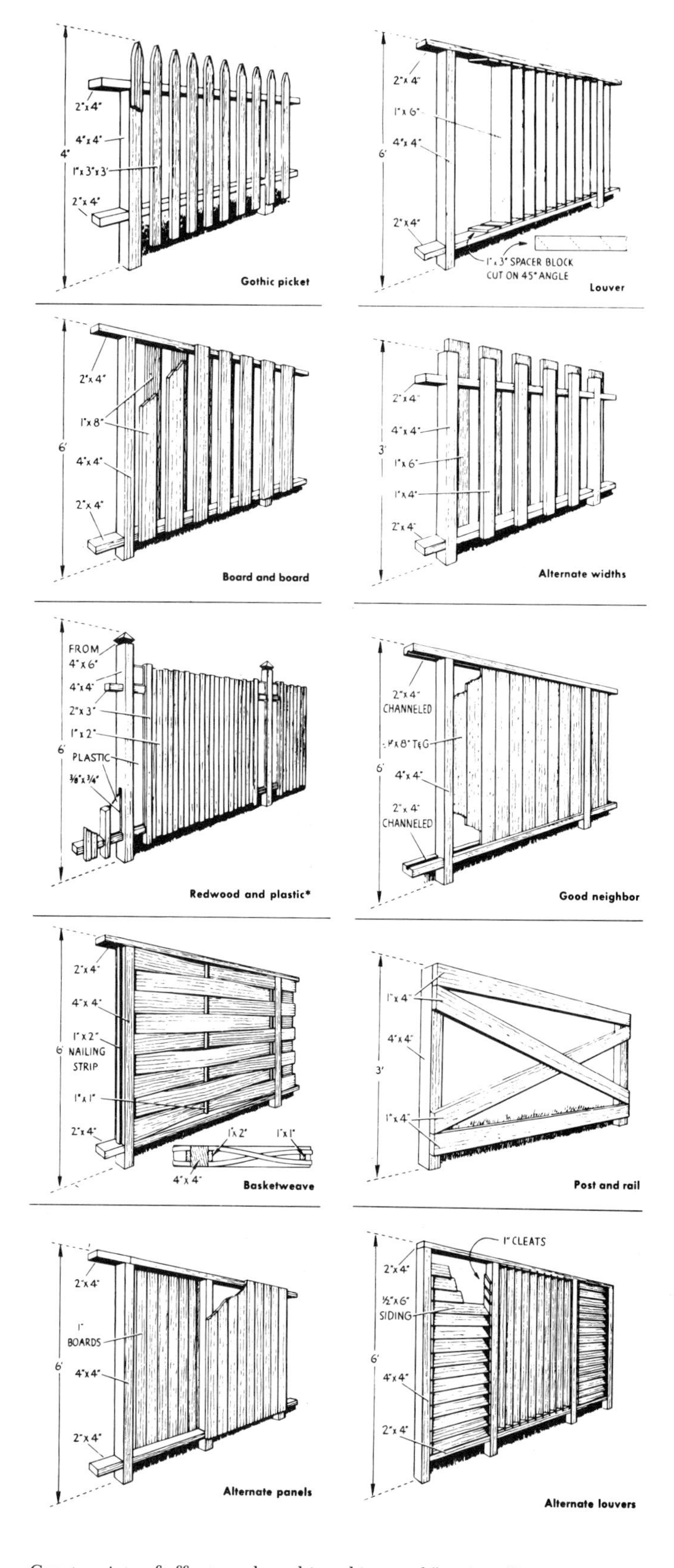


Great variety of effect can be achieved in wood fencing. Same creativity can be applied to numerous other materials, as noted in text at left. Illustration courtesy of California Redwood Assn.

Redwood screens impart oriental mood to California garden "conversation area." Fencing and plantings combine for privacy and comfort.

"Window fence" permits parents to lounge around barbecue while keeping an eye on poolside children. Open picture frames display hanging or boxed plants.

Serpentine fence enfolds plantings on either side of brick walk. Slat motif continues on house. Fences can be open for air circulation.

Diagonal boards in picture-frame panels create interesting barrier between patio and utility/storage area. Photographs courtesy of California Redwood Assn.

## Creating an Outdoor Room

The combined effect of using plantings and fencing is to create outdoor "rooms," areas defined for particular living activities. Outdoor living is, after all, an extension of indoor living. Just as a lot can be seen to be three-dimensional, so can such a defined area: it has length, width, and—in fact or in feeling—height.

The two photographs at the top of this page illustrate especially well how an outdoor room can be effected. The "conversation area," at the left, is a "living room" al fresco. The fence, at the right, is a wall complete with windows, with a "kitchen" and a "dining area" beyond.

Imaginative planning can work wonders for outdoor living pleasure.

New living room addition to old colonial incorporates harmonious new entrance hall.

Inviting arch-covered entrance approach leads from driveway through arch to courtyard.

# 3.
# The Entrance Says "Welcome"

The entrance to your house is an introduction to you and your family. At the same time it expresses your welcome to your guests. Its importance as a reflection of you and your family should not be overlooked.

On the facing page are two entrances that successfully express such a welcome, each in its unique way. Suggested in the top picture is inviting northern shelter, graceful and simple. Suggested in the bottom picture is warm southern hospitality, enlivened with abundant Spanish flair. Each entrance mirrors the homeowner's architectural preference and interest in good living.

This arched entrance hall of living room addition is interior of entrance shown on opposite page (top). Closet and vanity are to right on entering (seen through arch), and mini-kitchen with bar (through door to left) shares vanity plumbing. Entrance glass fills hall and living room with natural light.

## Entrance Requirements

Basic requirements must be met in order to achieve an inviting entrance. First, it should be obvious. When a guest arrives at your house, he should see at once where he's to enter. He shouldn't have to search for the way in or choose between two possible doors. From his parking spot—in the driveway, in a parking area, or in the street—the entrance should be evident.

Second, your entrance should be convenient. It should be directly and easily accessible to your guest, as close to his parked car as possible. The last thing you'd want would be an arriving guest to need a few minutes to get his wind back after reaching your door.

These requirements involve nothing more than simple consideration on your part for those whom you invite into your home—the thoughtfulness that's at the heart of hospitality.

The same consideration underlies entrance requirements for safety and comfort. These go hand in hand. Your entrance approach, whether a walk or steps or both, should be well lighted. Walk and step surfaces should be of a material—brick, stone, crushed stone—that's nonslippery in wet weather, especially in winter. The approach should be wide enough for two, preferably three, persons to walk side by side. The entrance itself should be similarly lighted and of the same rough surface. If possible, it should be covered against inclement weather. There should be a mat or other surface for wiping wet feet. Waiting for you to come to your door should be made as pleasant as possible for your guest.

Attractiveness plays a large role in your entrance. The approach and the entrance itself can be thought of as an appetizer, your house the entree. "What a lovely place you have!" should be on your guest's tongue before he enters your home.

An entrance approach can be as simple as a walk bordered by shrubs or as elaborate as a courtyard with a covered walk along a wall. Plantings along the approach should be planned for year-round enhancement, incorporating evergreens as well as flowering shrubs. The same is true for your entrance.

Your front door is the face your entrance presents to your guests, and as such it should be attractive. Generally, panel doors are far more distinctive than flush doors. Sidelights and door panes add character to a door and are of practical value, since they bring natural light into the entrance hall. Front doors come in a wide range of styles. So does hardware. Quality counts here.

A few words about entry into your home other than by your main entrance, about an entrance on the side or at the back of your house. Homes do have "family" entrances, those used daily and informally by both family members and friends. One such entrance is that from the driveway or garage to the kitchen, for ease when unloading groceries. Another might be that from an outdoor living area to an indoor living area, say from a patio to a family room. In these cases, the same entrance requirements apply—attractiveness, convenience, comfort and safety. In other words, show yourself the same consideration you would show your guest. Simply because you use these entrances on a constant basis, treat yourself specially.

Historic colonial has kitchen and office/guest room on first floor, two bedrooms on second. Large flagstone patio at kitchen family entrance is functional and handsome.

## The Entrance Hall

The entrance approach and the entrance itself are two parts of the three-part welcome that your home extends. The third part is the entrance hall. The entrance hall provides a desirable transition from the outside to the inside.

Your guest likes to be drawn into your home. He needs time and space to get his social bearings. He should have a private moment or two with you before joining the other guests in the living room. And he probably prefers not being on display as he enters. The entrance hall welcomes him with intimacy.

The entrance hall serves practical activities. Here hats, coats and overshoes are removed, hair is combed, make-up checked, and ties straightened. For these reasons, entrance halls should contain coat closets, mirrors, powder rooms, and table surfaces. All combine to prepare your guest to enjoy his evening in your home.

The entrance hall is practical in another way. As a room between the out-of-doors and other rooms, it serves as a buffer against cold, wind, rain, and snow. To suffer least damage from wet clothing, flooring should be of a material other than wood—perhaps brick or stone, for example. Carpeting, of course, is warmer and works well if there's an area at the door to wipe your feet.

For aesthetic reasons, an entrance hall shouldn't have a view of the private zone of the house, of a bathroom or a bedroom hallway. Views of the working area of the kitchen and of the dining room are also discouraged.

A few words about stairs. The entrance hall is a logical location for stairs. They should be placed not only with convenience but with safety in mind. A window at the bottom of a staircase is just plain dangerous. Similarly, stairs running down opposite the front door invite accidents. Stairs need to be lighted at top and bottom, the lights controlled at either level.

Entrance hall provides space for closet, table, and mirror. Simple solution to problem of door opening into living room.

Roof extension from living room bay protects entrance to this contemporary home. Chairs add welcoming touch.

This modern, realistic entrance is easily accessible from carport and drive. Roof overhang protects entrance.

Practical approach in this California home has added deck off drive to welcome guests. Note protected entrance.

Covered entrance serves to unify style elements and to give balance to this fine old home.

A front entrance can be warm, welcoming—even whimsical—as this unusual West Coast home makes clear.

## Realistic Convenience and Thoughtful Protection

Are you dissatisfied with the entrance to your home? Is it less than convenient—or downright inconvenient? Because of its inaccessibility, is it so little used that it's become ornamental rather than functional? Many a house has this problem. It's one that can be solved. With imaginative planning, you can relocate your entrance.

One New England family solved their entrance problem by including a new entrance in a new wing. At first, their problem was one of entrance approach. Guests were obliged to mount a fourteen-step fieldstone staircase from the road to the entrance on the front porch. The challenge is evident in the picture at the right. The approach problem was solved when they added a driveway to a parking area at the kitchen end of the house. The problem then was that guests entered the kitchen door instead of going around to the porch. The new wing (to the left in the picture above) did the trick. Guests are led from the parking area across a brick patio to a covered entrance.

Original entrance approach to farmhouse porch and front door presented no small challenge to guests. Steps number fourteen.

## An Entrance Hall Created in the Living Room Space

Having an entrance hall in a home is so valuable that it's worth "robbing Peter to pay Paul." An entrance hall area can be gained by reworking existing space, as was done in the two homes whose entrances are pictured at the right.

In each instance, the aim was to create an enclosed space in the living room that would provide intimacy for the pleasant business of welcoming guests.

Above, both a coat closet and a bookcase serve to define the entrance hall area. Note the common style of the two doors and the front door sidelights, which illuminate the area with natural light. The ceiling light fixture provides just enough artificial light at night to serve as a transition from outside darkness to the more brightly lighted living room. Note too the vinyl floor covering, durable, easily maintained, and most important for an entrance, impervious to rain and snow.

To realize the private entrance hall area shown in the picture below right, the front door was replaced by the window on the left and moved to the end of the room. A floor-to-ceiling bookcase in the living room screens the entrance from view. The louvered folding door unfolds to completely close off the entrance hall area.

The lesson to be learned from these two home improvements is that, with imagination, an entrance hall area can be created easily. And the investment can be modest. After all, in each case, the space was already there. In fact, each area was used as entrance space (in the second case this space merely shifted when the door was moved), so no living space was really sacrificed. A plus is that, in both cases, the dividers—the closet and the bookshelves—serve purposes of their own.

Much can be had for little.

Closet and bookcase combine to create "entrance hall" from living room space.

Front door was moved to end of living room, and bookcase was added to create entrance hall area.

## Large Entrance Hall with Den Addition

When this house was extended to turn a weekend/vacation home into a retirement home, a special feature of the addition was an entrance hall large enough to contain a piano.

The entrance hall connects the old living room with a new den. The den, served by a new bathroom, can be closed off from the entrance hall to double as a guest suite.

The entrance hall opens through sliding glass doors onto a patio at the back of the house.

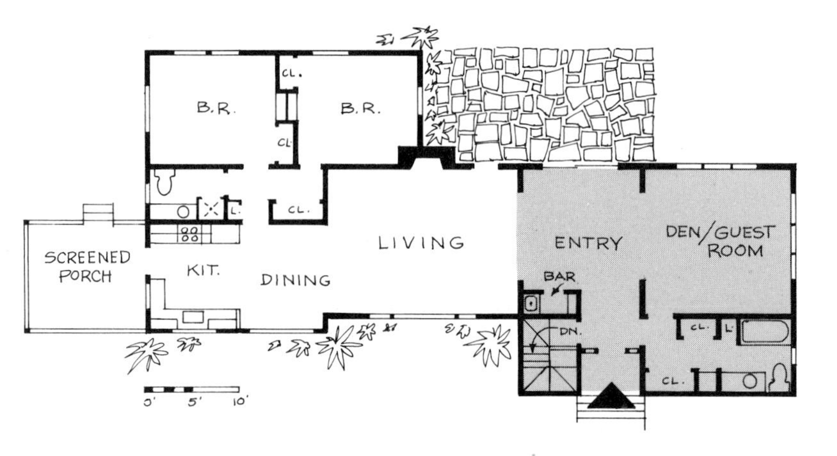

New entrance as seen beyond piano in large entrance hall. New den and bathroom that double as guest suite are to left.

## Keep It Practical

A happy result of a major remodeling project was this entrance hall that serves the living room, to the right of the camera, and the bedroom wing, to the right in the background. The entry space does much more than welcome guests. It is large enough to accommodate chairs and tables for spill-over entertaining and decorative elements, like the plant stand, and still accept a group of arriving guests with ease. The bluestone flooring is eminently practical. The large plate glass window gives the owners full view of the driveway and the entrance approach, as well as providing ample natural light.

And what a great out-of-the-way location for a bar! When entertaining, guests can fill their glasses away from the center of social activity.

Remodeled entrance hall offers spacious welcome to arriving guests. Note out-of-the-way bar at right.

## Elegant Entrance Hall Blends Old Home and New Living Room

When Mr. and Mrs. George Bates added to their fine old home, a major concern was to maintain the integrity of the original. Attaching the new wing at an angle (see page 36) accomplished this goal. The 25′ × 25′ original structure dominates the architectural whole. They succeeded all the more admirably by blending old and new in the interior with an entrance hall that is part of the addition but also extends the charm of the old house.

Central to the transition—although at the rear of the entrance hall—is a lovely curved staircase that leads to a hallway and a master bedroom suite on the new second floor.

## First Impressions

Most of us care what others think about us and try to make good impressions. We especially try to make good first impressions. This is so whether we're a boy meeting his girl's parents, a wife being introduced to her husband's boss, or a new family in a neighborhood getting to know the family next door.

Your entrance expresses you and your family and the way you live. It gives the first impression of your home. Of course you wish it to be a favorable one.

First, your entrance should say that you're a considerate host. You've made it convenient, comfortable, safe, and attractive. And you've made your entrance hall intimate—as a host, you have warmth.

The second thing that it should say is that you're you. Your entrance should reflect your personality through the choice of plantings along the approach, the color and style of the front door, the decor of the hall. The mirror might speak of your love for antiques, the watercolor show your appreciation of original artwork. A spiral staircase could announce your preference for the unusual.

The idea: convert old, cluttered carriage house into massive, multipurpose living room. The result: in view from balcony (see plan at right), country charm and good taste come together in striking example of livability. Sliding glass doors at far end of room flood area with natural light and provide ready access to peaceful country scene from 16′ × 23′ deck. Fireplace with raised stone hearth at left was added. Room arrangement provides multiple choices for small or large group gatherings.

# 4.

# The Living Room for Good Living

If your living wants and needs aren't being met by your present living room, you have every reason to remodel. The first step is to determine what the shortcomings are.

Perhaps the existing living room is simply too small or too dark—small because your family has grown, and dark because you don't use the picture window that faces on the street and makes your living room a fish bowl.

Often, it's the very location of a living room that's at fault. The picture window promise would be kept if the living room were at the back of the house with a view of the backyard (sliding glass doors opening onto a patio would put a mere window to shame). The rear location offers both privacy and harmonious relationship of indoor and outdoor living areas.

At present there may be a circulation problem. Is the room located between other rooms so that it's used as a main thoroughfare?

Still another problem could be that the room simply wasn't designed with furniture in mind. Perhaps there is only one place for the sofa, a poor place, against a heating unit. The only place for an easy chair may be in front of a window. The placement of the fireplace may attract people away from the living center of the room. Electrical outlets might be too few or inconveniently positioned. There may not be enough wall space for pictures.

A common reason for remodeling a living room is to make it fit your lifestyle more closely. How do you presently use the room? How would you like to use it? What will it *not* be used for? Who will use it most, and when?

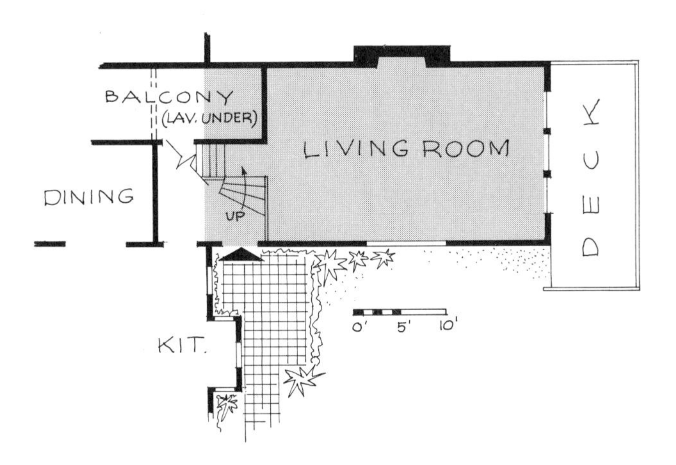


Added open stairway in old carriage house, just off entrance, leads to small balcony which serves most often as delightful play area for children.

## Informal and Formal

A living room is either informal or formal depending upon its use. Often, when it tries to be both, dissatisfactions surface.

An informal living room is used all day by the whole family for a wide range of activities. Mother relaxes there when the breakfast dishes are done. The small children play there with toys, games, and puzzles. After school, the older children use it to watch television or, better, read. Before dinner, both parents may have a cocktail, and after dinner, the entire family gathers in the living room to read the newspaper, study, play games, watch TV, or listen to the stereo.

Formally used, the living room is an evening room where the adults entertain. In this case, the family activities are carried on elsewhere, often in a family room.

If informal, a living room should be furnished with comfort, convenience, and durability in mind. The sofa and chairs could be the kind you sink down into; lighting would most conveniently be by table and floor lamps; and the floor surface should be one that resists wear, perhaps hardwood with a hard finish and durable rugs or indoor-outdoor carpeting. The room may have a television set, a stereo cabinet, and bookshelves. Importantly, the room should be oriented to the south for daytime light and sun warmth. And there should be considerable storage space.

A formal living room should also be practical, but in terms of entertaining. The emphasis, however, is on aesthetics in this case: fine furnishings, built-in valence lighting over the drapes with spotlights for paintings, a choice lamp here and there, and elegant carpeting. Neither television set nor stereo equipment should be in sight, although music can be piped into the room through unobtrusive remote speakers. Here, the room will be orientated to the west for enjoyment of the evening sun.

While these pictures of informal and formal living rooms are extreme, the point is that lifestyles determine living rooms. Some families entertain informally and make satisfactory use of informal living rooms. Others entertain formally in their formal living rooms and informally in their family rooms or country kitchens. Many families entertain so rarely that a formal room reserved for that purpose would be nothing short of wasted space. We all know of formal living rooms that seem to exist only for show.

Ideally, the average family could use two "sitting spaces," one for the children and one for the adults. The first would be a flexible room, to serve in turn as a nursery, a playroom, a room for school study, and a TV room or den. The second room—a formal living room—would be essentially for parents and their friends. Used primarily for entertaining, it would have an inflexible purpose, and wear and tear would be minimal.

## Take an Entire Side of Your House and Move It Out a Dozen Feet

Pushing out one whole side of their house has resulted in adding a living room with dining area and "the best of everything" for William Wilkinson and Alfred Conley of New Milford, Connecticut.

Having gotten away from "big city living to a casual way of living," they'd been operating their fund-raising consultation business for six months from a home that was just too small, for clients as well as for

At far end of porch is new entrance to new living room. Addition starts just below second-floor window.

guests. With imagination, they planned big and moved a thirty-four-foot-long wall out twelve feet. The old wall had miniature windows; the new wall has three eight-foot sliding glass door units that open onto a swimming pool area with a river below.

In adding on, the pitch of the roof was continued, and the ceiling of the new section follows this pitch. In the picture above, the sitting area with the horizontal ceiling was the old, narrow dining room, and the wall, to the right, was the exterior wall of the kitchen. A pocket door has replaced the old back door in this wall. It serves the dining area, in the foreground.

Designed by the owners, who did their own general contracting, the bright and spacious new space contains, in addition to the dining and sitting area, a second conversation area and a game table.

The old, small living room, located on the other side of the kitchen, is now a library.

Dark wood floors, white walls, and ample glass make for casual chic. Dining table is in background. New sitting area, former dining room, is off left.

## Converting a Two-Car Attached Garage into a Spacious and Cheery Living Room

Creative, constructive change in the home environment can become a richly fulfilling lifelong passion. For over two decades, the couple living in this old Connecticut home (he's an avid do-it-yourselfer; she's a clever and thoughtful decorator) have modified and adapted with unbounded enthusiasm. Today there is little resemblance to the original tiny farmhouse with its too-small rooms.

The first big project was to convert a two-bay garage into a living room large enough for lots of friends and a growing family.

A major undertaking, it required the right answers to well thought-out questions: What could and should be preserved? How could the new living space most efficiently and economically be heated? With the garage gone, where would the cars and tools be kept?

Our Connecticut friends chose to retain the original garage windows, in their strong horizontal pattern, giving the exterior facing the driveway an unusual and attractive appearance (photo above). Radiant heat installed in the cement floor was chosen as the best heating method (see before and in-process photos below). A new two-car garage and a badly needed workshop for the handyman in the house (see plans at right) became a necessary part of this same project.

Cleaning out old garage was first step before renovating.

Here tubing for radiant heat is being laid in cement floor.

With a brick fireplace, natural wood paneling, and a large picture window offering an idyllic view of a well-stocked mini-lake (also added to the property), the room has given the family pleasant extra living space. They would be quick to tell you that the finished product, pictured above, has added an important living dimension to the small home they bought "mostly for the lovely setting."

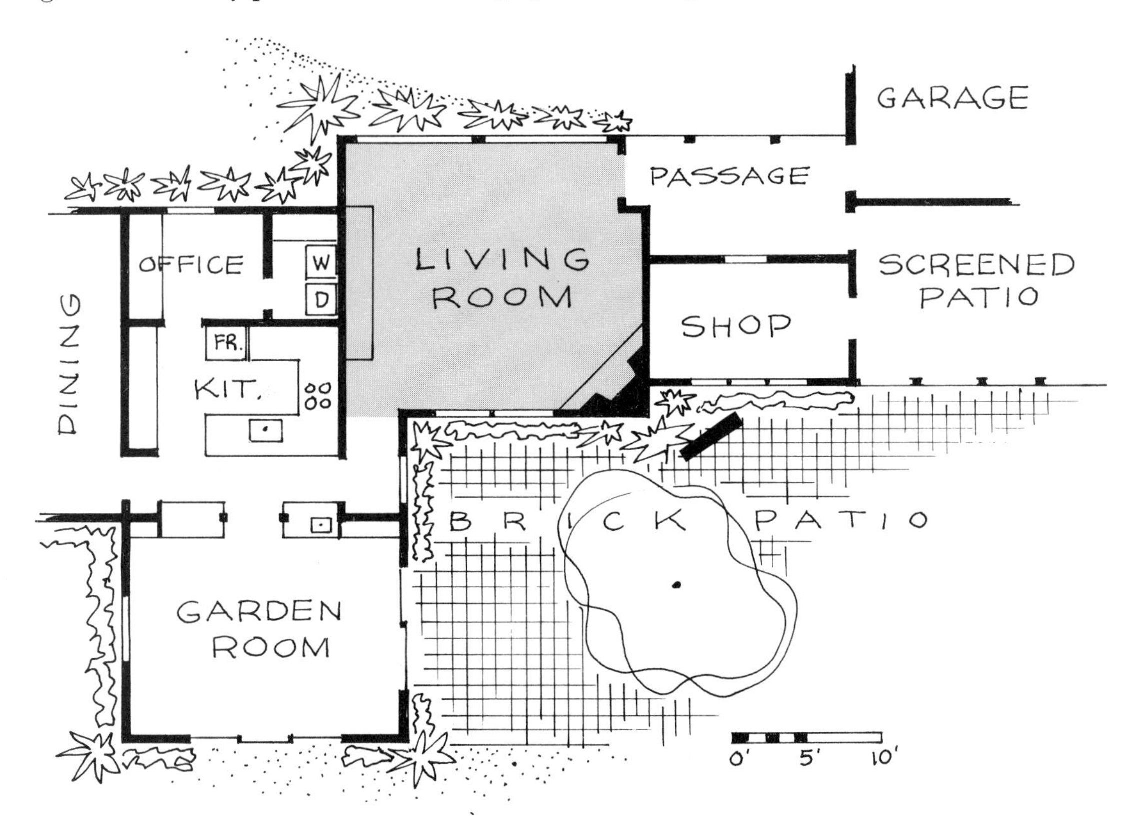

## An Architect's Skill Blends Old and New

The need or desire for more space is the single greatest impetus for change in the home environment. But when space is added to a beautiful old home, it must be done with loving care and consummate skill to preserve and enhance the original structure. It's a good time to call in your friendly neighborhood architect or residential designer. In this instance, architect Franklin B. Dailey solved the problem of blending old and new in a highly creative way when he placed this major living room addition on an angle to the original house, in perfect harmony with the gently sloping lot. The net effect is to de-emphasize the addition and its less formal covered patio and screen porch, while providing a balance with the kitchen-dining wing at right, which accentuates the classic lines of the old house.

Seen from road, new wing, at left, angles toward rear so it does not overpower house.

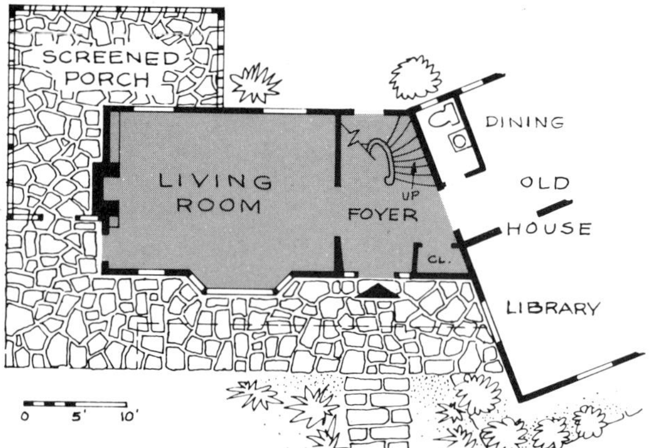

## Raise a Dining Area for a New Living Room

Remodeling the home of the Fred Scholzes of Sherman, Connecticut, required solving at least three living problems.

To begin with, rooms were poorly arranged, with the living room squeezed between the kitchen and the lanai/dining area. Setting the table while entertaining, Betsy Scholze was "forever stumbling over guests." Then, there was a problem of space and its use. Since the lanai floor was two steps down from that of the living room—with planters separating the two areas—guests at large parties tended to divide into two groups, up and down. A third problem was the presence of plate glass sliding doors across the lanai. When the temperature plummeted outdoors, it fell just as rapidly inside.

The Scholzes boldly decided to raise the level of the lanai to the level of the living room and to redesign the entire area, making the old living room the new dining area and the lanai the new living room.

Sledgehammer in hand, Fred Scholze himself demolished the planters (they stood along the ends of the lanai as well as between the lanai and the living room) and filled their depths with cement. A contractor was engaged to install joists over the lanai's flagstone floor for the new floor of plywood. Insulated sliding glass doors were installed, and plush carpeting laid.

Project began with Fred tearing down unwanted structures to let contractors build the new.

Enlarged living room, as viewed across reconstructed patio.

## Living Room Separated from Dining by . . . a Greenhouse!

If a single change in your home environment can accomplish more than one desired result, then you are, of course, way ahead in the remodeling game.

The young couple living in this beautiful contemporary home solved two problems with one brilliant stroke. The problems: the lady of the house wanted a year-round chance to exercise her green thumb; both the lady and her man wanted some separation of the huge space which originally embraced both the living room and a dining area. These photographs depict the striking solution to both problems: building a greenhouse *into* the home that juts out onto a deck area.

While serving its practical purpose, the greenhouse also adds an inexhaustible topic for conversation when dining or spending long evenings with friends before the living room fire.

Dining area is partially separated from living area by inside-outside greenhouse.

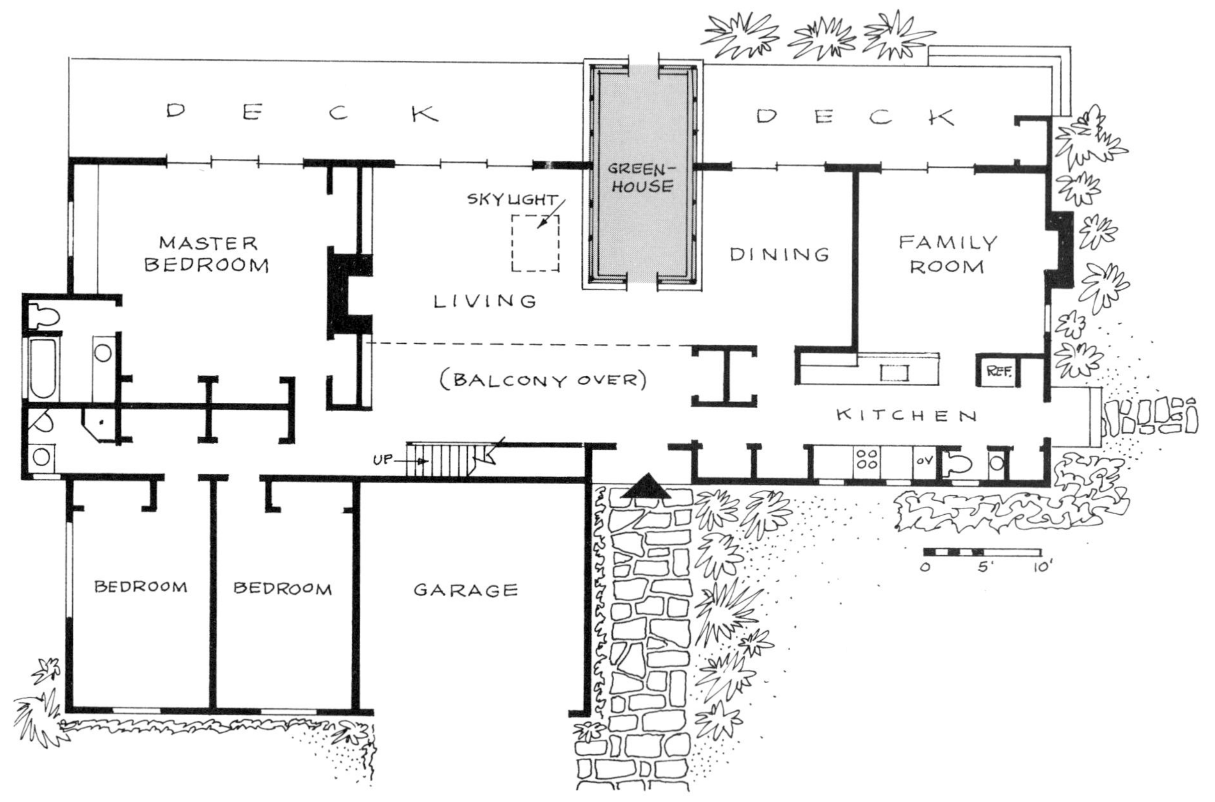


See page 82 for description of family room addition and kitchen extension.

Pleasant living room area is lit by sliding glass doors that open to deck. Greenhouse and large dormer light illuminates balcony over part of living area.

## Space Between Two Buildings Is Living Room

A basic enlarging concept enhanced by an architect with an eye for possibilities of elegance has made the home of architect Alfred Beadle of Scottsdale, Arizona, a showcase.

The international style house, designed by the architectural firm of Killingsworth, Brady and Smith, was built in 1957 and had been vacant for more than three years. To most prospective buyers, the house appeared too institutional.

Incorporated in the house design was the idea that the space between the two buildings could be made into dramatic living space by connecting them with a roof and walls of glass. In the house Mr. Beadle purchased, this space constitutes a 44′ × 30′ living room, with a music pit, dining area, and bar. In the picture shown above, the building on the left contains the kitchen, utility rooms, shop, and carport; the building on the right houses a master bedroom suite and two other bedrooms. (Note the exposed structural I-beams and the suspended accoustical ceiling panels.)

Mr. Beadle's changes included a new entrance near the swimming pool, the addition of an enclosed sculpture garden, and complete and tasteful refurbishing.

In his bright and airy living room, the architect has accommodated over ninety guests for buffet dinner parties.

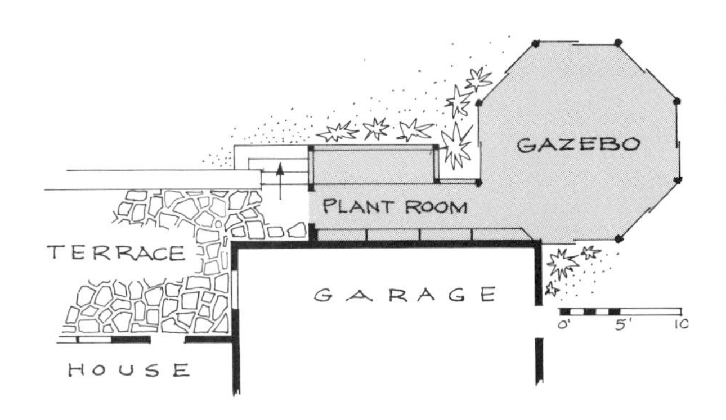


## Take the Living Room to the View

"When architect Dick Donohoe and I first began to talk," says the proud owner of this gazebo/living room, "all I wanted was a very simple plant room addition. But in the process of sharing and thinking and weighing and evaluating, my modest ideas were expanded considerably."

While his friends tell him the new structure "looks like an exclamation point on my house," the owner points out that it's a highly practical, utilitarian space.

The space is large enough for entertaining—in fact, it's the new location for the family Christmas tree—but most importantly, "it offers what is almost a 360-degree view of fields and woods which I can get from no other vantage point in the house," says the happy owner.

Passageway which leads into new living room from fieldstone terrace provides built-in book and utility space at left, and at right, plant table which easily converts into work surface.

The "exclamation point" on this house gives traditional exterior highly distinctive appearance. View from addition is panoramic, to owner's delight.

Door at right rear leads to "butler's" kitchen. Arch is entrance hall. Architect J. Robert Purdom.

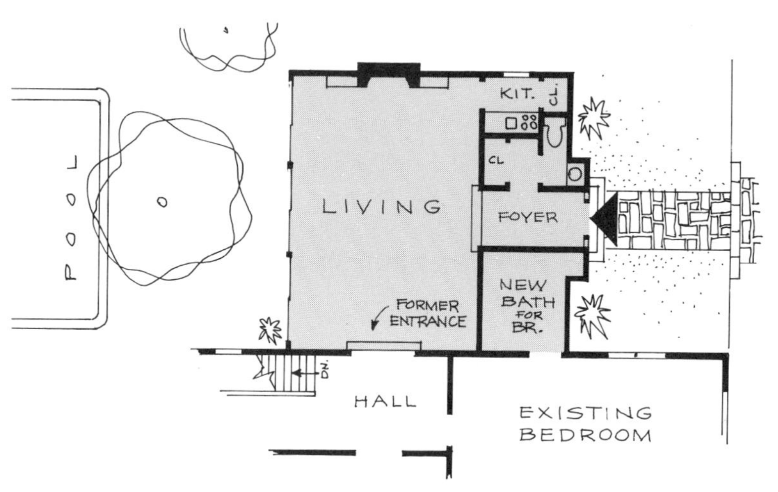


## A Second Living Room Includes New Entrance and Entertainment Kitchen

A new living room came with extras when Mr. and Mrs. Fred Mustard Stewart of Kent, Connecticut, added onto their home.

To begin with, the remodeling dramatically improved the entry into the old colonial. Guests now enter and pass through an arched entrance hall to step down into a bright, airy living room. Abundant natural light combines with the use of white paint on both walls and ceiling for brightness, and the height of the ceiling, sloped downward from above the arched entrance hall, creates a feeling of airiness.

A floor of brick from a friend's chimney adds a fine, rugged touch to the room.

To the right, on entering, are a closet and a vanity, and around the corner to the right is a mini-kitchen with a bar for entertaining. Its plumbing is conveniently back to back with that of the vanity.

Black vinyl beanbags are chairs in living room, which has free-standing fireplace. Recessed spotlights in ceiling cast shadows of arches onto wall.

Biggest outlays in total remodeling cost of $7,500 were $1,700 for plastering and $1,200 for shag rug.

Guests dine in tall chairs at leatherlike counter. Kitchen range, which rolls out on casters, hides furnace.

## Unlikely City Basement Converts to Chic Apartment

This unusual living room is part of the unusual apartment of Art and Trudy Detrich of Chicago. It is the story of a town house basement successfully turned into a contemporary city dwelling.

Art's father, an industrial exhibit designer, told his son he could have the basement of a two-flat building he owned to "create his own living environment." Art planned arched doorways leading to and from room-sized spaces with rounded walls and curved windows. He covered the walls with lath wire curved to suit, coating it with a gray structural fibrous plaster. Then he hired a plasterer to cover this inner structure with textured white plaster. Finally, he covered old radiators with filigree and hid the gas meter with a painting.

Studio addition has deck, which surrounds shade tree, that provides outdoor sitting area over sloping land.

## A Studio Living Room with Warmth

For years, this country cottage was a summer retreat for Mrs. Lillian J. Bragdon, an author of children's books. When Mrs. Bragdon decided to retreat there year-round, she turned to an architect to provide her with more living space. The result is a bright, cheerful, imaginative studio addition to an existing living room. One has the exhilarating experience of stepping from an old, low-ceilinged space into a new, lofty space.

Glass doors leading to a small deck, which surrounds a shade tree, tie the project together into a harmonious whole.

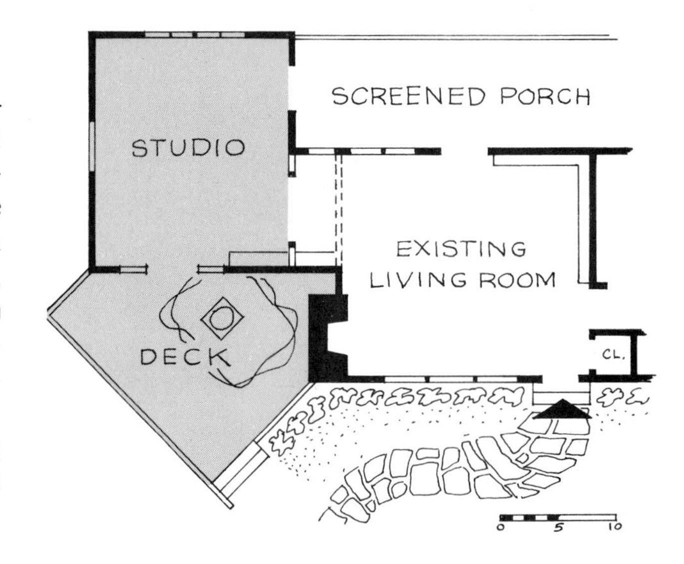

Glassed-in porch with glass-roofed extension for "greenhouse" plant area is now part of living room.

Windows at either end of "greenhouse" area open for exterior access to plants.

## Stunning Extension Gives Light and Air to Narrow Room

Closing in a porch with glass and adding a glass-roofed "greenhouse" extension to the porch, Kay Linz has opened up her living room to the out-of-doors. Natural light and airiness combine for expansive living.

Potted plants hang or sit on marble chips in watertight planters across the end and along one side of the new space. Books line the shelves under the planters.

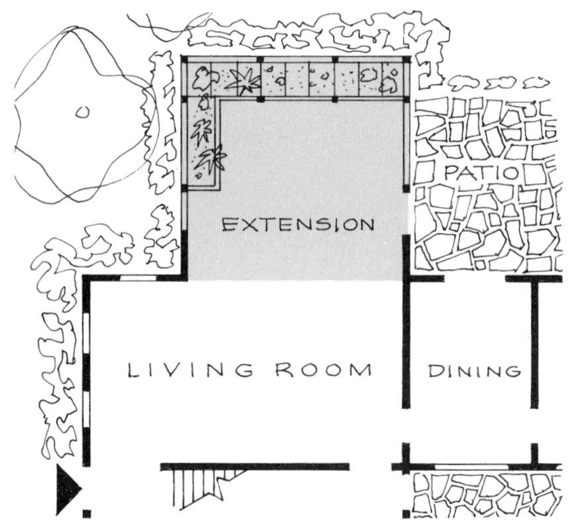


View from living room across new space. Boxed-in steel beam supports ceiling where living room ended.

Original parlor as seen from original keeping room, two of three areas combined to form spacious living room and dining area, to right.

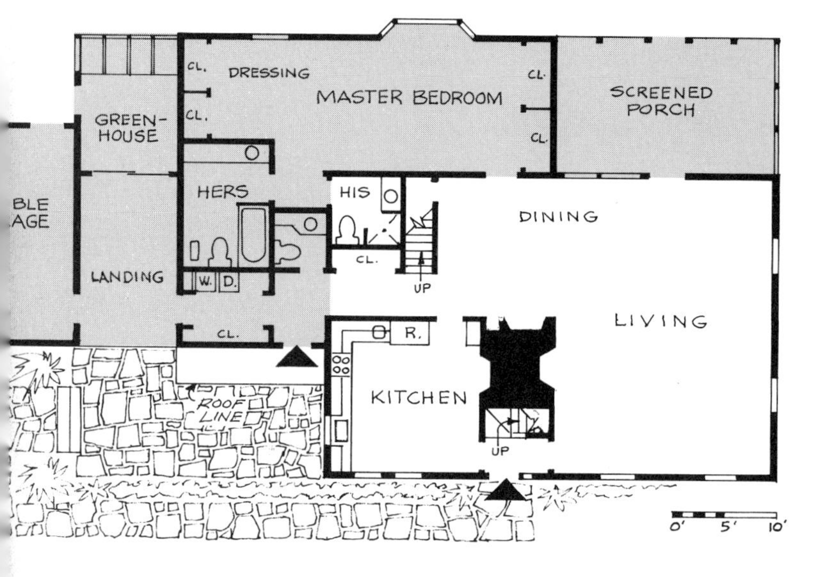


Plan shows opened-up living space in original house. Part of master bedroom was old "lean-to" farm kitchen. Note good arrangement of garage greenhouse, landing, laundry, storage, lavatory, family entrance. Bathrooms—"his" and "hers"—described on page 135.

## Old Central-Chimney Farmhouse Yields Generous Living Room

George Fink had known the summer camp in the Connecticut hills since 1928. Eighteen years later, he bought it, eventually settling into a house on the property. In 1974, learning that acreage adjacent to the camp with an old colonial house was for sale, he bought it. Suddenly Mr. Fink had a two-century-old home to remodel.

After engaging the services of two architects, the Finks decided to plan on their own. They invested ten months worth of imagination and determination in trying to make their new home meet their living requirements without injuring the historic integrity of the house. The Finks succeeded admirably.

Dining area was original kitchen of this old colonial home. New kitchen is through pocket door in paneled wall in background. Chestnut paneling was taken from barn on property.

New dining area, with living room proper in background, is shown below. To match original flooring in rest of room, similar boards were taken from an upstairs room.

A major achievement was the consolidation of three existing rooms—the original parlor, keeping room, and kitchen—into one spacious L-shaped living room with a dining area. Walls were removed, a sagging ceiling was leveled, wide-board original flooring was scraped of paint, and the fireplace was uncovered behind layers of plaster and rebuilt. In the dining area, where original flooring was lacking, original boards from an upstairs room were used to match those existing, and new boards replaced the old ones upstairs. The old stairway off the dining area was walled off. In the new living room area, the door from the entrance hall, painted white for years, was dismantled and taken down to the bare wood on the living room side to match the adjacent cabinet doors.

Today, the Finks have an airy, gracious living space with a sense of history.

## Standard House Gets New Summer Living Room from Walk-out Basement

With the services of designer William Corrigan, Dr. Laura Simms of South Kent, Connecticut, turned the basement of her standard house into rooms designed for summer pleasure.

A second living room combines old barn timbers, brick, and ceramic tile for a rich country feeling. The room contains a bar and, for those cooler evenings, an open hearth/wood-burning stove.

A utility/potting room serves a charming arbored patio and garden.

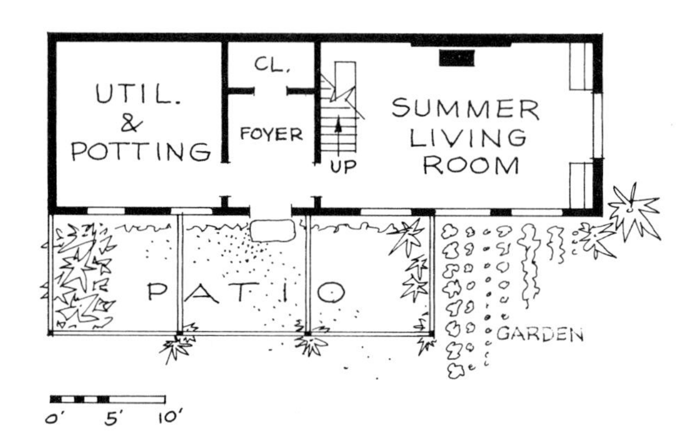

Ten-foot addition to this living room provided opportunity to add fireplace and two sets of eight-foot sliding glass doors. Ceiling beam shows where old house stopped.

A too-high ceiling is brought into scale wit decorative non-functional tie beams.

## Points to Keep in Mind

As a recapitulation, we've listed below the points to consider when creating a new living room, whether remodeling, relocating within present space, or moving to a new addition:

- A living room should be a dead end room, not a means of access from one room to another.
- It should be entered indirectly from the front entrance, through an entrance hall.
- It should have two exposures and enough windows for ample natural light. When possible, orientation should be to the south if the room is used during the day and to the west if it is used primarily in the evening.
- It should have a view of the outdoor living area in the back, not of the street and passersby.
- As an indoor living space, it should relate to any corresponding outdoor living space, such as a patio.

  (The last two suggestions are in fact a single suggestion urging that the living room be placed at the back of the house and not in the front. Like the front porch, front yard living is a thing of the past.)
- The living room should be designed with the placement of furniture, windows, doors, heating units, and fireplace in mind. Sofas and chairs should face the fireplace, the view, and the television set.
- As an attraction, the fireplace should draw people away from the entrance and into the room.
- Finally, the living room should have an overall purpose, based on the particular wants and needs of the individual family.

Modern, airy kitchen has five large casement windows on each side. Formica counter top section next to cutting board has knee space for counter snacking. Mrs. Kay Linz of Merryall, Connecticut, remodeled old country woodshed on her nineteenth-century colonial into kitchen. Old kitchen became dining room. Advantages of woodshed site were more space, large pantry behind stove area, cross ventilation, and opportunity for lofty beamed ceiling. Former kitchen was under bedroom. Chestnut custom-made cabinets enhance country kitchen warmth.

# 5.
# The Kitchen—Heart of the Home

The kitchen is the real heart of the home. A cliché? Perhaps, but there's truth in it. Think about it. What other room in your house is so central and so vital to your family's needs?

Consider how many hours each day a wife and mother spends in this room, providing her family with the sustenance—the three squares and more—psychologists call one of man's primary needs. Then consider how much love underscores her efforts. Students of family life have noted the family togetherness that results from the cooking, shared meals, and conversation that take place in the kitchen. It's a special part of the home, and "heart" is the right word for it.

For the family, then, and especially for the woman of the house, the kitchen should be designed as an efficient, pleasant environment. Workability and warmth are the goals.

## Planning

As with any remodeling in your home, the best starting point for creating a new kitchen is to take a good, long look at what you have now. What is wrong that wants righting?

Make a list of the problems. Is the layout, and so the traffic pattern, awkward? Is there insufficient counter space, too little storage space? Is the lighting poor, the ventilation poor or nonexistent? Are the appliances inadequate? Are the electrical outlets too few or inconveniently located? Is the decor dull or depressing?

Gather kitchen ideas through magazines, brochures, books, appliance centers, kitchen equipment showrooms, the homes of friends, model homes, and anywhere else you can think of.

Other end of kitchen shown on opposite page contains recessed stove under exhaust vent. Recess walls are lined with hand-painted tiles for touch of warmth and personality.

Then make sketches on graph paper (see Part Two, Chapter 1) based on your kitchen as it is now. Take these plans along when you visit an architect, designer, or contractor, or use them as the basis for more detailed plans if you are tackling the job yourself.

As essentially a work room, the kitchen is distinct from any other room in the house. Above all it should be designed for efficiency.

The most important consideration is that of work traffic flow. In a word, the fewer steps taken to bring a meal from the outside door, where the groceries are taken in, to the dining room table, the better. Many a mile is measured in a kitchen.

## Work Triangle

Planning experts talk of a kitchen's efficiency in terms of a "work triangle." This is the shape formed by joining the three major appliances—refrigerator, sink, stove—representing the three major work centers: storage and mixing, cleaning and preparing, cooking and serving. It's recommended that the sum of this triangle not be more than 22 feet, measurements being taken from the fronts of the appliances. The suggested distances are as follows: from refrigerator to sink, 4–7 feet; from sink to stove, 4–6 feet; and from stove to refrigerator, 4–9 feet.

The work triangle defines the actual work area of the kitchen, and ideally, this area will be free from other traffic flow in the home.

The work triangle is a "rule" that can be broken with successful results. We refer to it only to point out its intent. Your remodeled kitchen should be as you want it, whatever its geometry.

## Kitchen Shapes

Your needs and present space will determine the shape your kitchen takes. Discussed below (see diagrams on facing page) are the four most common kitchen arrangements. (Dotted rectangle represents dishwasher.)

The L-shaped kitchen is an excellent plan for a large space, and it lends itself easily to the inclusion of an eating area. Range, sink, and refrigerator can be conveniently located, and the continuous line of cabinets and appliances makes for ease of work. This plan can incorporate, nicely, a kitchen island for the range and sink or for a mixing center. To keep the work area free of general traffic flow, the L-arms shouldn't be broken by doors.

The single-wall kitchen is ideal for minimal space, as found in studio apartments and vacation homes. Careful planning is needed here to provide adequate working and storage space while maintaining convenient access to the range, sink, and refrigerator.

The galley or corridor plan adapts well to a narrow space (one at least eight feet wide to allow for a four-foot aisle). Here, again, work centers should be in close relationship.

The U-shaped kitchen is highly efficient, with the range, sink, and refrigerator located in the true "work triangle." In this plan, a five-foot-wide central area is recommended. U-shaped kitchens often adjoin eating areas, one arm of the U frequently serving as a room divider.

## Spaces

Next to work traffic flow in importance are counter space and storage space. An architect friend admits to heresy on both counts.

Traditionally, counter space is talked of in terms of minimum measurement. Our friend talks of minimums and of maximums. He recommends at least two feet of counter to the right and to the left of both the sink and the stove, adding that he believes any more than three feet is a waste of space. If the two appliances are on the same wall, he recommends at least two feet, but no more than three feet, between them.

He has a preference for full-size storage cabinets (seven feet high and two feet deep) over the conventional base and wall cabinets. His other "heresy" is a conviction that, in base cabinets, drawers are much more functional than shelves; they can be pulled out for access to back space.

We mention our friend to suggest that the best thinking might not always be the standard thinking. In other words, leave room for new ideas in your planning, your own and others'. For instance, what about open shelves, or hooks in plain view, for availability of spices and pots and pans?

## Lighting

Lighting in a kitchen involves considerations that are both practical and aesthetic—it should be efficient and pleasant at the same time.

Large windows are advisable for natural light, and a window over the sink is practically a must, both for the light needed in this busy area and for the relief and pleasure afforded by an outside view.

For practicality, artificial light should be so evenly distributed, and of such intensity, that you can see into all corners, those inside cabinets included. Lighting should consist of one or two central fixtures for general need, and individual fixtures for specific needs, such as lighting over the sink or counter space.

Aesthetically, low intensity lighting is pleasant in a kitchen. During dinner, a brightly lighted kitchen can be as distracting in the dining room as a darkened one, and a darkened one would hardly be practical. And after dinner, if only for snacking, light in the kitchen is welcome. For such reduced lighting, a dimmer control on the central fixture is recommended. Using individual lighting is a less satisfactory answer.

Efficiency and pleasure also dictate area lighting where meals are taken in the kitchen. This is all the more the case for the "country kitchen," a combination kitchen and dining room.

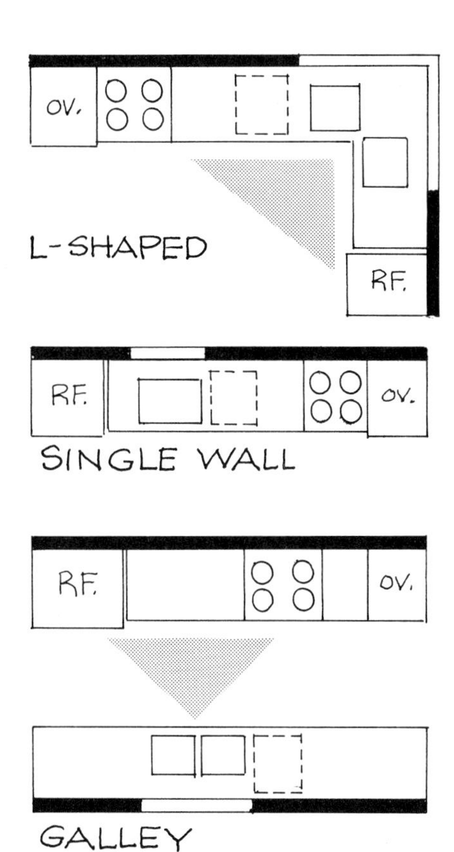


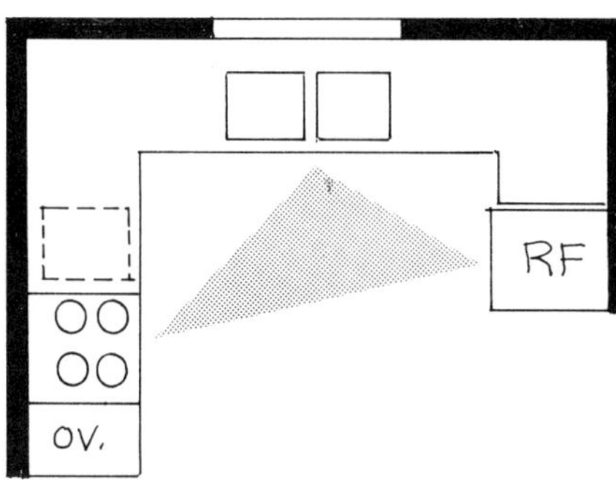


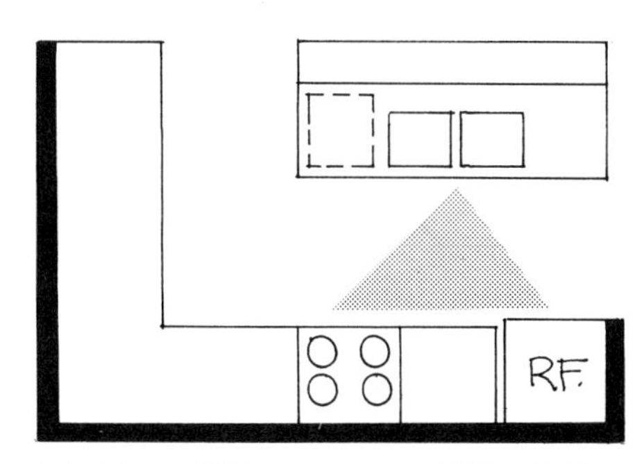


## Ventilation

Ventilation in a kitchen is a requisite for eliminating the moisture, smoke, grease, and odors that result in cooking. Vapors are best vented to the outdoors, although they can also be filtered indoors. Both an exhaust fan mounted in an outside wall near the stove and a ventilating hood above the stove ducted to the outside work well. Nonducted ventilating hoods filter the vapors and return the air to the room.

Efficient U-shaped kitchen, designed by David Jalbert, has end counter with knee space and stools for snacking. Window looks out on garden and mountain. Note skylight.

## Modern Convenience Plus Old Charm

As part of an ambitious overall renovation of a revolutionary era farmhouse, a library became a bright, spacious, thoroughly modern kitchen that retains the warmth of those early days.

Much of the warmth comes from the rich glow of the custom-made pine cabinets. The refrigerator, the dishwasher, even the range hood, are paneled to match.

The old fireplace on one wall adds to the comfortable, hospitable atmosphere. No longer used for fires, it's been adapted to contain an electric grill with an exhaust fan that draws fumes into the chimney flue. The bricks in the grill recess are new, made to look old by the owner.

The kitchen table is often used for informal dining while enjoying the view of the garden or the news on the television.

Generous 14′-square kitchen with L work arrangement has space for family dining. Refrigerator, paneled, is at left.

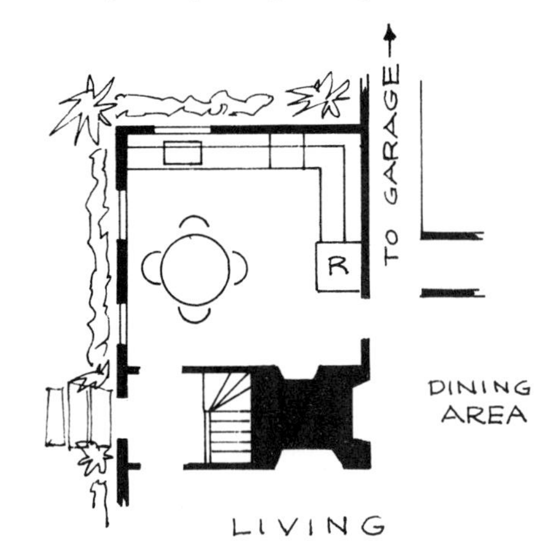

Clean, simple lines of contemporary kitchen are accented by colorful accessories and plants. Ovens at far left, refrigerator opposite.

## Interior Kitchen with a View

The kitchen of Dr. Todd Anderson breaks with tradition: it's an interior room, lighted by a plexiglass bubble skylight. Eight-foot-wide see-through openings on each side of the room provide easy access and sight lines to the dining room, the family room, the deck, the front entrance and hall, and on to the garage and driveway. Contemporary, clean lines and indirect lighting highlight the carefully chosen accessories. Butcher block counters under the openings add desired warmth to the room. In all, this kitchen succeeds as a "command post" core of the home.

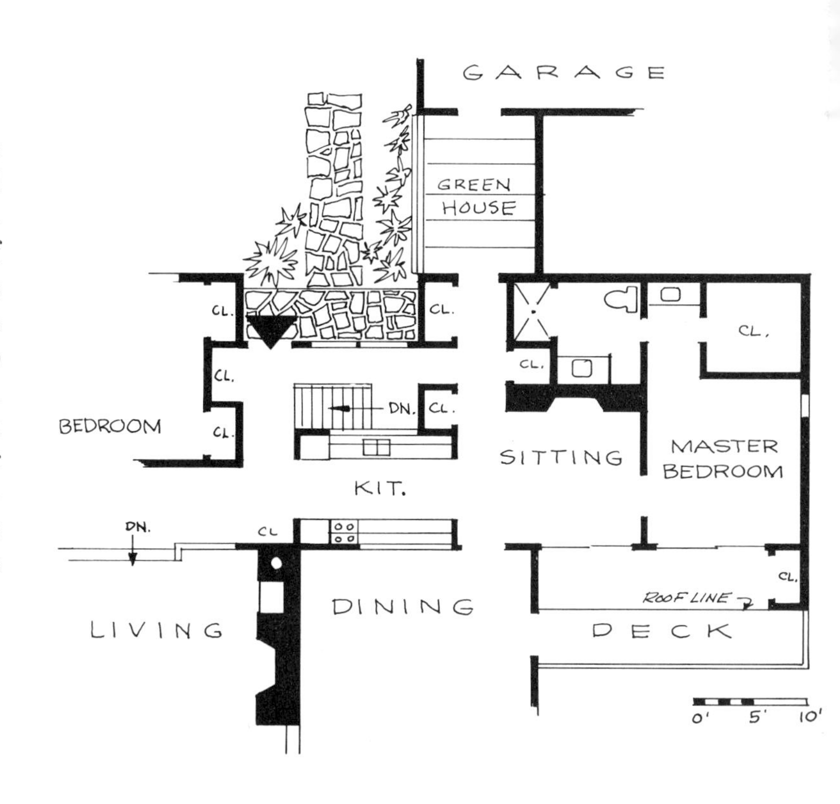

Old barn "posts" in original outside wall and exposed ceiling beams contribute to authentic country look of Neufeld kitchen. Note breakfast nook with table and seats.

## Letting Out a Too Tight Kitchen

When the Woldemar Neufelds of New Preston, Connecticut, remodeled their kitchen, they succeeded admirably in achieving all the modern conveniences while maintaining the fine old charm of their New England stone farmhouse.

They enlarged the kitchen by removing the outside wall and adding a small L-shaped area, pushing out 26 inches to accommodate a sink and dishwasher and five feet for a breakfast area out of the way of work traffic. The new wall contains large windows for abundant natural light.

A family of artists, the Neufelds wanted not only good design and order but the contrast of textures as well, and their new kitchen handsomely mixes old oak barn beams with enamel tile and butcher block counter tops.

"Letting out" their kitchen made room for an island counter with a second sink.

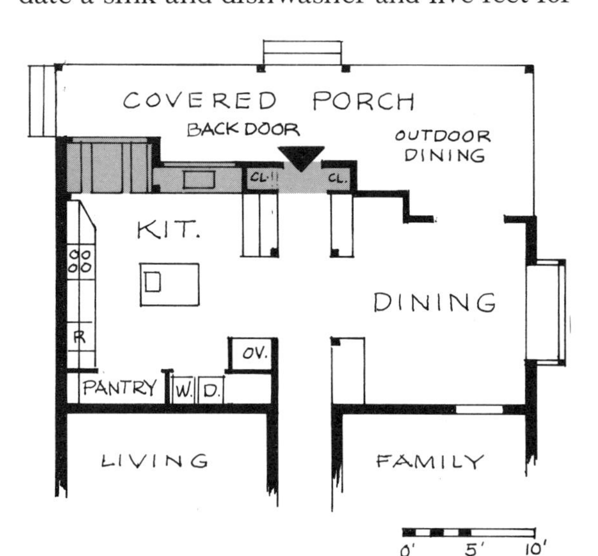

Entrance hall was added to provide closet space.

View of new dining room through new kitchen.

## Kitchen Goes into Breezeway

There was no dining room in the small home of Rev. and Mrs. William Penfield, but there was a breezeway connecting their house to their garage. The solution to the Penfields' problem was tailor-made. What they did was to add a kitchen to gain a dining room. They enclosed and insulated the breezeway, turning it into a kitchen with a cathedral ceiling, and converted the existing, larger kitchen into a comfortable dining room. The dining room now connects with the living room, hall, patio (through sliding glass doors), and the kitchen, and the kitchen connects with the garage, for the convenience of unloading groceries.

Closed-in breezeway, now kitchen is convenient to garage for delivery of groceries. New space without enlarging.

Note ingenious saving of kitchen space by placing refrigerator in recess extending into the garage.

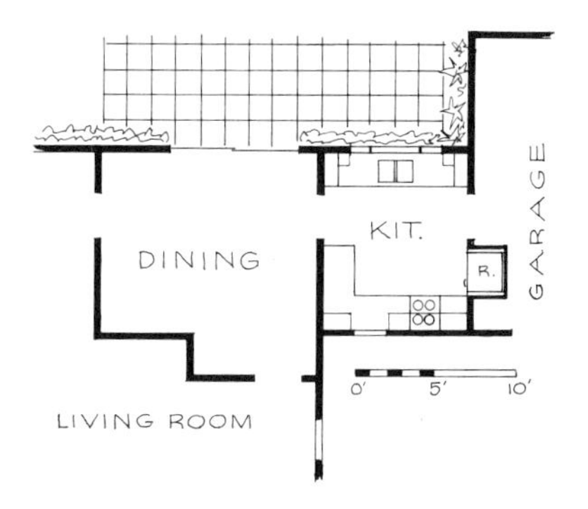

Butcher-block island is focal point of house, drawing family and guests into warmth of kitchen. From kitchen, family and dining activities can be overseen. Builder made cabinets and fan hood of red and white oak. Note window over sink.

## New Kitchen Planning Grew to Include Bedroom, Study, and Family Room

Often, planning for a small home improvement leads to planning for a larger one. The Anastasios of Princeton, New Jersey, began by thinking of a new kitchen and ended up with an addition that almost doubled the area of their home.

They were living with their two children in a small three-bedroom house that became almost unlivable when the children had friends over or they had weekend guests.

With a new, workable kitchen uppermost in mind, but also more space for the family, they explored options with architect Elizabeth Moynahan. They decided on a high-ceilinged addition with few walls and large sliding glass doors.

For under $20,000, the Anastasios got their kitchen, a new dining area, a family room, a new bedroom, and a study. In the existing house, an entrance hall and laundry were created from a small front bedroom. At the same time, a new furnace and a hot water heater were installed.

The new kitchen is L-shaped and contains a butcher block range island that is wide enough for eating. The fan hood over the island has lights as well and is of red and white oak, as are the kitchen cabinets. A unique feature of the room is its wall of oak flooring. Off the kitchen is a dining area that opens onto the family room, so that the kitchen is truly a center for family living.

Wall on right of kitchen made of No. 2 oak flooring. Owners call it their "floor on the wall." Builders said it couldn't be done, but it became their pride and joy. Wall now generates more comments than anything else in house. New 17′ × 15′ bedroom is behind wall.

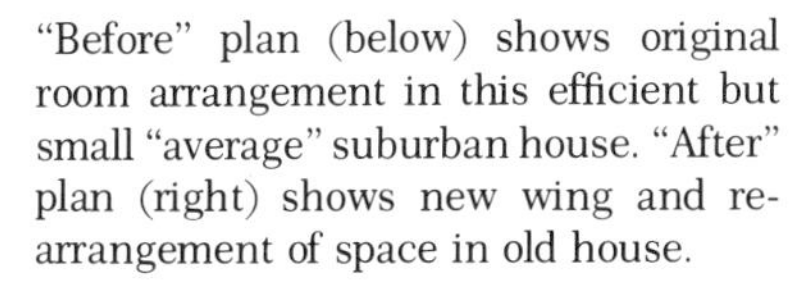

"Before" plan (below) shows original room arrangement in this efficient but small "average" suburban house. "After" plan (right) shows new wing and re-arrangement of space in old house.

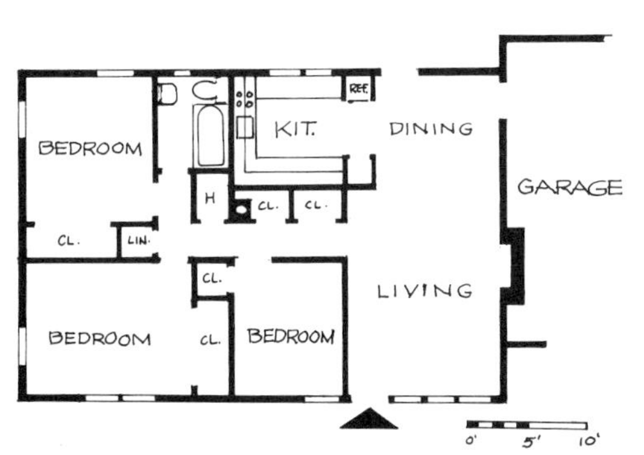

The Anastasios built back because of zoning laws governing distance from neighbors and street.

New family room has black couch over game cabinet. With cushions off, couch is work table for small children.

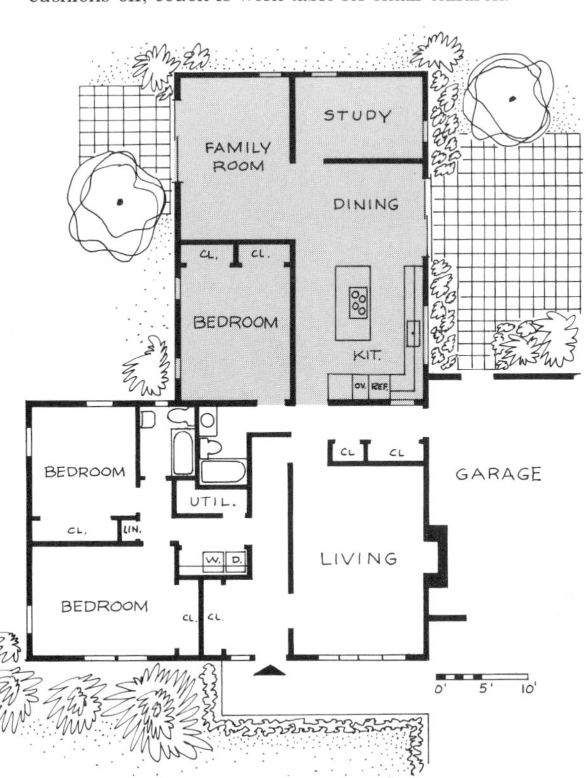

For growing young family, colonial kitchen turned living room becomes kitchen again, at least in feeling—with simple removal of a wall. Door to dining room is at left, beyond fireplace. Door to rear patio at right.

## New England House Gets Back Family Kitchen

The usual story of a family buying an old colonial house has them happily discovering and uncovering an oven next to the fireplace in what had been the kitchen of the house. The Ward Smiths, a family of six, uncovered a whole kitchen!

Here's what happened. When the Smiths moved into their colonial, the original kitchen (see picture above) had long since been converted into a second living room. A small, efficient kitchen had been installed in the original pantry. The new kitchen was walled off from the new living room but had connecting doors at each end. The Smiths, in a flash of inspiration, simply removed that wall, bringing the kitchen ambiance back to the room in which cooking had first been done in the fireplace.

The counter that had stood in the kitchen against the separating wall became a kitchen island with a new second sink. A new counter top was extended into the living room to serve as a snack bar.

At a reasonable cost, the Smiths were able to restore a space to its original function. Kitchen warmth is back in the living room—and the warmth of the living room fireplace can be felt in the kitchen. The arrangement suits the Smiths to a T.

New kitchen wing with chimney is in harmony with nineteenth-century architecture.

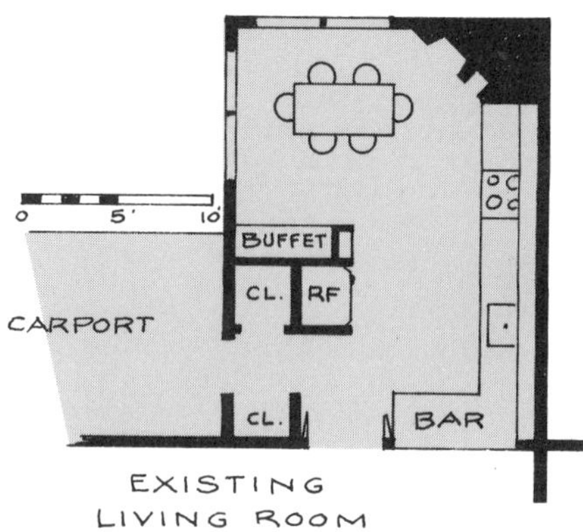


## Kitchen Wing Provides Country Dining "Room"

With an addition to the home of Mrs. Charlotte Pratt, a small corner kitchen was expanded to incorporate an informal, fireside dining area. Her country kitchen ambiance was achieved with used brick, old barn beams, and simple American furniture and accessories. The charming raised hearth is used for hibachi cooking, and the brick wall contains storage areas for wood and utensils.

Note the space provided by raising the ceiling half way to the peak of the gable L addition. Also note, in the plan at left, how the kitchen dining area has its own personality as a room, with windows on two sides for the lovely view.

## Putting Comfort Back in the Kitchen

When the Ted Schrieners retired to their compact, well-designed home in Arizona, they felt that something was missing. There wasn't any place for the sit-around socializing in the kitchen that they had always enjoyed when they lived in the Midwest.

Without relocating any of their plumbing or appliances, they removed a section of the exterior kitchen wall to add an "Arizona room," measuring 14′ × 24′. A concept of the Jones Construction Company of Sun City, the room is really part of the kitchen.

At one end of the room, sliding glass doors open onto a new covered patio. The opposite end of the room contains a hobby area with desk and cabinets.

A room air conditioner was installed in the new section to avoid placing an additional load on the central system.

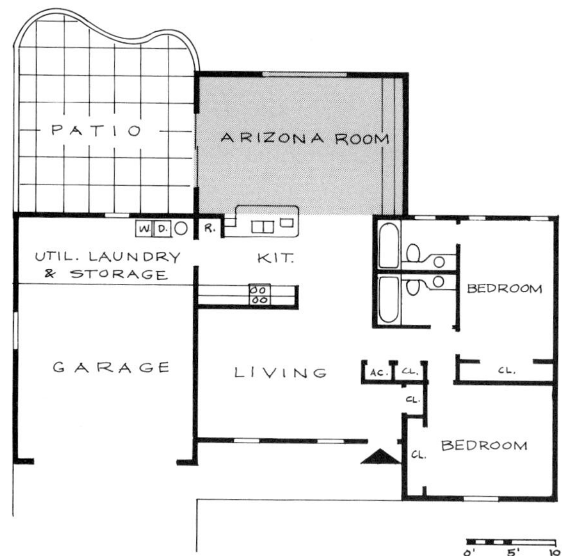

Family dining area is in foreground. For entertaining, table is moved into "Arizona room" and leaves are added.

Covered patio, off new room, offers opportunity for open-air dining. Decorative cement block "privacy wall" pleased neighbors.

## Small Kitchen Becomes a "Happy Corner"

When sportsman and painter John Cleimer saw the small, dark corner kitchen with a "great view," he knew he wanted to buy the house and add sitting, dining, and greenhouse space. The result was an opening of the kitchen out onto a living area that feels less like a kitchen than the outdoors he loves so much—and it is a year-round area for enjoyment. Although the kitchen itself was changed only by removing the window over the sink and enlarging the opening for a pass-through, the effect has been to create a sunny garden retreat.

Outdoors comes indoors in this view from Cleimer kitchen of greenhouse addition.

From outside, addition is only greenhouse, but on inside, it's so much more.

New-addition atmosphere provides special pleasure when "just plain sitting."

In Donohoe kitchen, wood and stone textures complement white of appliances and cook-top with backsplash paneling.

## Enlarged for Charm, Modernized for Efficiency

The striking modern country kitchen of architect Richard P. Donohoe and family is a far cry from the laundry and farmhand washroom it was in the closing years of the last century. It's a far cry, too, from the small, functional kitchen that shed had become when they moved into the farmhouse a few years ago.

The Donohoe touch began with a seven-foot addition to the twelve-by-twelve room. To capture the morning light and a view of the garden, the new far wall is angled at forty-five degrees and contains an eight-foot-wide glass door. Since the Donohoes enjoy variety in dining, the addition incorporates an eating area that supplements the dining room. Friends and family take pleasure in its special charm.

The Donohoe touch continued in the woodwork. The earlier cabinets were made of oak plywood. The new ones, as well as the walls, valences, and shelves, are made of cedar—rough-sawn planks ripped from four-by-four posts on sale at a nearby lumberyard. The flooring of natural-cleft flagstone on plywood subflooring is complemented by counter tops of the same bluestone, rubbed smooth. These textures and colors are shown off against the white surfaces of the major kitchen appliances, including the cook-top with its backsplash paneling.

The architect made a "conscious selection of white" for the appliances, believing it to be the color that permits the widest range of general color selection. He notes that white appliances are more easily replaced because they are standard, and that choosing white lets you buy appliances from different manufacturers with no concern for matching.

Eating area in kitchen addition looks onto garden and receives morning light for added pleasure at breakfast.

Architect Richard P. Donohoe champions drawers instead of shelves for base cabinet storage space for easy access.

Evident in the new kitchen are the architect's preferences for floor-to-ceiling cabinets instead of base and wall cabinets, drawers in base cabinet space, open shelves, and wall hooks for utensils. A Donohoe lighting touch completes the kitchen—two levels of fluorescent lights on four switches in valences above the counters and cabinets.

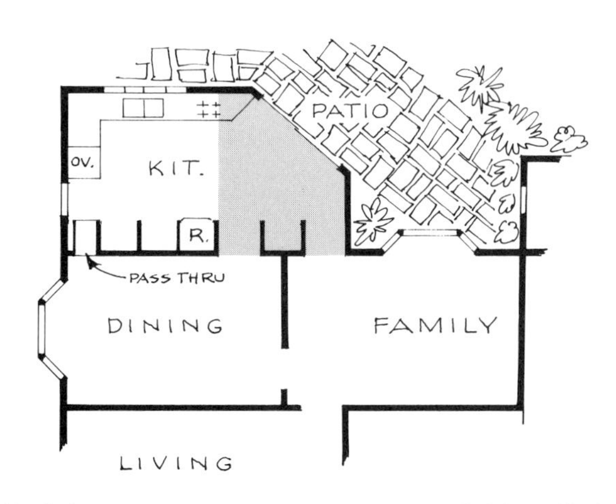


Shaded area shows kitchen addition, with angled far wall of sliding glass doors. Former kitchen was totally remodeled.

Former entrance from formal dining room to kitchen now doubles as pass-through and cabinet for wines and liqueurs.

## A Kitchen Must Be Cheerful

A modest remodeling investment paid off handsomely for Mr. and Mrs. Peter Mullen. The Mullens' kitchen had a single exposure and insufficient natural light. By doing no more than opening the interior south wall to the dining room, the kitchen gained another exposure and twice as much daylight as before. The eating counter itself does double duty as a serving counter. For formal dining, bi-fold panels close off the kitchen from the dining room. Note how designer Bill Corrigan's decorating scheme blends the separate room areas.

Certainly unique to Mullen house is addition built to look like an entrance that serves as dining room china closet. "Entrance" adds to attractiveness of back of house as seen from lake.

## Family Outgrows Kitchen Breakfast Area . . . Encloses Porch

"Like father, like son" dictated the home improvement of Mr. and Mrs. Larry Greenhaus and family. When the Greenhauses' son grew to eye level with his six-foot-six father, the "eat-in" kitchen area proved too small for the two of them. To solve this dilemma, the Greenhaus family closed in their porch and installed year-round heating. The porch end off the kitchen is used for family dining, the other end for sitting. MaryAnne DiMarco was the designer.

Old, dark kitchen with high ceiling is given airy, arbor effect with dropped ceiling of plastic panels laid on stained 1″ × 4″ pine framework covering fluorescent lighting.

Authentic old barn door on old chestnut board wall slides to open up buffet end of kitchen to dining room. Door is conversation piece.

## A Potpourri of Kitchen Thoughts

As suggested earlier, decoration should play a major role in the kitchen. As the work center of the home, it needs to be a pleasant place to be—bright, airy, colorful, and interesting.

Think wood! The kitchen is the warm spot of the house, and nothing is as warm as wood. Consider not only wood for cabinets and shelves, but also wood paneling for walls. Even think about paneling as veneers for major appliances, for refrigerator doors or dishwasher fronts. In an "old-feeling" country kitchen, modern conveniences can be so camouflaged. Consider the distinctiveness of random-width wood flooring.

Think brick! Natural, or painted white, brick has that earthy feeling of tradition, of "roots," and its texture works so well with wood. Think brick for both wall and floor surfaces. And tile! Tile, on wall or floor, adds special accent.

Consider using shelves to display collections of pewter, copperware, glassware—and wall racks for objects for food preparation. Copper, aluminum, stainless steel, together with today's wide range of enamel finish hues, offer possibilities for exciting color combinations. Keep backgrounds simple.

Think, too, of plants, especially flowering plants! What gives a room more life than growing things? Plants are so easily cared for in the kitchen.

Don't fail to consider displays of art work! Why not a painting or two, or a mural? Or a craft creation, an example of decoupage or macrame?

Two kitchen space suggestions! One, think about having a "planning center," an area where a woman can sit down and read her cookbooks, or write out a shopping list, or balance the checkbook while the dinner cooks. And include a telephone within easy reach. Two, think about providing seating for the friend who joins the housewife in the kitchen for a coffee klatch.

Room expanded upward! Floor of unused maid's room was removed to achieve elegant vertical space in dining room of this two-hundred-year-old farmhouse. Huge suspended globe fixture supplements candles for dining illumination.

# 6.
# A Dining Place That Satisfies

Much of what we discussed about living rooms is equally true about dining rooms. Once again, it's a matter of informal versus formal.

## Formal Dining

When we take our meals in the dining room, we can be said to be eating formally since we're in a room specifically set aside for that activity. We eat informally in the kitchen, in the family room, or in the living room—perhaps in front of the TV—or buffet-style with guests, on the patio or deck, or at the picnic table in the backyard. And there can't be a more informal meal than breakfast in bed!

This isn't to say that we can't have an informal meal in the dining room. Hot dogs, potato chips, and soda, even at the dining room table, is hardly a formal meal, nor is bacon and eggs eaten under the splendid dining room chandelier while clad in pajamas and bathrobes.

The point is that a dining room is a room reserved for dining.

A family does or doesn't need a dining room depending on whether or not it wants to have its meals in such a special room. To the degree that the need or desire is there, having a dining room becomes practical. It can be a basic necessity or a luxury—or even a waste of valuable space.

As with a living room, a dining room has a formal purpose in entertaining when your guests follow an elegant progression from cocktails and good talk in the living room to dinner and continued conversation around the dining table. Mellowed guests mellow all the more with a gracious meal in the warm glow of candlelight. The return to the living room for after-dinner drinks or coffee before the fire tops the evening.

## Dining Room Planning

For the family who enjoy entertaining in this manner, there are dining room requirements to keep in mind.

First of all, the room should be large enough to comfortably seat all your guests at the dining table. A rectangular table requires at least three feet of space between the table and the walls of the room or any other piece of furniture in the room. A round table requires a bit less. Accordingly, a 3′ × 5′ rectangular table for six would call for a room measuring 9′ × 11′ if the room had no cupboard, sideboard, or other furniture.

Special lighting is called for in a dining room. As mentioned earlier, candlelight is the warmest. Electric lighting should take its cue from candlelight and be as soft and warm as possible, illuminating both the dining table itself and those surfaces involved in preparing or serving the meal. Electrical outlets for hotplates and other appliances should be conveniently located.

A fireplace in a dining room creates an especially elegant dining atmosphere. However, it must be at a comfortable distance from seated guests. Heating units, too, shouldn't be uncomfortably close to the table.

Formal dining insists on privacy. While it should be adjacent to the kitchen, the dining room shouldn't offer a view of the kitchen, at least not of the work area. The sight of dirty pots and pans on the stove or dishes in the sink is less than appetizing. A swinging door between the rooms provides an ideal screen. If there's a pass-through from the kitchen to the dining room, it should be of sufficient height to obstruct unattractive sights or have some means of closing it off. Similarly, if a dining room opens onto a living room, the opening should be positioned to discourage visual intrusion.

## More and More the Dining Room Is a Dining Area

The alternative to a separate dining room is a dining area that's essentially part of another room.

A dining area is often set off at one end of a living room. Here, as compensation for any loss of intimacy, diners can enjoy a pleasing openness. Entertaining, from pre-dinner cocktails through dinner to after-dinner socializing, can flow easily and naturally from one space to the other and back again. Imaginative decorating can either blend the spaces or give each a personality of its own. Furthermore, the dining area can share pleasant features of the living room, from its fireplace to its view.

Another common eating area is found in the kitchen. Such an area is invaluable, even if there's a formal dining room. The very convenience of a kitchen eating area recommends it certainly when there are children to be fed.

An expansion of kitchen eating space is the country kitchen, in which the dining area is an integral part of the cooking area. Here, as in the earliest American houses, the warm, heart-of-the-home atmosphere pervades.

By definition, the family room lends itself naturally to informal eating. Even a bedroom can include a special eating space. An architect we know has an alcove in his bedroom that opens onto a deck for romantic meals with his wife.

Of course, outdoor areas can be reserved for eating: a deck or gazebo, not to mention a screened-in porch or breezeway.

Whether a family has a formal dining room or not, having more than one dining area adds spice to the pleasure of sharing a meal.

Architect Alfred Beadle's dining area is in living room, bordered by walls of glass at either end. Kitchen pass-through makes for convenient serving, can be closed to screen kitchen working area from diners' view.

For William Wilkinson and Alfred Conley, living room with dining area was result of extending side of house. Ceiling continues roof pitch. Kitchen is off dining area, to left in background. Dining patio is one step down from sliding glass doors.

Ample window space floods Plumb dining area with natural light. View through windows is of wooded hillside. Note how table at right, against living room sofa, serves to separate dining area.

## Living Room Pushed Out to Make Dining Area

In the Plumb home in western Connecticut, extending the living room ten feet afforded a formal dining area with its own identity as a room.

In the original weekend vacation home, meals had been served at a sawbuck table in the kitchen breakfast area. The new dining area meets the requirements for year-round living.

At the same time the dining area was added, the kitchen was enlarged to almost double its former size. A bonus was added closet space in an existing bedroom. (See plan, below right.)

Ten-foot addition for dining area includes new space for kitchen, in foreground. Kitchen almost doubled in size.

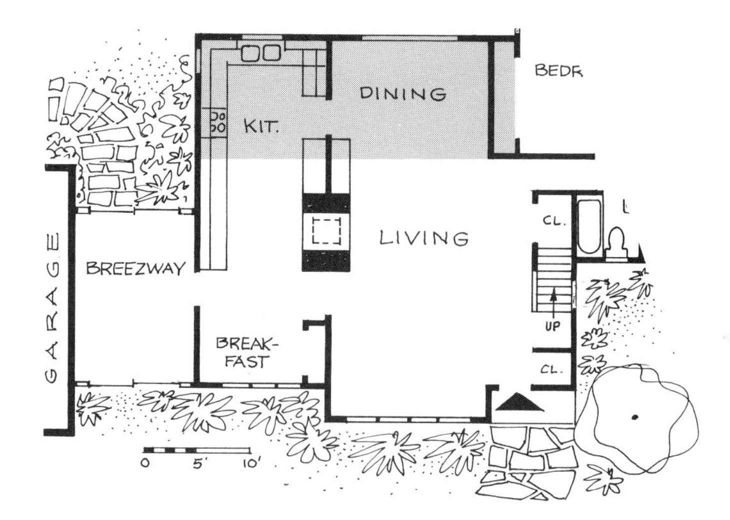

French doors, at left, in Neufeld dining room open onto porch. Wall in foreground was removed to open room to hall. Note generous bay window, filled with plants in winter.

Wooden extension (formerly a shed) of stone house contains dining room and kitchen. Covered porch is new addition.

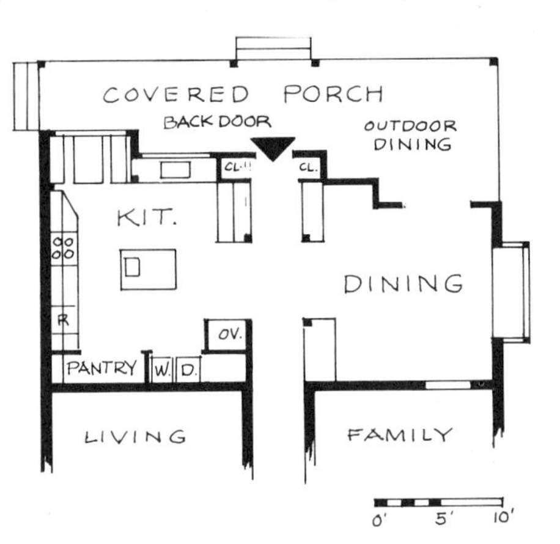


## A Special Room For Dining Preferred by Many

A shed area, added years ago to this stone farmhouse, is today a spacious, elegant dining room.

Highlighting and lighting the room is a large cantilevered bay window, filled with plants in winter. A beamed plaster ceiling, wide-board flooring, and traditional wood furniture (including a dry sink) contribute solid warmth. The white-painted wainscoting, wall surfaces, trim, and French doors increase the overall brightness. The owners' personality is reflected in the handsome ceiling light fixture and the art work on the walls. The French doors open onto the porch and outdoor dining area.

A window in the old dining room (to the right in the picture above) was removed to become a sculpture bay. The old dining room is now a family room.

Wall of mirrors adds light and sense of doubled space to new dining room. Ceiling beams and studs give "arbor" effect.

Vinyl flooring practical, as swimmers enter room from pool and room serves for parties. Note outdoor effect of skylight.

From breakfast area, French doors lead to dining room, white door in background to bathroom.

## New Dining Room and Guest Room Fit Neatly into Place

When architect Gabor Lorant decided to add a dining room to his family's home in Paradise Valley, Arizona, he realized that two of the needed walls were already standing. The L-space between the kitchen and breakfast area and one of the boys' bedrooms was tailor-made. Since the kitchen overlooked this area containing a garden and patio, it had served well as a supervised play area for the three Lorant children when they were small. But they were in their teens now.

This L-space was in fact larger than needed for a dining room alone. The addition could also include a guest room and bath, for visiting grandparents or for the children's school friends spending the night or changing for the pool.

Simply, and with marked effect, one interior wall of the new dining room was finished with mirrors. For ease of maintenance, vinyl tile floors were installed throughout the addition, since swimmers enter this area from the pool and it doubles as a party room. The outdoor effect of the dining room is heightened by a twelve-foot sliding glass door unit, skylights, and an exposed beam ceiling. Looking from the kitchen pass-through across the dining room to the pool area, Mrs. Lorant can still see her children at play.

Pocket door to guest room bath makes it accessible to dining room and outdoor activities area.

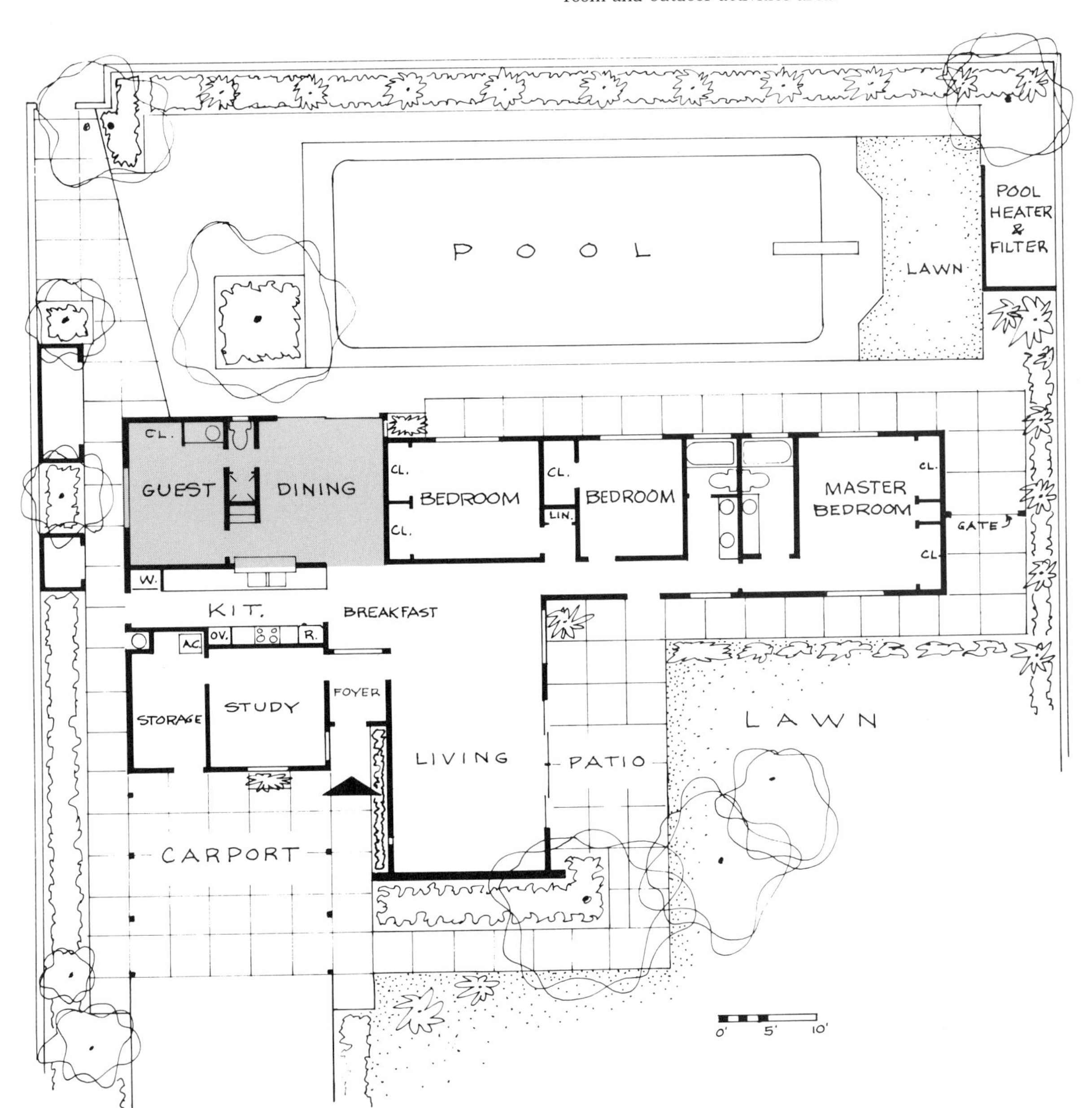

Addition ties in neatly with house, protects patio.

Old Vogt kitchen ended at vertical beam to left. Extension of kitchen to new dining room required entirely new kitchen ceiling.

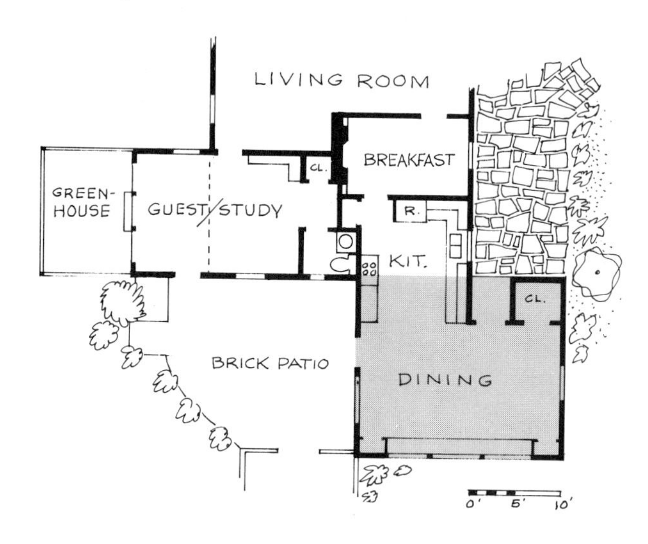


## New Dining Room Wing Stretches the Kitchen

It all started with cakes—decorating them, that is.

Maureen Vogt, wife of psychiatrist Dr. Walter Vogt of Sherman, Connecticut, had spent four years studying the art of cake decorating and three years giving lessons in cake specialty work. A decision to "go into business making cakes" with a friend led to remodeling her present kitchen to provide work space for up to a dozen people at a time. The result was a new kitchen built to professional specifications—and a whole new dining room wing as well.

Highlighting the new dining room is a cherry table measuring 8½′ × 5′. Oak beams span the room under the high ceiling.

To either side of the long window area are display cases for cake demonstration dummies, and under the window seat are a total of eight drawers. The display cases are lighted, as is the window seat, the latter with fluorescent lights for hanging plants. Independent lights on dimmer switches and attached to the beams shine up and down.

Dining room table, here set for eight, can serve as cake decorating surface for as many as twelve workers.

1951 "Number 2 Ranch" Levittown house as originally built.

Original carport is now new entrance and dining room.

### From Carport to Dining Room!

Imaginative remodeling abounds in Levittown, New York, the private housing community founded in 1947 for families of World War II veterans. The houses, mass-produced (in five years, 18,000 of them were built—a rate of 150 a week) and nearly identical in appearance, have from the start encouraged creative improvements. Today, the Jerry Worthington home bears little resemblance to the original, 1951 "Number 2 Ranch."

Enclosing their carport (see picture above left), the Worthingtons have added an entrance hall and a dining room. They have also extended their kitchen to the front of the house, and their living room to the back, adding a study at the rear.

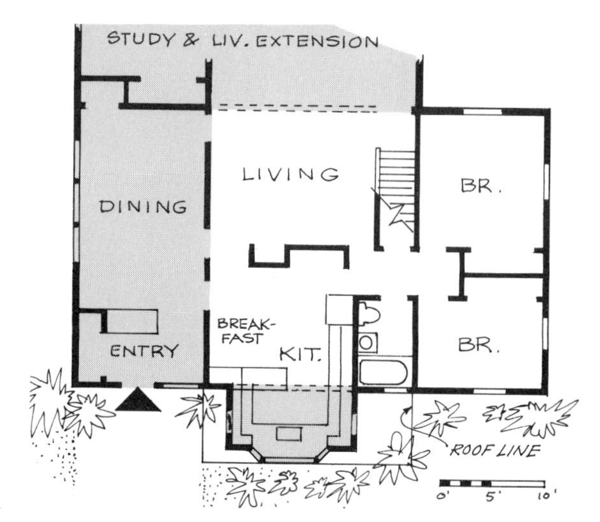

Gracious dining is now enjoyed where car used to stand. Stained-glass windows, at left, were created by Mrs. Worthington. Buffet, foreground left, separates dining room from entrance hall. Guest closet is at left.

## Dining Room with a View Was Formerly a Porch

A desire to extend special summer pleasure into the other three seasons was the basis for home improvement in the home and office of architect Frank Dailey.

The summer enjoyment was that of dining on the porch with a stunning view of a lake. It was decided to enclose the porch and make it the dining room, shown below. Today, through a large window, diners enjoy year-round an ever-changing outdoor scene.

Originally, the Daileys sat down to dinner in a dining area at the kitchen end of the living room. That area now contains a piano. In the remodeling, the doorway from the dining area to the kitchen became a pantry.

Enclosing the porch has actually enhanced the outside appearance of the Dailey house.

Frank Dailey's house, now with enclosed porch.

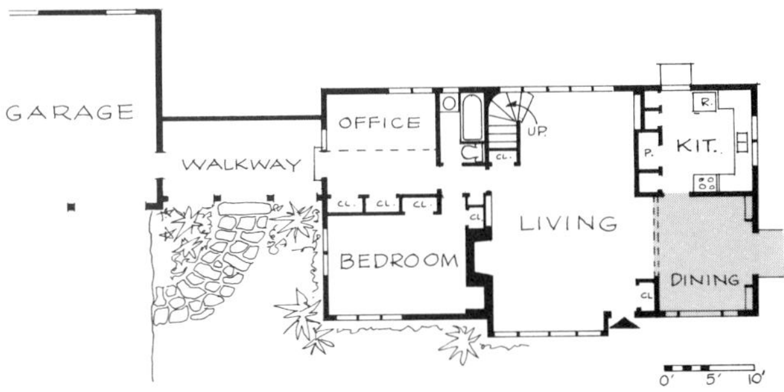


Dining room, below, was formerly porch. Window offers breathtaking view of lake. Glazed door with sidelights lends brightness and airiness to room.

## Dare to Be Different When Dining

The enjoyment of a meal involves more than the meal itself. Atmosphere plays a major role in dining pleasure. We all have restaurants we treasure as much for the ambiance as for the cuisine. For that matter, we sometimes eat out for the atmosphere alone since the food may actually be better at home. We simply like a change of scene when dining.

Dining area variety can be had in the home as well to let you break everyday mealtime routine.

Look for possible new dining spaces in your house. Is there space for a small table in front of the fireplace in the living room? Is there room before the window in the bedroom? Would the richly paneled study be a likely dining area? How about dining in the greenhouse? Be daring when you look!

It might not be the top of the world, but it's pretty high, and dining here on a summer's evening is exhilarating!

Dining is a lush experience in this greenhouse home with tropical paradise of ferns, plants, and bamboo—all year!

## . . . And Enjoyed from the First Cup of Coffee in the Morning

Days get underway with coffee. You can make that first cup special—the day a special day—by having it together in a special place.

That sun-warmed window area in the bedroom might be just the place (bathrobes the attire). It could be, season and weather permitting, the patio or deck, even the pool area. If coffee has always been served in the kitchen breakfast area, why not serve it in the dining room for a change?

Have a different morning!

For morning coffee, dramatic view of city below is thoughtfully provided in this guest room of a Boston apartment.

This "garden room" off a kitchen is a special place to enjoy a cup of coffee or tea—or a meal—no matter what the season.

Coffee served in a formal dining room traditionally used for dinner only can be an elegant change from kitchen coffee.

Kitchen-oriented and ideal for young children, this family room in the contemporary home of the David Helprins is seen across kitchen sink counter. Simple, rugged furniture, fireplace, television set, and family dining/game table add up to inviting informality. Efficient kitchen, below, has open contact with family room. White walls and paintings, instead of cabinets, unite this space with that of family room (see plan opposite page).

# 7.

# A Family Room for a Happier Family

In a real sense, today's family room is a return to yesterday's "sitting room," that room in the home in which the family would gather after supper and chores to be together before bedtime. While Father filled his pipe and Mother threaded her needle, the children did their school lessons or played a quiet game. Unlike the "parlor," the sitting room was informal and warm.

The family room today serves much the same purpose. It's a comfortable room for all to share. It's also, of course, a modern room, usually containing the television set and stereo equipment. And it's often a room for informal snacks and meals. For this reason, a family room is wisely located near the kitchen. Such location has another advantage; since the kitchen is the "command post" of the home, the "commander" (Mother) can know what the troops are up to in the family room.

For parents, the family room can sometimes be a lifesaver. When they need privacy and quiet, not to mention order, they can retreat from their children in the family room to be alone elsewhere—possibly in a living room that stays private, quiet, and orderly only because there's a family room.

The very use of a family room requires that it be furnished simply and ruggedly—in short, practically. Planning for wear and tear should be the rule.

The recreation room, a more isolated area for family activity, will be discussed in the next chapter as a room distinctly different from a family room.

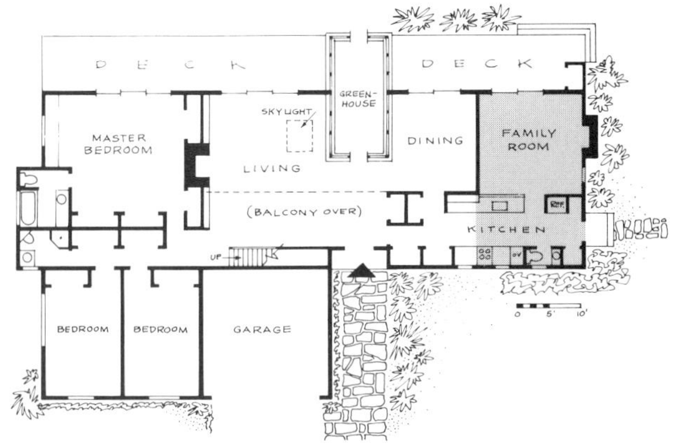


Note family room access to deck, bath, and back door—with no traffic through either living room or dining room.

Family room addition (see opposite page) included extension of kitchen and a half-bath.

Rear deck was extended to serve added family room. Covered buffet is at left.

Mrs. Peter Stearns practices at one of two pianos at bay window end of new family room–music room addition. Room is large enough for recitals for music-loving friends.

## A Special Family Room for a Special Family Use

The Peter Stearns family of Sherman, Connecticut, is a musical family. Peter is a composer, pianist, music teacher, church organist and choir director, and the owner and director of a music publishing company. His wife, Marcia, is a pianist and singer. The Stearns' older daughter, Gloria, 16, plays the violin, and their younger daughter, Ethelyn, 14, like her mother, plays the piano and sings.

When the family planned an addition to their woodland home—formerly a church dating back to 1853—the new space was to be a family room, and their living room was to become a music room.

Feeling themselves "landlocked" at first, they thought small. But, with the services of an architect neighbor and friend, they were able to realize a new room measuring 18′8″ × 27′4″—a room large enough to be a combination family and music room. The living room became a library.

Stearns' addition as it harmonizes with old house in the background.

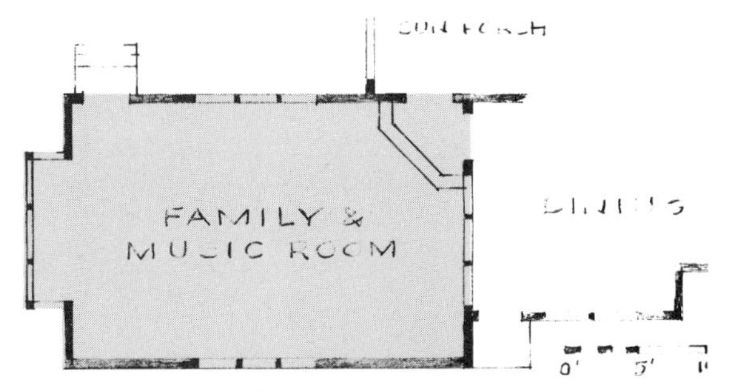


Steps lead up from the Stearns' new family room for access to both dining room and porch. Note windows between dining room and new room.

## Old English Comfort for Basement Family Room

In the basement below their living room, a commercial pilot and his wife have created a strikingly handsome family room opening onto a brick terrace. They call it their "moot hall," from the Anglo-Saxon word meaning "to meet."

Dominating the room is an oversized fieldstone fireplace. Furniture is rugged. A cowhide rug on the simulated brick flooring adds Old World charm to the room. Natural lighting floods the room through the ample window space.

Beyond the furnace and utility area, the other half of the basement is closed off to form a "his and hers" workshop.

The remarkable fact is that the couple did it all themselves!

This family room has direct access to brick terrace under deck. Note wood supply for large fireplace in "moot hall."

Old English solidity is conveyed in fieldstone fireplace and heavy wooden furniture. Cowhide under table adds primitive touch to otherwise thoroughly civilized room. Couple made their new room—all of it—by themselves.

## From Modest Garage to Colonial Comfort

For the Phil Birkets their family room is not only a place to dine and relax but one in which to display, use, and enjoy their new hobby—collecting American antiques.

Garage, breezeway, and family entrance were incorporated into the Birket family room, and their small, "problem" kitchen was opened up to the new living space in the process. (The pitcher and bowl, in the foreground of the bottom picture, rest on the counter that divides the family room from the kitchen.)

Family dining is gracious at the colonial dropleaf table, and the old wood-burning stove economically heats the room. The Birkets enjoy a special comfort.

DINING
KIT.
FAMILY ROOM
CL.
LIVING RM.
0 5' 10'

Family entrance to breezeway will be softened with appropriate plantings. Former garage, now family room, at right.

Warmth of Americana, including genuine heat of old stove, pervades Birket family room. Use of antiques adds to enjoyment. Meals at the colonial table are special meals in special ambiance. Photo taken from former problem kitchen.

Looking down stairway from bedroom floor into family room. Stairs to right lead down to kitchen.

Two-story wing, with family room above garage, ties in tastefully with lines of this fine old colonial.

## New England Colonial Gets Garage—Plus

When Dennis Murphy inherited the old family home in Litchfield, Connecticut, his first thought was, "A nice place to visit, but I wouldn't want to live there." He liked his efficient ranch house.

But his wife and the two Murphy boys loved the tree-shaded street in the old part of town, and they all remembered the warmth of the house.

When they moved in, there was quite a bit of refurbishing to do. The only addition they planned was a two-car garage, but Mrs. Murphy suggested that a two-story addition would look better in their neighborhood of fine old New England homes and would also give them a good-sized space for a family room.

The difference in grade level where the garage was to be added was turned into an asset. The family room is six steps up from the kitchen and six steps down from the bedroom floor—inviting either way.

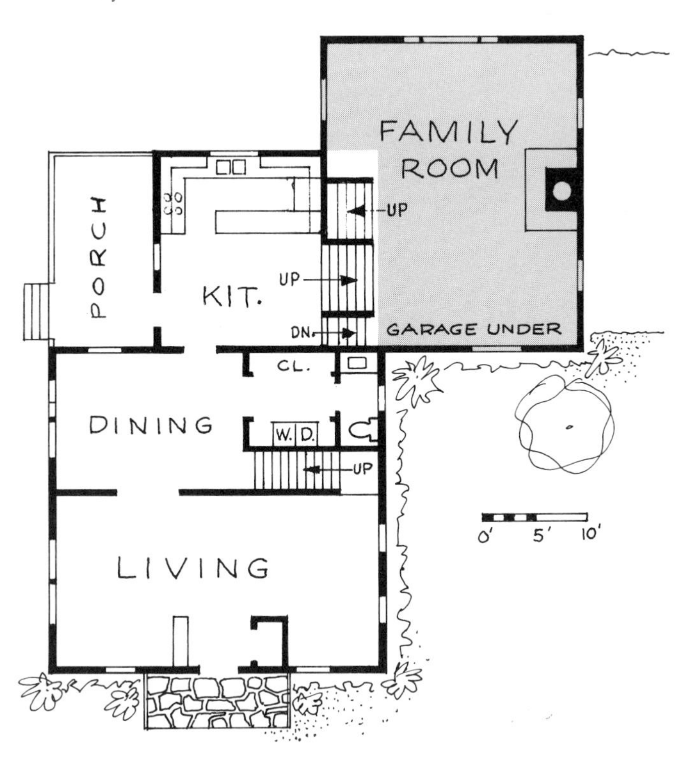

Though small in size, Jalbert family room is large in usefulness, serving as library, TV room, dining room, and entertainment center.

## The Many-Faceted Family Room of the David Jalberts

Where once a woodshed stood, there now stands the most used room in the Connecticut hills home of Mr. and Mrs. David Jalbert.

This family room also serves as library, television room, and informal dining room. Modest in size (12′ × 16′) but elegant in ambiance, it's the room where people naturally cluster at a party.

As can be seen in the "after" picture bottom right, the converted and enlarged wing makes use of the patio as a private outdoor living area. The doorway (the back door of the house) leads through a good-sized back entrance hall directly into the kitchen.

Woodshed before becoming Jalbert family room.

Woodshed turned family room with remodeling.

## The Family Room for Entertaining

For the family with children in their preteens, a family room begins to serve a special dual purpose.

As children grow socially, they come to need a place of their own in which to entertain friends. A family room is just such a place. The young people might play a quiet game; they might watch TV or listen to records; they might have a snack, even a meal; or they might just lie around and chat. What's important to them is that they don't have to share space with grown-ups—it's a comfortable way to be. More and more as they grow older, they'll need this independent condition.

When adults entertain, too, the family room can be put to good use. If a family entertains another family, it can be a common place of retreat for all the children while the adults enjoy the living room. If adults entertain other adults, and the children aren't present, the family room can serve as an additional area for guests to gather, an overflow space for a large party. Guests like to move from group to group and from room to room.

If the social affair is an informal one, entertaining could be confined to the family room, with neither the living room nor the dining room needed to be used.

Of course, the best entertaining in the home is the family entertaining itself—which is what the family room is essentially all about.

Usually the most economical new family living space is to be found in basement. Curtained recess with back light suggests sliding glass doors. Fireplace is electric. Photograph courtesy of Armstrong Cork Company.

# 8.
# And . . . a Recreation Room

Not every family needs, or wants, a recreation room, but many a home would do well to include one. If you have children, whether toddlers or teenagers, such a casual place for them to "rattle around" in is a definite plus. It's even more valuable if family members love games and indoor sports, pursue hobbies, or like to entertain informally. For a wide range of family activity, a recreation room can multiply the pleasure possibilities of your home.

## Modest Investment

One of the biggest selling points of the recreation room is the modest investment involved in adding one to your home. You probably have the space for it already—perhaps in your basement or attic—space currently being wasted. (Since improvements in either area don't enlarge your house in most cases, taxes won't increase.) Furthermore, such a project offers an opportunity for creative planning and do-it-yourself work. In a recreation room, the imperfect joint or the extra nail hole can be shrugged off as no big thing.

The pictures above and opposite tell a dramatic attic story. Designed by Louisa Cowin for Armstrong Cork Company, this playroom for two boys was given a Tom Sawyer–Huck Finn atmosphere.

The first step was to install batt insulation between the rafters. Next, a durable ceiling was formed by nailing on furring strips and stapling over them wood-grained "planks." The columns and beams, nonstructural and less expensive than solid beams, are 1″ × 4″ pine stock nailed together, to give the room architectural interest as well as the look of strength. The picket fence makes a unique headboard for each bed and, for window access, opens at the center on hinges. The storage bins, bed platforms, rugged desk, "raft" center table, and easy-to-clean, tough floor coverings make this out-of-the-way room a joy for boys and parents alike.

## Planning the Recreation Area

The cardinal rule for the planning of a recreation room is to make it indestructible!

Begin by listing all the family activities the area will be expected to accommodate. Then plan the size, shape, sub areas, access ways, and furnishings. Ideally, the recreation room should be flexible and capable of meeting the changing needs of your growing family.

Access should be easy and safe. For attics, if possible, make a narrow, steep stairway wider and less steep. An outside stairway with a balcony or landing at the attic floor level might well be considered if it can be put at the back of the building, and will not detract from the appearance of the house. A balcony would be pleasant to use in fair weather, and the stairway would be added convenience. A dead-end basement is highly undesirable and can be opened up with a stairway to the out-of-doors. On a hillside lot, a downhill grade level door should be installed, even if this involves removing soil to achieve a ground level slightly lower than the basement floor.

Best recreation room floor coverings are vinyl-asbestos or cushioned vinyl tile, waterproof indoor-outdoor carpeting, and pattern-dyed polypropylene carpet (psychologists claim that carpeted surroundings encourage civilized behavior).

Durable walls can be created with tough paneling or vinyl or scrubbable wallpaper. For washable painted surfaces, use enamel paint, which comes in glossy or satin finish.

Ceilings should be light in appearance, and since you're probably starting with rafters or joists, recessed and flush lighting fixtures would be practical. Don't skimp on insulation, especially in an attic room. In a basement room, it's needed in the ceiling to reduce noise.

Ideal furnishings will be sturdy, durable and washable, yet comfortable. Vinyl-covered upholstered chairs and couches meet these requirements. Consider multiuse furnishings such as a convertible sofa, a backless bench for seating from either side, and square seat cushions that can be laid out as "sectional" furniture. A recreation area is a good place to use old or second-hand furniture, but built-in counters or desks should have plastic surfaces. Clear polyurethane applied to wood or painted wood surfaces makes a tough finish.

The most pleasing color schemes for a recreation area are light and bright, particularly for a basement. A decorating "theme" is fun, but it's well to remember that a family's activities change as children grow, and decor tastes change with them. Color schemes should be adaptable.

Light from the outdoors can be gained in attics with added dormers, skylights, or more economical windows installed in the gable ends. In basements, where windows may be small, block and even cement foundations can be pierced for more window area. An enlarged basement window in a windowwell can be hooded by glass to serve as a greenhouse or hot frame. In any case, plan ample artificial light for a recreation room. Flush fluorescent ceiling fixtures are efficient and economical. "Fake" picture windows with indirect light on painted or photographic murals can be effective.

A rec room should have its own climate controls. Auxiliary heat, a fireplace or a wood-burning stove, could be considered. A small electric wall heater might be enough for a basement. Certainly, a basement should have a dehumidifier. An attic should be equipped with an exhaust fan system, as should cooking areas and lavatories in the basement.

Plan on generous storage areas in both attic and basement renovations.

Remember that recreation means freedom to move about, in and out. If possible, a recreation room should open onto an outdoor living area. If you're converting a garage into a recreation room, consider retaining a garage door that can be opened onto a patio on the cement apron.

The recreation room is to be enjoyed. Use it in good health!

"Treehouse" playroom for children uses available garage loft space. Note fun means of access, positioned out of way. Gable window serves to light playroom and to offer view of drive. Attractive feature is out-of-the-way privacy.

Points to keep in mind for attic hobby area. Plan generous storage space; use gable end windows to avoid more costly dormer additions; ceilings can be painted, or insulation with panels between or covering rafters can be installed.

Attic retreat, remodeled and furnished for reading, TV watching, and fireside conversation. Free-standing fireplace at left is pre-fab from mail order house, requiring roof-top chimney kit. Hole was cut in ceiling and roof. For noncombustible hearth, shallow box was built, lined with asbestos, and filled with pebbles. Scheme illustrates how much can be had in so little space—available and otherwise wasted space at that. Photograph courtesy of Armstrong Cork Company.

Former garage is now recreation room for family's twelve children. Picture window wall replaced overhead doors. Entrance from new mud room is in background to left. Note recreational facilities and rough furniture meant to take abuse.

## Semi-Attached Garage Turns into Teenage "Rock" Room

The problem was music. With a dozen children in the family, there was little time when the stereo in the living room wasn't playing the sounds teenagers love to hear. The solution for the parents was a place the children could call their own, for music and for other youthful activities. The oversize, two-car garage was converted into a "rock" room, with stereo, TV, and furniture built to take the wear and tear.

The overhead doors gave way to a wall with a large picture window. An entrance mud room was added when the breezeway was enclosed to join the garage to the house. The mud room contains a long work bench, a storage closet for tools, a built-in coat rack, and bins for boots. At the same time, the garage was extended ten feet at the back for a separate, concrete-floored room for more rugged activity. Both rooms are heated electrically. A powder room hallway provides access from one room to the other.

Game end of recreation room has snooker pool table and bench for model building. Note recessed lighting in ceiling.

Converted garage as seen from former driveway, now basketball area. Entrance/mud room was added when breezeway was enclosed.

## Basement Bonanza

This basement space was transformed from a clutter collector to an Irish pub. Called a "Hibernian Hideaway" by the designer at Armstrong Cork Company, it's a recreation area for the older "boys." A separate ping-pong room is located at the other end of the basement.

A recreation room is a good place to carry out fun ideas. Note the whiskey-barrel game table base in the background. Fabric borders stretched over plywood framing outline the small casement windows, and lace café curtains make them look deceptively large. Second-hand chairs, spray-painted and padded with denim cushions, and the vinyl-asbestos floor tile in Oak Knoll heighten the pub effect.

Before remodeling, this unfinished basement was "catch-all" for family paraphernalia.

With imaginative renovation, former basement becomes enchanting retreat for family and friends. Clever, inexpensive decorating ideas are key to spirited Irish pub theme. Photographs courtesy of Armstrong Cork Company.

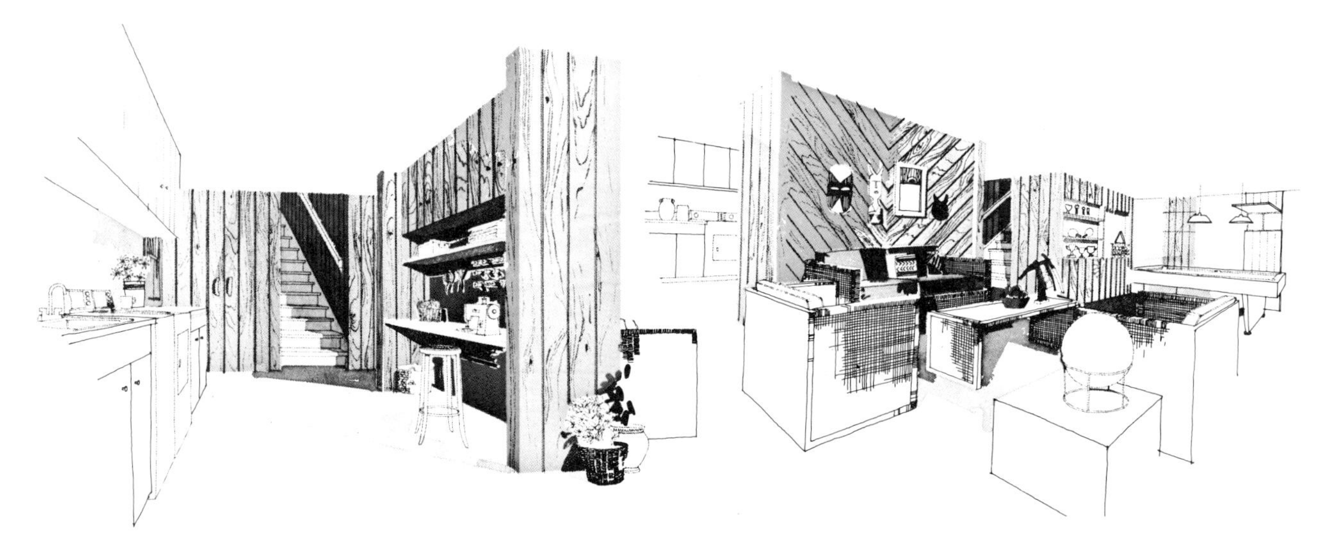

## Multipurpose Basement

Planned as a multipurpose space, this small ranch house basement has been divided into two distinct areas—a work area and a recreation area.

The work area, top left, is screened from the rest of the basement by a partition which contains the sewing center facing the laundry. Cabinets, shelves, and pegs above the sewing counter hold fabrics, equipment, and sewing aids. The laundry is located opposite the sewing center, with enough room between the two for easy movement. Stairs and the utility room are in the background.

The recreation area, top right, is subdivided into a game space with a billiard table at one end, and a sitting space with sturdy furniture for conversation and TV watching.

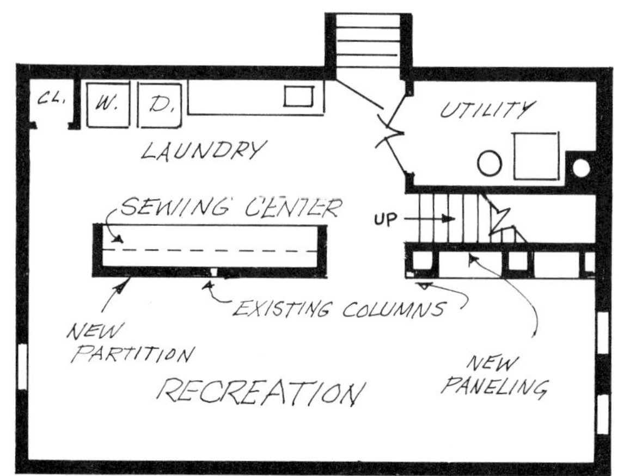


The plan drawing above shows how the partitions have been placed to include the existing pipe columns, leaving the remodeled area free of any obstructions.

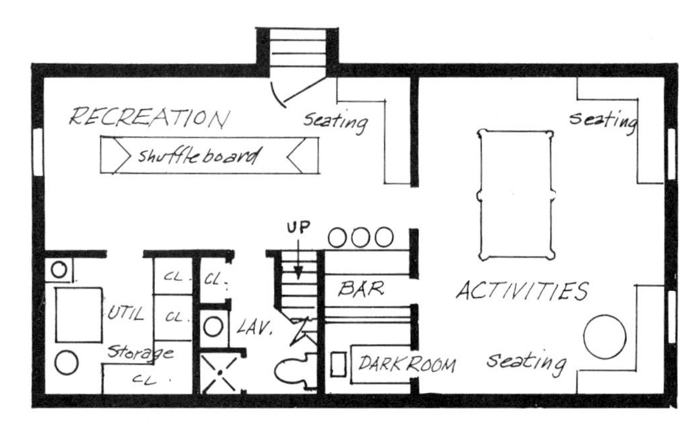


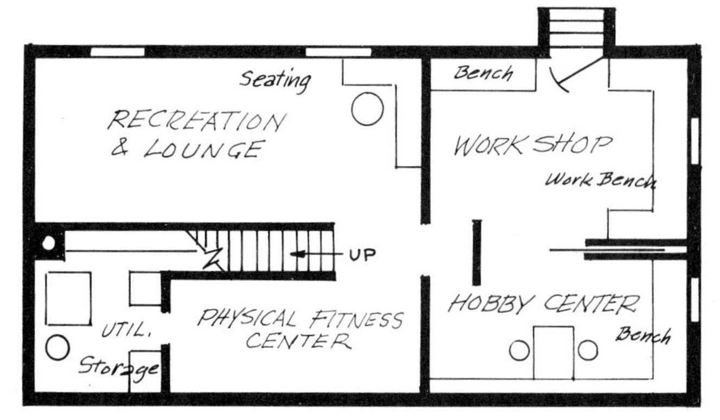


Typical plans for basement recreation activity. Note, in each case, how most important activity is given largest space and how various activities are separated from each other. Note especially, at right, how partition and pocket door separate workshop. Both plans indicate that basement space—in part or in whole—is space to be used for family work and play.

## Activities and Space Considerations

A recreation room, as has been noted, is an area in the home for games, indoor sports, and hobbies. It's a room for fun with the family and with friends.

Activities can include everything from the currently popular TV-video contests to the enduring challenge of Monopoly or Scrabble, from pool through darts to ping-pong, from model building to model railroading. The successful recreation room plans distinct areas for different activities.

Boys' end of this basement makes most of available space for multiple youthful activities. Note convenient and economical storage of sports equipment and games on wall. Note, too, reading and study table in background. Recessed lighting evenly illuminates ping-pong table. Photograph courtesy of Armstrong Cork Company.

Special planning is required for both pool and ping-pong. Since each involves player movement, space for the movement needs to be provided. There's nothing as frustrating as drawing back a cue stick only to strike a wall, unless it's slamming into a wall with a paddle in your hand.

Standard pool or billiard table sizes are, from large to small, 5′9″ × 10′9″, 5′3″ × 9′9″, and 4′9″ × 8′9″. A minimum of five feet of space around any size table is recommended. The areas, then, for the activity should be roughly 16′ × 21′ for the largest table and 15′ × 20′ for either of the smaller ones. It's worth noting that pool and billiards are also spectator sports, if only for the player awaiting his turn. Thoughtful planning provides sitting space. High benches along a wall or tall stools make for excellent viewing.

For table tennis, standard table sizes are 5′ × 9′ and 4′ × 8′. Here, recommended space around the table is seven feet at the ends and four at the sides for the larger size, and five feet at the ends and three at the sides for the smaller size. The areas would be 13′ × 23′ and 10′ × 18′ for the large and small sizes respectively.

Another indoor sport commonly found in recreation rooms is shuffleboard, which also requires special planning. Dimensions are 52′0″ × 6′0″, with recommendations of two and a half feet at the ends and two feet at the sides. Indoors, the court is usually shortened.

Whatever the activity, be sure to plan storage space for materials and equipment. You'll want ample shelves, drawers, and bins for them to be out of the way when not in use but conveniently at hand.

If the recreation room is to be used for adult entertaining, planning might well include a bar and eating counter. If so, plan the bar as near to existing plumbing as possible. An indoor barbecue is a plus in any recreation room.

A reminder! Keep in mind that ideally a recreation room is flexible, to change as the family grows. Plan, for example, so that the model train area can become the "pub" area. Don't lock yourself in like the parents who furnished their children's playroom with Lilliputian-size furniture—built-in!

Good living and repose is expressed in good patio planning. The outdoors invites lounging, dining, exercise, good health.

# 9.
# Decks and Patios... Where the Livin' Is Easy

The deck and the patio, perhaps more than any other living space you plan, should express freedom.

Here, nature works with you. Your deck or patio starts partially or fully open to the sky, and most patio sites are free from confining walls. Naturally, you'll start with one wall—the house. Two walls, or an ell, can be an advantage in providing privacy and protection from wind and afternoon sun. Some part of the deck or patio should, of course, provide protection from the midday sun and from rain. Don't deny yourself the delight of sitting outside through a brief shower on a hot summer day! Overhead protection could be in the form of a large umbrella, a canvas panel, an awning, or an extended roof overhang.

Freedom from upkeep is also important. Stone, brick, and natural and stained wood surfaces need little care. Sealers preserve exposed wood. Rugged furniture, shrubs, and perennial plants all contribute to that invitation to relax.

Combination deck and patio invites freedom of movement by its uncluttered look and generous proportions. Privacy and party possibilities are included in design. Photographs courtesy of California Redwood Assn.

Before: Undistinguished front yard of this average-looking California suburban house lacks charm and needed living space. After: Low-cost redwood deck creates comfortable outdoor living area and attractive entrance approach.

Before: Unattractive and unused backyard. After: Deck with storage unit buffet adds outdoor dining area and lounging space, at the same time concealing air conditioner and drainage ditch.

Before: Backyard of this suburban house lacks character. After: Simple 10′ × 12′ barbecue deck adds outdoor space and a look of quality. A deck can be your most economical and enjoyable addition. Photographs courtesy of California Redwood Assn.

When a deck is this close to the ground, extra freedom is expressed by no railing. Ease of maintenance is obvious.

## The Deck Offers Instant Escape

The new deck space, above, adds a new dimension of freedom, the greatest gift that a patio or a deck gives a home. The untreated wood gradually weathers to a soft, driftwood gray, in this case complementing the seaside scene.

Wood, as the picture to the right illustrates, is just as much at home inland. Stained here, it blends into its forest setting. Wood decks are the obvious solution for outdoor living on difficult hillside sites.

Generous 640 square feet of versatile living space out of a previously little-used sloping back yard.

This city roof garden, one of many attractive sitting areas at the Wilfred Gargen public relations penthouse office in Manhattan, is available as a locale for clients' advertising photographs (see page 13).

This deck can be reached from kitchen, dining room, and family room. Sheep wire temporarily attached to pipe railing ensures safe use of deck by toddlers.

Deck adds elegant outdoor living to development home. Note sliding glass door access from family room. Kitchen door is at the left. Photograph courtesy of California Redwood Assn.

Cool patio was converted from carport to include open deck for sunning and better view of Sun City, Arizona, golf course. Great Western Remodelers executed this stylish extra.

A patio plus is effected through the use of transluscent fiberglass reinforced panels, for light with shelter. Construction is simple, benefits on hot or rainy days obvious.

Retractable awnings protect deck from midday sun. Sliding glass door leads to dining room, family room–kitchen, and living room.

New Orleans style serpentine wall of old brick enclosed this patio. Gates open onto outdoor activity areas.

## Outdoor Living Is Compatible with Any Architectural Style

A flagstone or brick patio with appropriate shrubs will go with modern, conventional, or period house styles. Cement and patio tile look fine with a modern home. Astroturf and indoor-outdoor carpeting can add an element of luxury to any patio.

Don't skimp on size. Trees and planter beds can be incorporated into your design. Large potted shrubs should be considered, too. Cement well-tile pipes make good planters for small trees. They come in 24″, 30″, and 36″ diameters and in various lengths starting at 18″. They can be painted to blend with your color scheme.

When adding a deck or patio it's often possible to plan access to it from more than one room. A deck or patio will give a family the most service when it can be reached from the following rooms:

A. The kitchen. Outdoor dining when the weather is inviting is always a treat. Breakfast in the morning sun—what a way to start your day! For entertaining, whether it's cocktails or a cookout, you should have access to your kitchen.

B. The family room. The usable space for family and youth activities is expanded by easy access to a patio or deck.

C. The dining room. Access to the deck or patio is great for cocktails before dinner, and especially for expansive entertaining.

D. The bedroom. To be able to step out of your bedroom onto a patio or deck for a morning stretch or deep breathing—perhaps even a few push-ups—is always exhilarating. And breakfast on the patio with your spouse and a few well chosen plants—not bad!

E. Bathrooms? Yes, we've seen an increasing number of walled garden patios that are reached only from the bathroom. The sunbathing possibilities are obvious. Often, a picture window on the tub wall contributes to the back-to-nature enjoyment.

Lofty pine-paneled ceiling gives this new bedroom spaciousness, while sliding glass door and large windows permit abundant natural light. Door opens to balcony with expansive view of countryside.

# 10. The Bedroom—for Comfort and Joy

The bedroom, more than any other room of the home, should offer comfort, quiet, and security.

Bedrooms are special rooms. We start and end our day in them and spend a third of our life in them. We share them as we share no other room. Bedrooms require special planning attention.

## Problems of Space

Most bedroom problems are those of space—existing space is either insufficient or inefficiently used.

Any bedroom should have room for more than just bed and bureau. Small children need room for play, for a toy box or shelves for games, puzzles, and books. Older children need room for school work—for a desk or table and chair and bookshelves. Adults, too, need room for a dressing table, a desk and chair, an easy chair. An 8′ × 10′ bedroom has space for a single bed and little else by way of furniture.

Another space consideration is important. For just plain convenience when making or changing a bed, there should be space on either side of a bed and at its foot to work. A bed with one side against a wall is an everyday and a once-a-week headache. A double bed with a side against a wall is nothing less than an obstacle course for the inside sleeper!

Bedrooms, like living rooms, should be planned around the furniture. The furniture, notably the bed, whenever possible should dictate the placement of windows, doors, and closets. Windows should be planned so that no furniture is put in front of them. Beds especially should be away from windows to avoid drafts. They should also be away from heating units, which should be located along outside walls, preferably under windows.

## Lighting

Lighting in the bedroom is simply planned. A table lamp for general illumination should plug into an electrical outlet controllable by a wall switch at the door. Bed tables need lamps. A floor lamp will serve an easy chair. Reading lamps over the bed are convenient. Outlets in the bedroom should be planned not only for lamps but also for such appliances as hairdryers and electric blankets, not to mention television sets.

## Closets

Ample closet space is a bedroom must. For each adult using the room, there should be a closet six feet in width. Children, especially smaller ones, can often share a closet using two clothing rods, one over the other. Bifolding closet doors are best, since they open for full access to closet space. A ceiling light in a closet is advisable.

## Bath and Dressing Room

A bedroom with bath is convenient, and one with both bath and dressing room is downright luxurious. The privacy, comfort, and convenience of a bedroom suite are powerful arguments for its consideration. Furthermore, a dressing room relieves a bedroom of closet requirements, so that the addition of a dressing room to a bedroom enlarges a bedroom. Certainly, any planning for a new bedroom in the home ought to include a long look at such a luxury.

The best floor cover for an adult's bedroom is carpeting. It's warm, soft, and quiet, and easy to care for. Carpeting throughout a bedroom suite is elegant. While a more durable surface might be wanted in a child's bedroom, it should be pointed out that carpeting offers cushioning for tumbles.

## Other Considerations

Bedrooms should be as bright and airy as possible. Long windows and cross ventilation help achieve these conditions. Bedroom orientation is important. In general, orientation to the northeast is best. You wake to sunlight and go to sleep in coolness. Unless you have air conditioning or stiff ocean breezes, orientation to the south results in too much heat in summer. The same is true with a western orientation, which also makes a bedroom cold in winter.

## A Route for Escape

Consider a master bedroom suite designed, furnished, and decorated to be that place in which to "retreat," to get away from it all.

We have all felt the relief, when on a trip, of settling into a comfortable motel room to spend time unwinding from the day's driving before turning in for the night. There was no need or desire to go out, and, showered and dressed for bed, it was almost luxurious just to lounge around—sitting at the desk to write postcards, lying on top of the bed-clothes with a good book or magazine, or maybe sitting in an easy chair watching the local news.

How much better such carefree use of a room would be if it were your room, planned in every way by you for you. T.V., radio, stereo, choicc of reading matter, *your* chair—even a hobby area.

And a snack or drink only as far as the kitchen at that!

Bedrooms can vary dramatically. In house formerly a barn, bedroom addition is part of "everything" room. Sitting area in foreground has fireplace, behind camera.

This bedroom suggests security of a fortress. Deep textures of cut stone wall, sculptured carpet, carved wooden divider (at right), and quilted spread combine for masculine solidity.

## Desire for Greenhouse Leads to Master Bedroom

For the Cleveland Feussiniches, it all began with plants. In the early summer of 1970, Mr. Feussinich promised his wife that by winter she would have that greenhouse she'd always wanted. By fall, his wife's wish was one for a greenhouse–breakfast room, a "garden" room. Mr. Feussinich himself had long wanted a darkroom. Planning for their wants, the couple expanded their thinking—the end result being a two-story addition to their fine old home that contains not only the garden room and darkroom but a new master bedroom with bath and walk-in closet as well. The designer for the addition was J. T. Sadler, Jr.

The new bedroom suite, above the garden room, is airy and bright (see the opening bedroom photo). Distinctive in the room is the high ceiling paneled in pine. (The addition sports a hip roof.) A sliding glass door unit on the south wall for sunlight and warmth opens onto a balcony containing planters and offers a splendid view of the countryside. Large windows on the east and west walls add brightness. Furniture is limited for an increased feeling of spaciousness. Wall-to-wall carpeting adds both elegance and comfort.

With the addition, the former master bedroom (see plan) became a welcome guest room. A smaller bedroom was converted to provide hall space and space for Mr. Feussinich's darkroom.

The Fuessinich experience—from plants to a two-story addition—attests to the solidly good sense of "thinking big" when thinking of home improvement. Needs and desires were established with time and care, and the happy conclusion was a realized plan that met each and every one. How much more than a greenhouse they have to enjoy!

Two-story addition contrasts dramatically with lines of old colonial. Maximum use of glass opens rooms to the outdoors for bright, cheerful living.

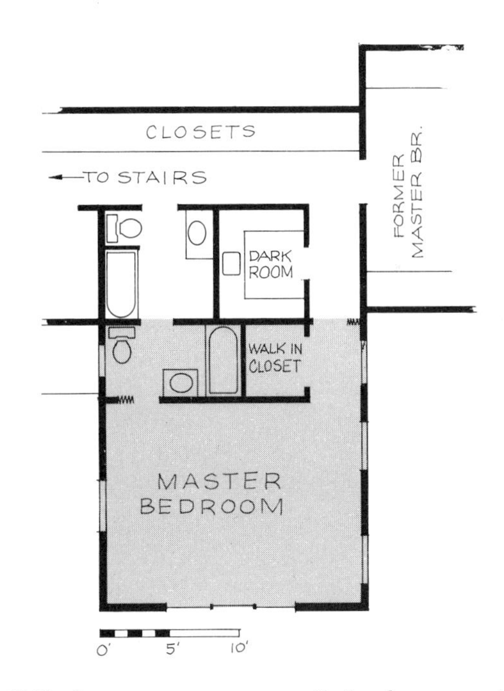


Old bathroom serves new rooms. Pocket door connects with new bathroom for housekeeping convenience. New darkroom plumbing hooked up to old bathroom plumbing.

Barn doors open one wall of bedroom to screened porch and valley view. Gentle pitch of beamed ceiling directs interest to view and adds to feeling of spaciousness.

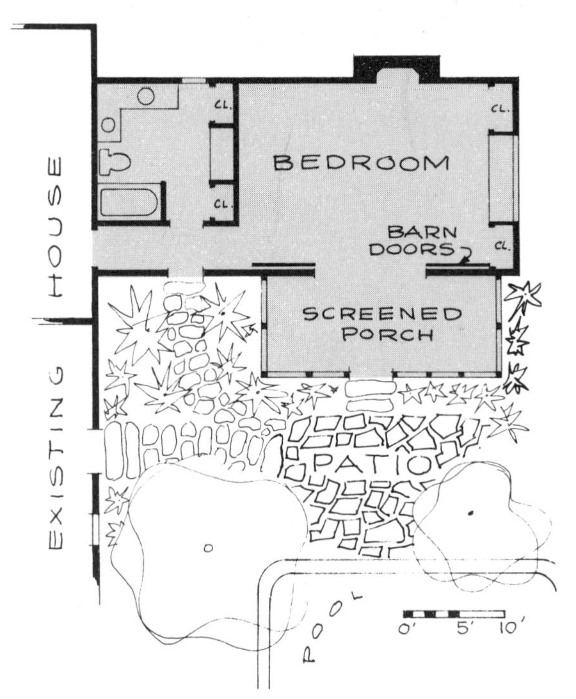


## Sliding "Barn Doors" Open Bedroom Wing to View

Mrs. Charlotte Pratt's love for the outdoors—for gardening and swimming, for reading or entertaining on a patio—determined the design of her bedroom wing addition. The generously proportioned wing, with sliding "barn doors" on the view side, lets all of the outdoors in. A screened porch, planned for protected sitting, soon became a favorite informal eating place as well. The

Barn doors, between bedroom and screened porch, are weather-stripped for snugness in winter. Note fireplace on opposite wall.

Bedroom wing, with shed roof, blends with old country house and provides additional privacy for patio of used brick.

porch overlooks the patio, gardens, the swimming pool, and a distant valley.

A fireplace and comfortable chairs make the bedroom a cozy retreat for reading or just relaxing, no matter what season.

Included in the new wing is a large master bath. Note in the plan the easy access to the bath from the patio and pool.

The screened porch serves as a weather break in the winter and a place to keep firewood free of snow and ice. The porch floor is bluestone flag in cement.

## Small Antique House Gets Big Master Bedroom—Harmoniously

When the George Regans decided to enlarge their country weekend house for full-time living, and perhaps retirement, the first improvement was to be a larger bedroom on the ground floor. The addition could also include a downstairs bathroom. Originally, the small farmhouse had neither.

Designer Bill Corrigan planned the tasteful addition on a back corner of the house.

New bedroom wing blends gracefully with small antique house. Glassed-in porch at opposite side of house helps balance architectural appearance.

Bedroom addition has bow window on south wall, making it always sunny and cheerful.

So located, the new space would be subordinated to the old, even though the addition was almost as long as the main house. Happily, only one window, in the dining room, was lost in the process.

With the new master bedroom, the two small upstairs bedrooms and bath now make ideal guest accommodations.

The new bath has linen and storage closets, and the laundry is concealed behind folding doors. The current trend is to place the laundry near the bedrooms; it makes good sense.

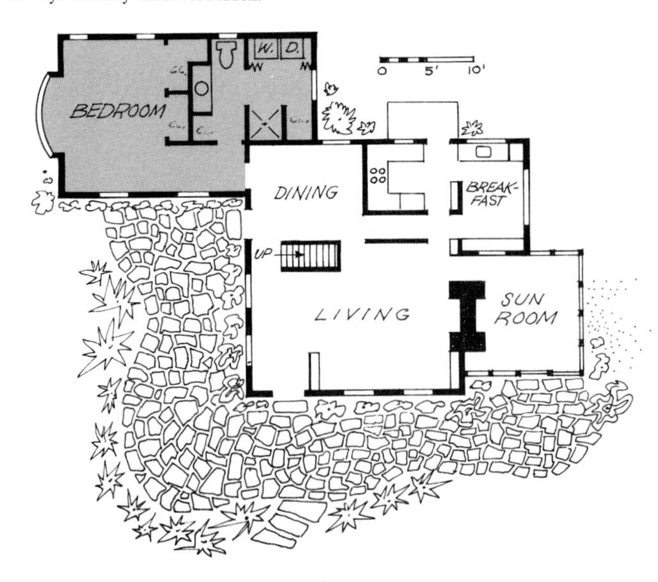

## Raising Half the Roof to Get Balcony Bedroom

When the Irwin Strongwaters moved their bedroom to the balcony of their hillside "Chalet" vacation home, they opened up their house to exciting new living space.

Originally, the balcony had been usable only as a storage loft. With the remodeling, half of the roof was raised to provide height enough for the bedroom area, a dressing area, a bathroom, and a study.

On the main floor, walls came down for a greatly enlarged living room with fireplace, a dining area, and a new kitchen open to the living room and with access to the deck and an eating area. The main floor bath was relocated, and access to the balcony—spiral staircase replacing stairs—moved to one side. A second spiral staircase, tucked neatly into a corner, leads to a lower level. Entry, which had been through the kitchen, is now into the spacious living room.

Under the new roof on three sides, rows of windows brighten the whole interior.

House with raised roof as seen from road.

Expanded living room with open kitchen in background.

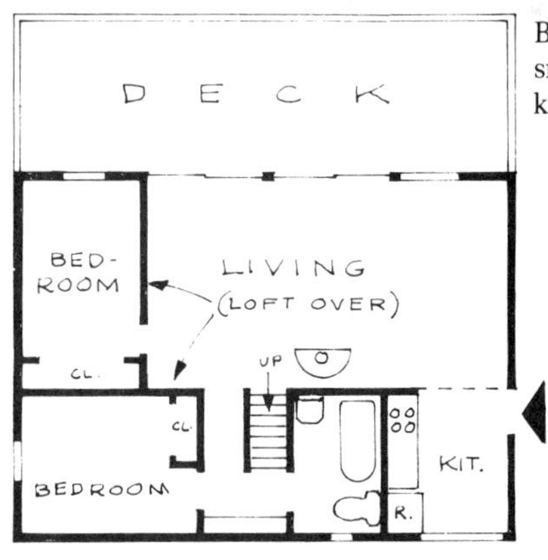


Before: under storage loft were two small bedrooms, bath, and "camp" kitchen in entrance area.

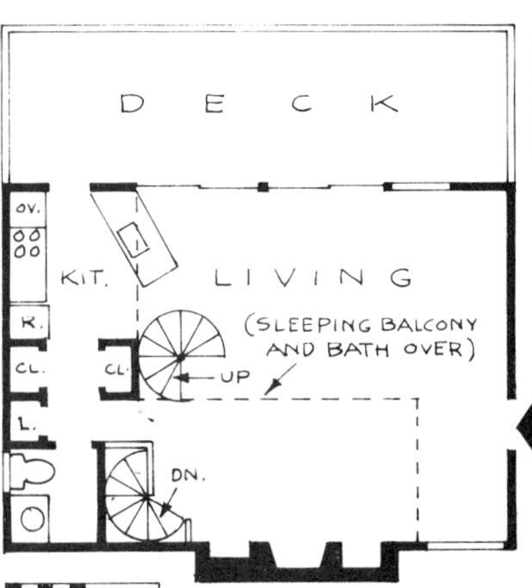


After: kitchen is open and has access to deck. And, except for bath, rest of this level is one big living room with huge fireplace under balcony.

New master bedroom has wood stove, bi-fold louver shutters, and skylight with simple window shade to control light. In background is door to deck with "hot tub."

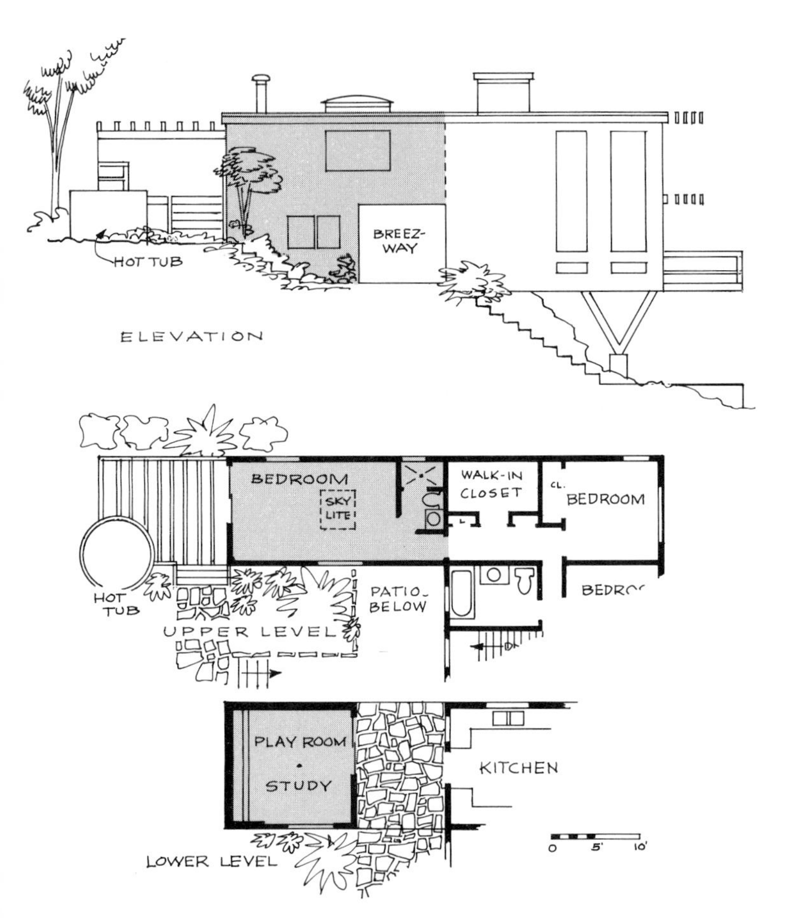


## Bedroom Wing Planned for Comfort and Health

Just off Grizzly Peak Boulevard, overlooking the city of Berkeley and the Pacific Ocean, Dr. and Mrs. Harold S. Newman added a master bedroom and bath to their home that separates them from the activity of their children. In the process a good contemporary house became an exciting indoor-outdoor environment.

Architect Peter Schneider took advantage of a steep slope, designing the new bedroom as a bridge from the second story of the existing house to the uphill terrace. Under the "bridge" is an open breezeway off the kitchen, and across this space is a playroom which will someday become an office or studio for Mrs. Newman's interests.

Installation of hot tub is supervised by architect while owner looks on in anticipation.

Hot tub is flush with bench on far side. Hydro-massage jet stirs water. Bedroom door at right.

Behind dresser wall is master bath. Through door is short hall to existing house with linen, storage, and walk-in closets on left. Note angled bathroom door for "softer" corner.

Beyond sliding glass doors on the uphill end of the bedroom is a deck. An oriental, redwood "hot tub" provides relaxing and therapeutic bathing experience, for both family and friends. Plans are for the deck to be expanded to wrap around the six-foot-diameter tub.

When the new space was added, a small, 8′ × 11′ bedroom was converted into a large walk-in closet and access hall to the new bedroom with linen and storage closets.

Simple lines of new master bath are brightened by generous skylight over white countertop.

Bed arrangement offers convenience for dressers on different walls. Below, guest room makes room for master bedroom closet.

## Two and a Half Small Rooms Combine for Master Suite

The challenge for the Dennis Murphys was to convert an old Victorian home, inherited from parents, into a house that would both function for a family with three small children and reflect good taste and adult comfort. They wanted their bedroom, too, to be a reflection of their love of elegance and fine living.

Neither of the two front bedrooms had closets. To retain the size of the room that would serve as the master bedroom, a generous walk-in closet was created from space taken from the other room. The other room, now a guest room, also gained a closet.

A small third room became the master bath, the ultimate in luxury with a 5′ × 7′ tub (described in Chapter 12). The master bedroom itself has a vanity sink–dressing table, equipped with a retractable spray nozzle for shampooing, and theatrical dressing room make-up lights. Swagged drapes and a boldly patterned bedspread put the focus where it belongs.

## Bachelor Bedroom—Simple and Open

When Allen Heimlick and architect Hal Caulfield focused their creativity on the simple farmhouse shown below left, the result was a bachelor bedroom with bath that is bright and warm and that opens onto a porch sitting area.

The bedroom, above, is on the upper level of a connecting building between the house and a barn, which is now a studio. The sliding glass doors lead to a porch at the rear of the house. On the opposite wall is a room-length, built-in dresser with a mirror in the center and casement windows on either side. To the right is a dressing area and bath, and a hall leading to the library, kitchen, and dining room.

Two good-sized bedrooms on the upper level of the house are now attractive guest rooms.

"Before" picture shows farmhouse from rear. Entrance is at other end on lower level.

"After" picture shows porch facing backyard. Sliding glass doors to master bedroom are at right.

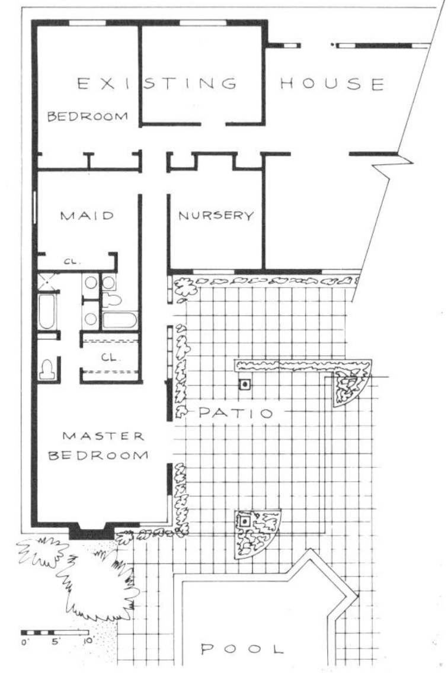

New wing addition, top, encloses and shades patio area at poolside. Natural wood and fireplace add charm to new master bedroom. Glass French doors at left, open onto patio.

## Bedroom Suite Addition Includes Swimming Pool

A new bedroom wing, with a new swimming pool, makes for gracious living in the home of Tom Brown of Phoenix, Arizona.

The addition, designed by architect Dave Mitchell, was attached to an outside wall of the maid's room (see plan). Utilizing the closet space of the maid's room, a hall from the house to the new suite was obtained. New closet space was provided in the maid's room, and by extending into the new wing, a maid's bath was also added.

Ingenious recessed cribs save nursery space, can re-convert to closet when children grow.

Master bedroom as seen from doorway. Bath is to right. Closets on either side of bed (see plan).

## New Bedroom Wing Respects Historic House

The fine old colonial home of writer Pierre Sichel dates back to Revolutionary War times. When he and his wife Edna decided to add a master bedroom and bath to their home, they turned to a designer friend and neighbor, Wilson Ware. His plans fully respected the Sichels' wish that the addition fit the original structure. As constructed, the new blends faithfully with the old, from roof to stone foundation. One concession to living needs are the large windows at the end of the wing, at the back of the house.

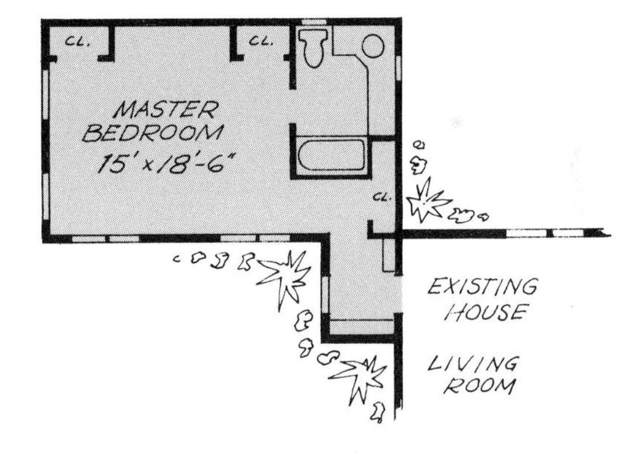

Sichel colonial as seen from road. Master bedroom addition is at right, stepped back and camouflaged by trees.

New wing as seen from rear of house. Note stone foundation matching original. Shed roof connector adds to interior charm.

## Garage Converts to Boys' Dorm

The Michael Casadeis were fond of their small "starter" home and didn't want to move. Also, to buy a larger house when their children would be off to college in a couple of years just didn't make sense. So, in one bold stroke, Mr. Casadei converted their oversize one-car garage into a dormitory for his two sons with a cot for overnight guests.

The family car sits in the driveway: "You don't get any more trade-in allowance on a garaged car," says Mr. Casadei.

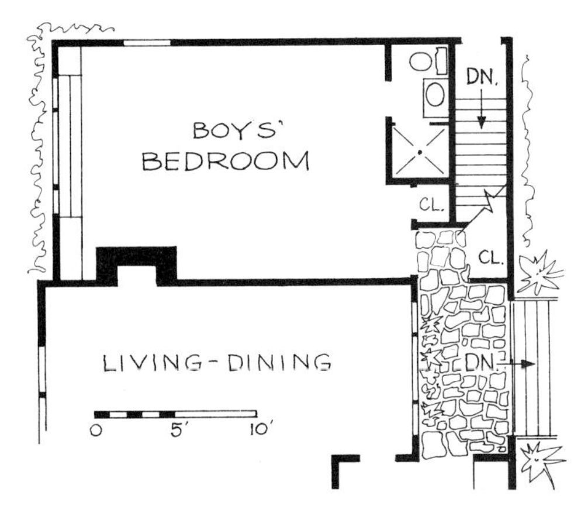

Former garage door opening now contains windows, with radiators below.

## Dormers Open Up Attic Space

Architect Frank Dailey added three good-sized bedrooms to his Connecticut home (see page 79) overlooking Lake Candlewood by simply constructing shed dormers on each side of this conventional gabled home. Before and after pictures below.

Ceiling in master bedroom shows new dormer line with old roofline beyond.

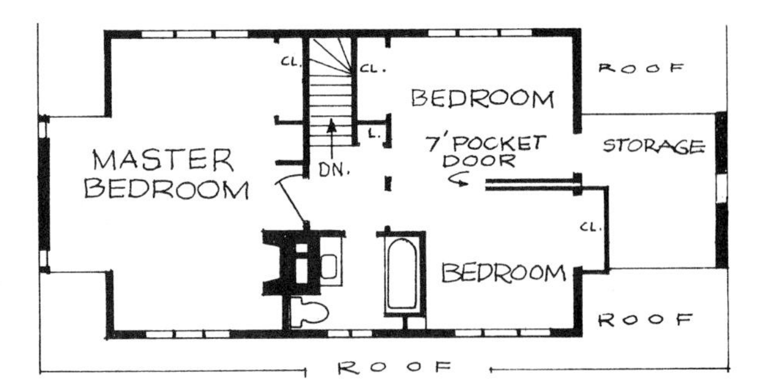


Attic at right, where old roofline was retained, is storage area. Note long pocket door separating boys' rooms.

## Another Dormer Idea . . . the Maisonette

Here, an attic dormer solves the problem of limited expansion space by extending a parents' bedroom to form a study-sitting area and a study-work area. The new space is accessible via a stair-ladder located between two doors on one bedroom wall.

Off the sitting area is a balcony.

The construction is simple. The original ridge remains, as do the original plate and the ceiling joists. The new dormer is built up from the plate where the roof and wall meet. The new floor is placed on the ceiling joists. Illustrations courtesy of the Georgia Pacific Corporation.

## Thoughts When Planning New Bedrooms

A new bedroom in a home, whether added or remodeled space, is one of the soundest home improvement investments that can be made. An extra bedroom is the selling point with the widest appeal, especially among young, growing families. This just isn't the case with a new recreation room, even a new family room. A few suggestions concerning new bedrooms follow.

### Privacy

Remember that the bedroom belongs to the private zone of the house. Avoid locating a new bedroom anywhere but in an area of the house that's away from general traffic and noise. A new bedroom wing, of course, will be its own such zone.

### Orientation

As suggested earlier, make every effort to orient a new bedroom with sunlight in mind, both for comfort and for pleasure.

### Other Rooms

If the bedroom is an addition, consider the likely returns, personal and financial, of an investment that includes bath and dressing room. If it's a remodeling project, consider adding such rooms in the process.

### Thinking Big

Think big by thinking of the whole floor plan. The best idea might not be to enlarge the existing bedroom but to enlarge the study to become the new bedroom, letting the existing bedroom become a new study. With a wider view comes a wider range of possibilities.

### Use of Outdoors

With eyes wide open, look for an opportunity to relate the new indoor space to outdoor space. Bedroom doors can open onto private gardens, patios, or decks.

### Size and Design

Finally, plan so that those space problems already mentioned never arise. Plan a bedroom that's large enough, and plan with furniture uppermost in mind.

Attic over New England living room converted to airy, elegant, and very quiet guest room. Room is located away from family's bedroom area for privacy.

# 11. A Guest Room to Make a Guest Feel Special

Consideration of the guest room begins with consideration of the guest himself. The single aim of the guest room is to make the guest at home in your home. Requirements are none other than those for the master bedroom—comfort, quiet, convenience, and above all, privacy. In short, guests are special people and deserve special attention.

Ideally, a guest room is in effect an apartment, sufficient unto itself. A guest should feel that he can be there and do what he wants to, without intruding on you and your family. Of course, it's understood that much of his living in your home will be with you, that he'll share your living room, your dining room, your family and recreation rooms, and indirectly, your kitchen. He'll share your yard as well. But he'll also have his own home within your home where he can be pleasantly alone.

- A guest room should be located in the private house zone and, if possible, privately within that zone. Not only should a guest be isolated from the main house circulation and sounds, he should be removed from private ones. If his bedroom doesn't have its own bath, he should have access to one without having to pass others in a hallway to get to it. And he shouldn't (as in a popular television series) have to hear all of the "good-nights"—he certainly shouldn't have to exchange them! In larger houses the best guest rooms have direct access to the outdoors, even to an enclosed guest sitting area.
- Comfort centers on the bed; it should be a good one. For couples, twin beds are better than a double bed. Comfort should also encompass an easy chair, a desk or writing table and chair, a night table, a light for reading in bed, and ample closet and drawer space. A television might well be provided.
- Locks on doors and locks and screens on windows should give a guest a feeling of safety. A guest, of course, should have his own key for any guest room door to the outside. A thoughtful touch is to let him know that you have another so that, should he lose his or drive off without it, he needn't be unduly concerned.
- Finally, there's the room itself. A guest room, like a bedroom, should be designed, furnished, and decorated to please. Brightness, airiness, good furniture (not cast-off pieces!), relaxing colors, rich textures (a special painting or print can only make a guest feel special)—all express the welcome you're extending.
- And don't forget the little things: the extra towels and blankets, the carefully chosen magazines and books, the flowers, the bowl of fresh fruit with a knife and plate beside it. Little things make the big difference.

To build guest house, Arizona broker Hans Mathiesen went "all out" over dry wash on lot.

## Poolside Guest Room Plus Patio

When Mr. and Mrs. Joe Walters of Sun City, Arizona, agreed that Mr. Walters needed an office-study, their first thought was to add a small room to their garage at the back of their house. Discussing the idea with Pete Jones of Jones Remodeling and Construction Company, they realized that such a location—with a great view of their swimming pool and gardens and the golf course beyond—was too good, even distracting, for such a room.

The Walters' rethinking resulted in an entirely different use of that very location. Off their huge (16′ × 45′) covered patio, they added a small guest room with a bath that serves the patio and swimming pool as well. A small bedroom in the far corner of their house was made to function as the office-study. At the same time, they installed a sliding glass door in the kitchen, turning the patio into their favorite informal eating area. The patio was extended and carpeted. The guest room itself has sliding glass door access to the patio and its own air conditioner. A ceiling fan was added to the patio.

The cost was under $7,000 for the addition (and approximately $1,000 for extending and carpeting the patio).

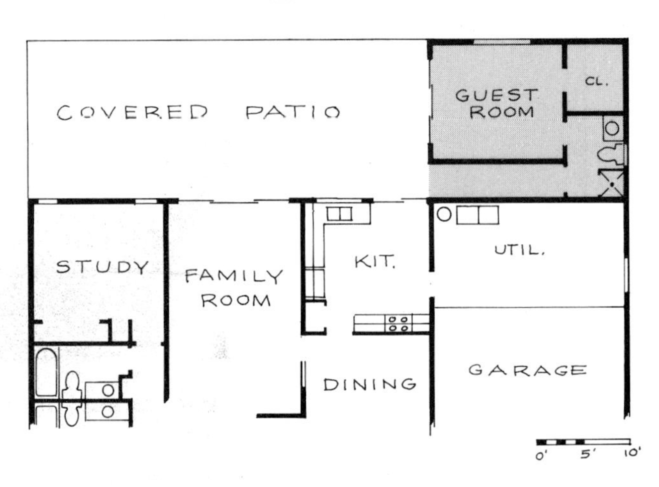

## Cozy Guest Room and More from a Two-Car Garage

The Mullens had a beautiful home on Lake Waramaug to entertain weekend guests but, with five active children, not a bedroom to spare. The need was obvious.

Designer Bill Corrigan earned his fee, planning a conversion of the Mullens' attached two-car garage into a charming guest room with a view of the lake, a guest bath, and a recreation room right off the kitchen.

Notice, in the plan, the second washbowl in the guest room. The tub is screened from the entrance to the guest room by an opaque plastic bi-fold door (see photo above right).

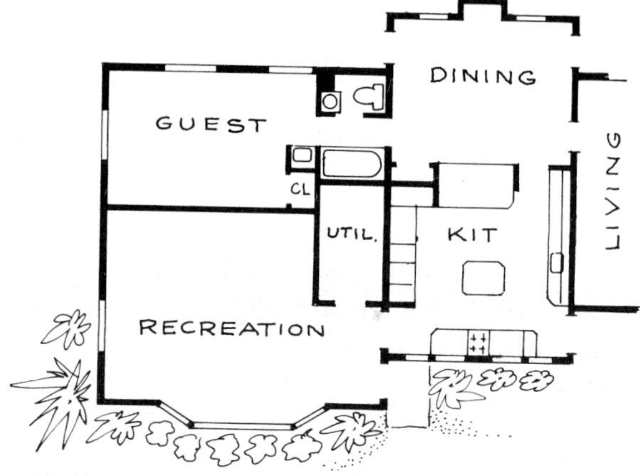

Vogt home before greenhouse and guest room extension and dining room-kitchen addition.

Door to right of cellar door is to new study/guest-room space. New dining room and enlarged kitchen are at right.

## Guest Room/Study with Step-Down Greenhouse

When the Vogts enlarged their kitchen and added a dining room (see page 76), they added a greenhouse to their home as well. In the process, they expanded existing space to provide a study for Dr. Vogt, a psychiatrist, that can double as a guest room. The greenhouse is just a step down from the new space.

As can be seen in the pictures below, the new space extends upward to the roof line. The upper wall section was the exterior wall of the house. Two windows in a second-floor guest room offer a view of the greenhouse.

## Streamlined Elegance

Deep in the hills of northwestern Connecticut, a communications couple who wish to remain anonymous have converted a barn into an elegant weekend home. For their lucky guests, they've planned a small, simple, clean-swept hideaway that's only two hundred feet from the house but hidden behind a rock ledge.

The amazing thing about this "guest house" is not that it doubles as a cabana for the pool but that it's under the one-car garage. Three sets of six-foot glass sliders make it seem larger than its $12' \times 24'$ dimensions. At one end of the room are a bathroom with shower and a clothes closet. The room is furnished to look more like a sitting room than a bedroom, with a small writing table and chair behind the camera in the picture above.

It would indeed be easy to feel special in this choice spot.

Irregularly shaped pool fits contours of ledge. Rock gardens at left provide spectacular view from guest hideaway.

This guest living room is part of top floor suite that includes bedroom, bath, and small kitchen and is now rented to owner's sister. It shares common entrance with rest of house.

## Guest Facilities Present Future Income Possibilities

Something to keep in mind when planning a guest suite is the second use possible when extra income might be welcome.

When Tom Golodic restored his brownstone in Jersey City (see page 164), he put its top floor to just such a profitable use, above.

Below, the Louis Pantes added a mother-in-law wing that could someday be a rental suite (see plan). A private exterior door would then be added.

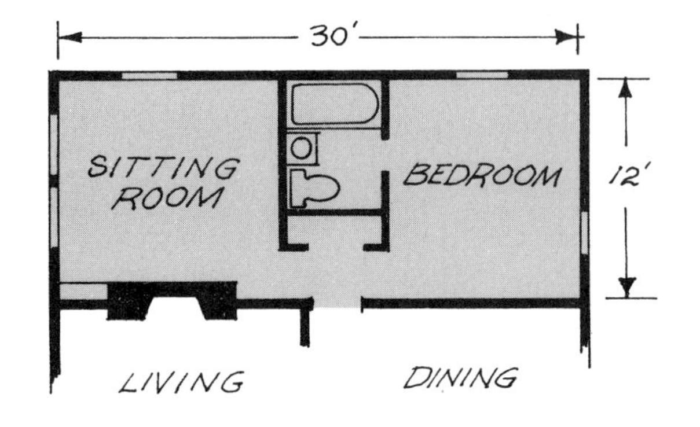

Matching siding and roof pitch make wing suite, to left, asset to appearance of home.

Comfortable sitting room, completely separate from bedroom (see plan) makes suite "little home."

## Garage Addition Expands into Guest House

The need for more garage space and a desire for a private guest suite combined in this country doctor's home improvement.

The doctor added a bay to his existing garage, utilizing the space over the bay and extending the construction to create an apartment having a balcony bedroom, a living room with dining area, a Pullman-type kitchen with bar, and a bath.

While the ceiling of the bedroom, over the new bay, follows the roof line, that of the rest of the suite is conventional, thus providing attic storage space above. Closet space is located under one end of the balcony.

Entrance to guest suite is around corner at right. Access from driveway is via flagstone path.

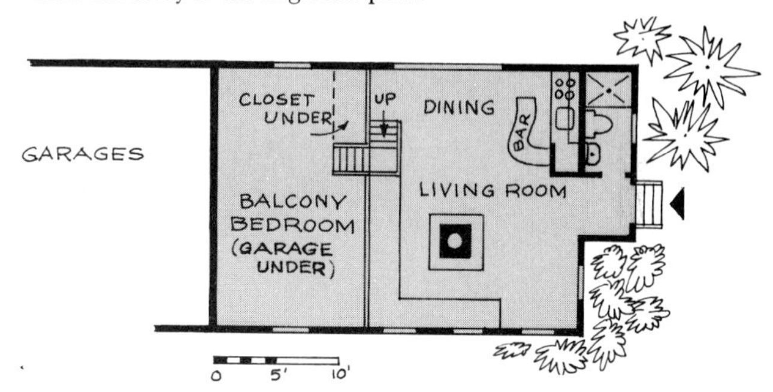

Living room has built-in banquette seating that wraps around free-standing fireplace. Balcony bedroom is over new garage bay. Efficiency kitchen with bar is off to right. Space above conventional ceiling used for storage.

Light, re-sawn hemlock walls and ceramic tile floor make small and potentially dark space seem light and spacious in living room of guest suite. Dining-kitchen area is in background. Skylight is directly over camera.

Before: Unevenly spaced posts fill residual space below existing carport. Imagination and courage made stunning guestroom.

## Enlarging Downward Makes Guest Suite

Thinking of adding on, the Martin P. Weissmans of Oakland, California, with the talents of architect William B. Remick, AIA, of Piedmont, decided to add down—and the result was stunning.

In the steeply sloped space under an existing attached carport was "fit" a multilevel guest suite, complete with a private outdoor living area consisting of a deck projected into a thick eucalyptus grove.

In area just over five hundred square feet, the suite is an entirely self-contained unit, totally independent from the house.

Sleeping level continues use of light walls for feeling of light and space. Living level is to left below. Steps down to entry and dining area are behind camera. Suite, under carport, is self-contained, independent—fully private.

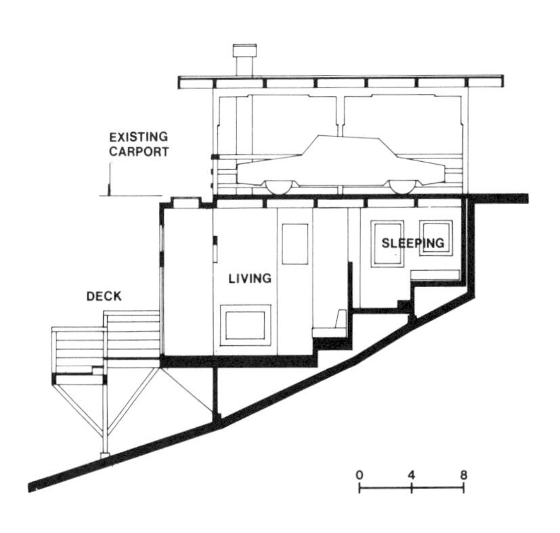


Elevation shows how space under carport works. Note stepped-down levels: bed, floor, seating, floor.

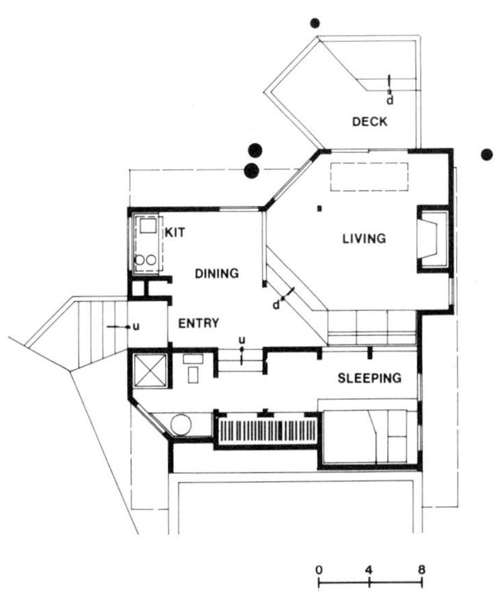


Plan shows ingenious use of space. Note entrance, dining, kitchen cluster, and bath-closet arrangement.

Here bathroom conveniences extend into master bedroom, so two can wash at same time. Vanity, with theatrical lighting, has sink with hair-rinsing nozzle.

# 12.
# A Bathroom That Indulges

As is the case with every new room, a bathroom can be placed in either new or remodeled space. An existing bathroom, another room—even a closet—can become your new bath.

## Bathroom Use and Location

Two big questions need to be answered when adding a new bath. The first is who will use it, and the second is what is the best location.

If it's to be used exclusively by the parents, the right location would be off their bedroom, accessible only through the bedroom. If it's also to be used by guests, it should be accessible both through the bedroom and from the living zone of the house. If the children will be the real users, it should be close to their rooms. And if it's for guests, it had best be off the entrance hall.

A new bath is most economically located above, below, or next to an existing bath and its plumbing, but convenient location for intended use should be the prime consideration. A further word on placement: a bathroom shouldn't be placed so you can see directly into it from another room. If such a view is unavoidable, plan the layout so that the toilet can't be seen.

## Bathroom Space

Hopefully, your new bathroom will be large enough to meet your requirements. A full bath, for use by two persons at once, should be at least 5′ × 7′. The size of the room will dictate the size and types of fixtures. Keep in mind that room is required to move around in, too. A half bath can be squeezed into the minimal space of a closet or in the small space under a stairway. Planning half bath fixtures is especially critical because of space limitations. There are, happily, space-saving corner fixtures that make planning easier.

## Bathroom Fixtures

Tubs, washbowls, and toilets come in a variety of grades, as well as in various sizes and shapes. Don't cut corners when choosing bathroom fixtures. Remember that these fixtures are meant to be permanent—so quality counts. This isn't to say that you shouldn't shop around for the best prices.

Bathtubs are rectangular or square. Common sizes are 5′ long by 30″ wide by 16″ high, and 4′ square by 16″ high, respectively. Enameled cast iron is considered better than enameled steel. Either material should be acid-resistant. Sunken tubs, though elegant, are less convenient to clean. Today, tubs in combination with showers or showers alone are available in fiberglass-reinforced plastic.

Like bathtubs, washbowls offer a wide range of shapes and sizes: the rectangular 20″ × 24″ size is common. In order of best and most expensive to cheapest, materials used are vitreous china, enameled cast iron, and porcelain-enameled steel. As with tubs, the finish should be acid-resistant. Washbowls can be free-standing, wall-hung, or built into a counter top or cabinet. Counter top space is convenient for placing toilet articles, and cabinet space is valuable for storage.

Toilets are differentiated by flushing action. Most often preferred is the reverse-trap model, although the siphon-jet toilet is more efficient. The cheapest is the wash-down, the best and most expensive is the quiet-flush. Off-the-floor toilets are the easiest to clean around but cost more. Discuss model advantages and disadvantages with a plumbing contractor.

Just as you should shop wisely for fixtures, you should shop wisely for fixture fittings. Brass content speaks quality. A manufacturer's middle grade is usually a safe bet.

## Walls and Floors

Ceramic tile is considered the best covering for bathroom walls and is often used for bathroom floors. Around the tub, it should run from floor to ceiling. Elsewhere, it can stop three or four feet up the wall. For moisture resistance, nontiled wall space is often covered with plastic-coated wallpaper, and plaster wallboard surfaces painted.

Bathroom floors, if not tiled, can be covered with pure sheet vinyl for the finest of plastic flooring. Less expensive resilient materials are vinyl-asbestos tile and linoleum, but these materials are of inferior quality. Wall-to-wall carpet makes an elegant and safe floor covering. In a children's bathroom, however, it may take quite a beating.

## Other Considerations

Lighting in the bathroom is critical. It's important that you have enough light to wash, brush your teeth, comb or brush your hair, or shave. Lights to either side of the mirror are the most effective for these activities. A light above the mirror might also be used. The lighting shouldn't be uncomfortably bright. Fluorescent tubes tend to be harsh and are best in a warm tone. Any light shining directly into the mirror should be avoided. Another area light to consider is a waterproof light over the tub or shower. General artificial illumination can be provided by ceiling lights, by concealed lights, or by a suspended ceiling with warm-tone fluorescent tubes and light-diffusing glass or plastic panels.

The best natural illumination is that offered by a skylight over the washbowl and counter area. Daylight can also filter through windows fitted with louvered shutters for privacy.

Electrical outlets in the bathroom should be conveniently located for shavers, hairdryers, and portable make-up mirrors. Since the bathroom heating requirement is minimal, a single unit is usually sufficient, but it should be placed away from the toilet.

Storage space is important in the bathroom. A cabinet under the washbowl or over a tub or toilet is handy. Corner cabinets work well in small rooms, and open shelves for towels are practical. A recessed medicine cabinet with sliding mirror doors is practical.

A word about color. It's wise to choose the colors of fixtures, wall tiles, and floor coverings with the future in mind. These are, in effect, permanent features of the bathroom. Tastes change. Loving flaming red today can be hating it tomorrow. It's better to be on the safe side and curb extravagance. The choice of wallpaper, paint, shower curtain, and towels can provide ample opportunity for daring.

A final suggestion: inform yourself of bathroom innovations. Fixtures not only abound in variety but come as entire bathrooms in packaged "kits." Such a prefabricated unit might be the perfect new bath for you.

Shelves of plants and sliding glass door unit "wall" that opens to wooded hillside combine to make this bathroom distinctive. Room is high above ground level for privacy. Railing shown is temporary, as deck or enclosed addition with "hot tub" is contemplated. Bathtub, in this 6′3″ × 11′ room is four feet square. Photo taken from vanity wall.

Luxurious master bath features 7′ × 9′ tub. Walls around tub are covered in black plastic to complement smart black and silver paper on walls. Arched window gives "touch of class." Master baths are plusses to master bedrooms.

Concealed door, with towel bar doubling as pull, opens to similar door in other bath. To left of door is concealed medicine cabinet.

Linen cupboard above toilet tank makes use of available space. Valence light here, as above vanity, provides diffused linear illumination.

## Remodeling Restores Access

The much needed modernization of two upstairs bathrooms provided the owners of this old farmhouse with an opportunity to solve an access problem at the same time. Originally, the space containing the baths had been a hallway joining the two sides of the second floor. When the baths were added, with a wall between them, the only way to get from one end of the upstairs to the other was either by going through a bedroom or by going down one staircase, across, and up another staircase. In remodeling the baths, the owners ingeniously installed concealed doors, back to back, in each room. The doors, flush with the walls and of the same material, have door pulls.

Modernizing the baths involved total reorganization of the fixtures, as well as complete replumbing (as both baths had floors raised six inches to allow for pipes, the floors were simply lifted). Shown, at left, is one of the new baths (the lower one in the plan below). Walls and cabinets are paneled with rough-sawn cedar. A revered, eighteenth-century window was left in place and cased by the paneling. The floor is of white, unglazed ceramic tile, as is the shower area, not shown. The vanity counter top and backsplash are of natural-cleft bluestone. The vanity has a fixed mirror wall with valence lighting above.

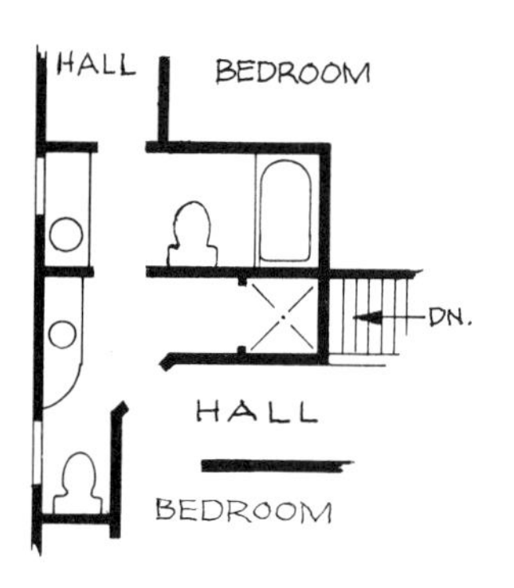

## "His" and "Her" Baths—An Attainable Luxury

When the George Finks remodeled the lean-to kitchen of their colonial farmhouse into a master bedroom, they made the most of the opportunity to include not one but two master baths, one on either side of a short hall space.

Mrs. Fink's bath is nothing less than luxurious (above, right). Large and bright—with recessed lighting in the ceiling and a window in a ceiling opening—it has a vanity with a full mirror that runs the width of one wall. The tub and shower, off to the left, is walled with marble. Bathroom fittings are gold-finished. Plush carpeting adds comfort.

Mr. Fink's bath, above left, is handsome. Its outstanding feature is a washbowl enclosure of antique tulip wood, saved from elsewhere in the house in the course of its overall renovation. His bath was formerly the kitchen pantry.

## Consider Outdoor Access

If your family enjoys outdoor living—and especially if you have a swimming pool—be sure to include access to your new bathroom from the outside. Access can be direct or through a hall or a dressing room, requiring only one exterior door.

The picture below shows a door to a pool area installed in an existing bathroom.

## . . . And an Outdoor Shower

The lean-to bathroom addition, below, by architect Victor Stimac, has a second door opening to a patio. At left in the picture above is a shower head, a simple outdoor extra enjoyed equally by children and by gardening parents.

## Thinking Small

Having another bath or half bath can mean the difference between family friction and family harmony. Most houses built before 1960 are "underbathed." A little ingenuity, possibly with professional assistance, can often fit in a bath where it had never been considered possible.

Under-stairs space of 2′ × 5′ includes convenient ground-floor lavatory. Small corner washbowl is space saver.

Three-foot square tub and shower makes full bath for kids in this 3′ × 5½′ space.

Concealed lighting on mural in "false" window adds romantic touch to small interior bath.

## Various Bathroom Layouts

The arrangement possibilities of the basic bathroom fixtures—tub or shower, washbowl, and toilet—are many indeed, as suggested in the illustrations below. Various too are the shapes and sizes of bathroom fixtures. (Today, there's even a so-called "soft bathtub," a plastic fold-up unit housed in the base of a vanity!) Given this planning flexibility, as small a space as a closet can become a half bath.

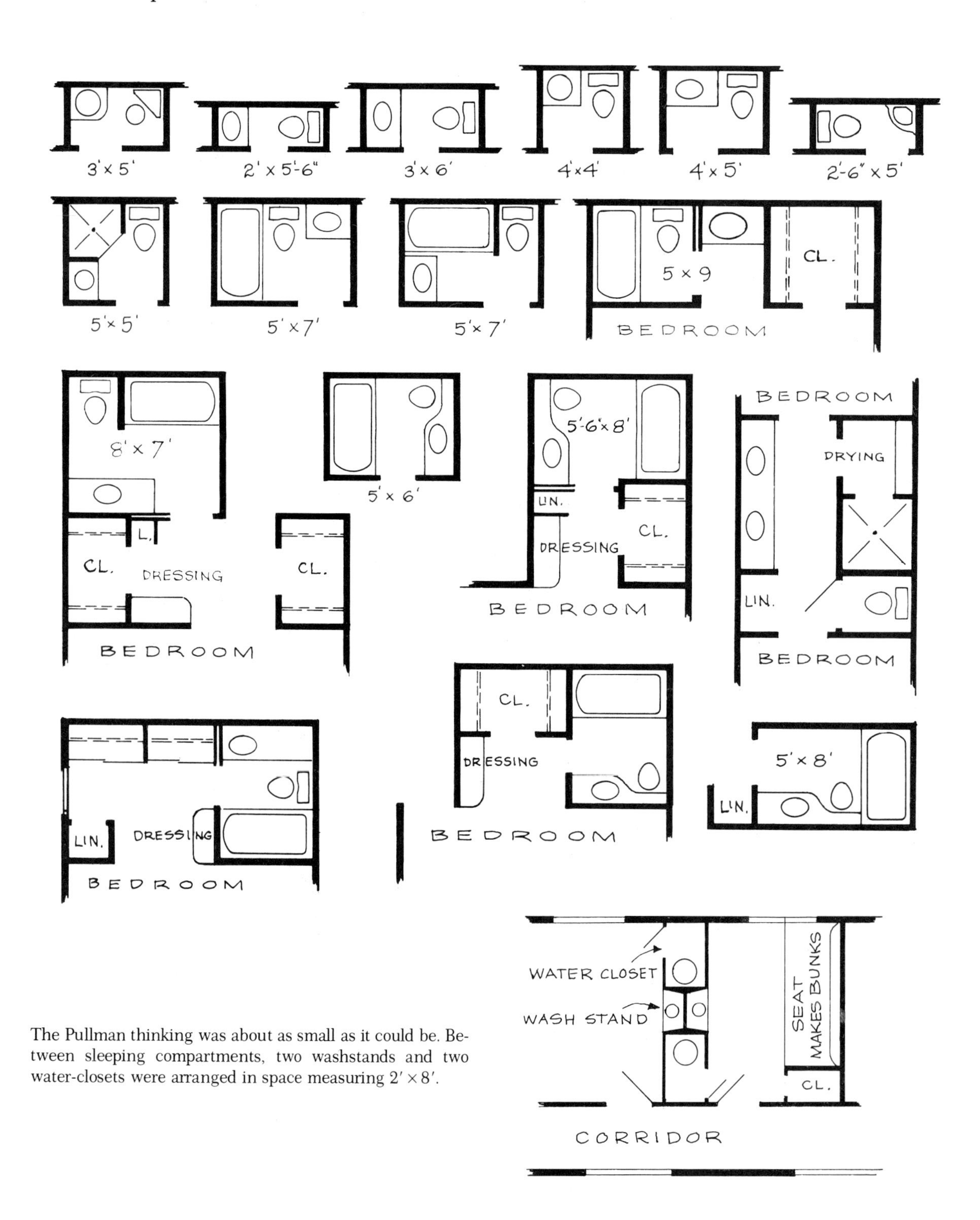


The Pullman thinking was about as small as it could be. Between sleeping compartments, two washstands and two water-closets were arranged in space measuring 2′ × 8′.

## Bathroom Decor

Entering a bathroom can be a happy surprise. The famed architect Frank Lloyd Wright said that every room should be a fresh experience. Why not the bathroom as well as any other room of the house?

Special attention is required when decorating the bathroom. Since it's undoubtedly the smallest room in the home, a little bit goes a long way—decor statements can be loud. This is all the more the case in a small bathroom. Following are a few suggestions.

Mirrors can work magic, giving an illusion of much more space than there is. A fixed mirror running the full length of a vanity does the trick, especially when bold wallpaper on the adjacent wall is reflected in it.

Dramatic effect can be achieved by the use of matching wallpaper and shower curtain, available at paint and wallpaper stores. The colors of the paper and curtain should be picked up in the other colors in the room. Fixtures can be either white or another compatible color.

Walls and flooring needn't be conventional. A friend's bathroom is paneled in chestnut from a tannery (filled with holes where the hides were tacked up) and has flooring of old, used brick. The vanity and washbowl cabinet are made of chestnut from old telephone poles.

Lighting fixtures today are so varied that lighting can be unusually decorative. Soap dishes and towel rods offer creative possibilities.

No longer is the bathroom the cold white room suggesting nothing but cleanliness—nor should it be.

Marble-patterned commode top, candle sconces, ornate lighting fixtures, and "tortoise shell" plastic wallpaper combine to create stunning guest bath.

Simple, thoughtful decorating gives old bathroom new life—up-to-date yet nostalgic. Note use of wall covering on old iron tub.

Many creative solutions to space problems can be found in homes of architects and artists. Bill Remick, AIA, of Piedmont, California, has a small work "nest" that extends out over part of the deck and thrusts into the living room on the high side of his shed-roofed contemporary home. Boxed-in stairs and balcony add strong design excitement to high-ceilinged room. From this vantage point, Bill enjoys a view of the Pacific, a skylight over his drafting table, and above-it-all communication with his family below.

# 13.
# The Home Office, Studio, or Shop

Special activities, avocational or vocational, call for special spaces in a home. Mother may paint still lifes in an attic studio. Father might refinish antique furniture in a garage workshop. Or perhaps Junior develops and prints film in a basement darkroom.

Those who work at home need special areas, too—a woman who sews slipcovers and drapes for additional family income, or a man who operates his real estate business from his home.

For whatever reason, for pleasure or for profit, everyone should have a room or an area in the home in which to follow his interests. This space can be meant exclusively for one activity, or it can be used for several purposes. The space may be any of the normal rooms in the home put to use for a special activity.

## Space and Privacy

Jobs and home businesses have the most obvious claim to home space. Furthermore, the job or business area in a home all but demands to be removed from the family living area, to be inviolable, sacrosanct. An architect friend of ours divides his house into distinct living and working sides. A painter friend has a Do Not Enter sign on the door leading from his entrance hall to his studio and at one crucial creative time went so far as to nail that door shut. There's good reason why artists' studios are separate, even isolated, buildings on the lot. Independence of activity applies as well to the woman of the house who writes or runs a profitable crafts business.

Hobbies, too, deserve to be privately established and located in the home. Someone pursuing an avocation has a right to expect to be left alone. He or she can hardly hope for privacy if the room or area isn't situated privately in the home. Mother's still lifes will be anything but still if the children are playing hide-and-seek around her easel. Father's antique furniture will never be refinished if it has to be moved all the time to make room for the second car. And Junior's photographs will hardly survive sudden openings of the darkroom door to get a jar of preserves.

Any room or area of the home, then, should be so located that it offers seclusion for the activity it's to serve. Basements, attics, and garages are likely locations. Additions can be tailor-made, wings all the more so. Unattached buildings are ideal, but they require at least some autonomy in the form of wiring or plumbing.

The most common course taken by families who need hobby or job space is to make use of existing home space. An unneeded bedroom can become a studio or an office. A basement area can be partitioned off, space in the garage or attic appropriated. For that matter, an unused living room can be converted, as can a recreation room after the children have grown up and moved away.

Finally, as suggested earlier, space can meet more than a single need, if one activity doesn't intrude on the other. A man can paint while a woman sculpts in the same studio. And, also as suggested, space can be used for different activities at different times. A woman can sew in the family room when her husband is at the office and her children at school.

Former garage is now office for small-town chiropractor.

## Converted Two-Car Garage Makes Professional Office

When Howard Hess, chiropractor, moved to a small Connecticut town, renting an office in the village was essential in building his practice. As he became better known, however, he realized that he didn't need his "shingle" on Main Street. He decided to have his office in his home.

Since three growing children overran the house, Dr. Hess eyed the garage for conversion into a home office.

"It worked out better than I thought it would," says Dr. Hess. "You can't beat the commuting time, and I see much more of my family!"

His chiropractic office contains a foyer, a waiting room, two dressing rooms, a bath, which doubles as a darkroom, an adjusting room, and private office space.

Notice in the plan that the "foyer" has a door at each end. The family can still use this service entrance to the kitchen and not be seen by the patients in the waiting room. What is more, the breezeway next to the garage—now the office building—is a storage and service area for both operations—family and business.

Certainly, a business in a home that so respects the home is good business. Dr. Hess' office in his home is a clear improvement on his Main Street shingle.

Attractive waiting room is to left of entrance and entrance hall. Healthy plants and bright colors enhance area.

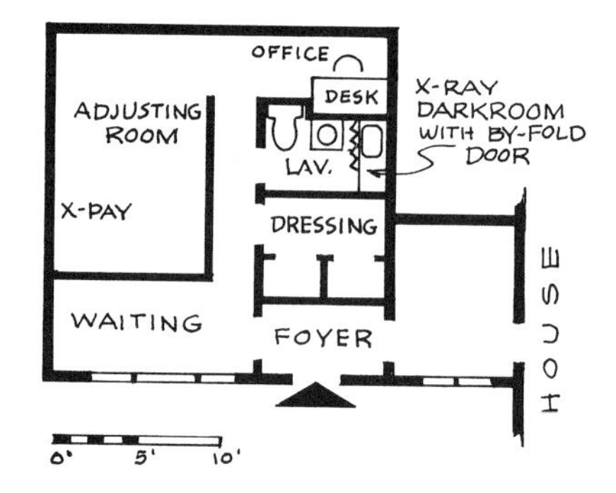


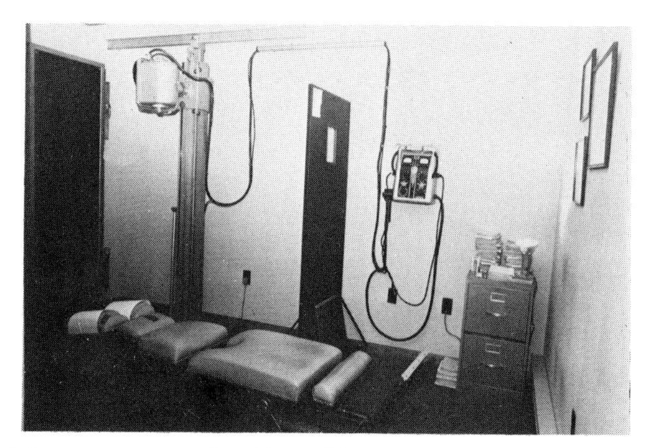

Adjusting room, with table and X-ray equipment.

Crafted figures climb in silhouette against glass south wall of Mitchell living room–studio room.

Central staircase to second floor balcony and to third floor highlights open-air ambiance of Mitchell home.

## Creativity Fills Creatively Added Space

The living area off the living room in the early nineteenth-century home of Henry and Rachel Mitchell of Sherman, Connecticut, doubles as a studio for Mrs. Mitchell, noted for her creative crafts.

From road, Mitchell house has traditional look.

The high-ceilinged room was opened to the living room and to a balcony, by the removal of an entire wall. Outstanding in the room is its south wall, made of glass. Natural light floods the airy interior of the house. Awning-type windows provide ventilation.

In her studio, as elsewhere throughout the house, Mrs. Mitchell's art work adds imaginative, personal touches.

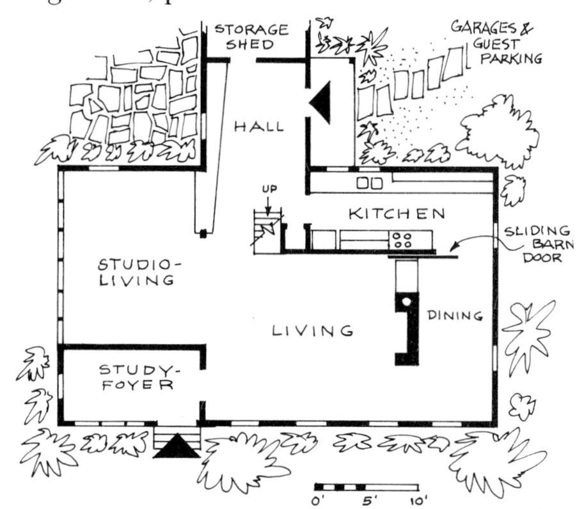

New studio wing, at right, is at ground level; garage is at driveway level below it. Studio balcony overhangs garage.

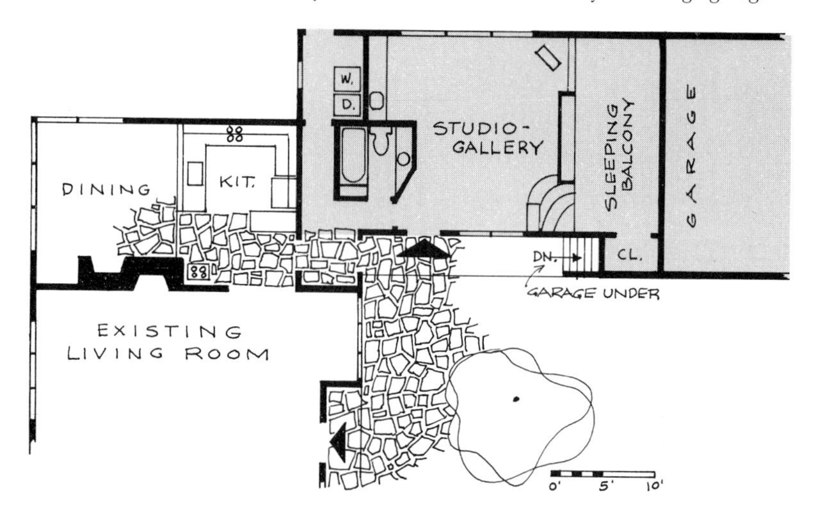


## Artist's Studio, Gallery, and Sleeping Balcony in New Wing

When artist and illustrator Ed Castro decided to build a two-car garage, he thought "studio, too." Instead of putting the studio over the garage, he worked out an ingenious plan that put it on ground level, with the garage placed further out on the slope of his land. Cars, on driveway level, sit in the garage with their hoods neatly tucked under a balcony in the studio.

The balcony serves as a sleeping area for both visiting grown children and guests. A full bathroom has more recently been added just off the studio. For overall convenience, the studio has direct access to the patio at the main house entrance.

Studio working area has large north light, and sink counter off to left. Balcony sleeping area is to right.

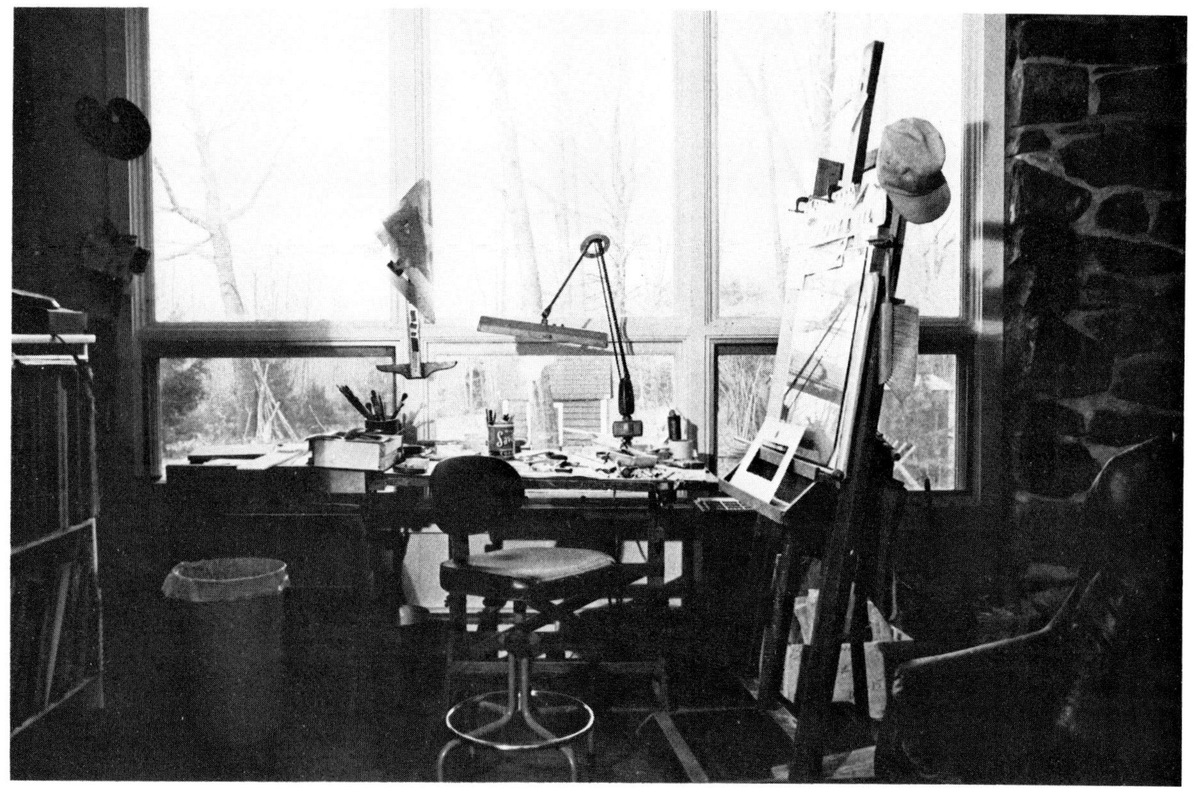

Textures—fieldstone, antique barn-siding, slate—work handsomely in gallery end of Castro studio, where artist's work is displayed. Balcony is beyond display wall. Seating opposite stove is comfortable.

Sleeping balcony, over garage space, has open see-through to studio below.

## Live-In Business Suite Adopts "Air Space" for Showroom

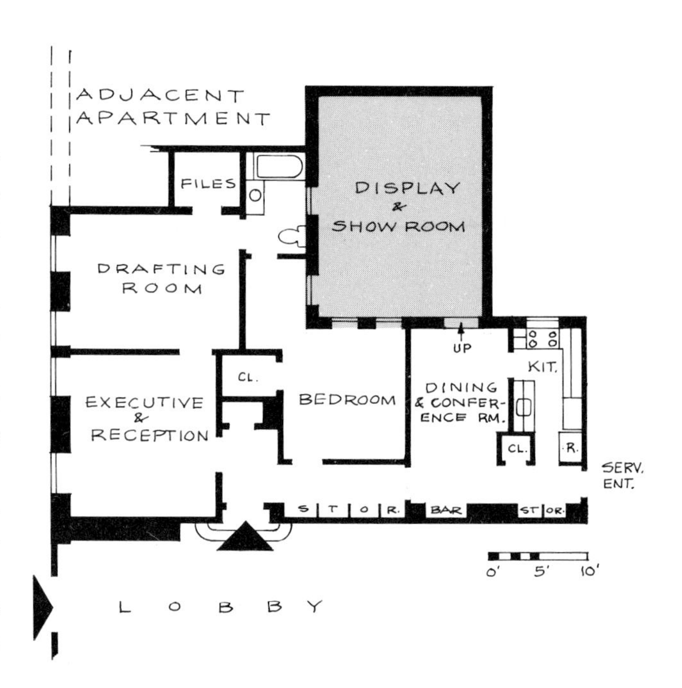


For interior designer J. Ray Baker of New York City, it's not a matter of having an office in his home but one of making his home in his office.

Two and a half years ago, Mr. Baker, a leading designer of hotel interiors, operated his business out of his apartment in the city. Wanting a business suite, he asked a friend who deals in such properties to keep an eye out for one. The friend had already seen one, a suite formerly occupied by a doctor—and just across the street from Mr. Baker's apartment.

Mr. Baker purchased this cooperative space in a residential building, and within

Added showroom, taking advantage of unused and unattractive air shaft terrace space. Steel beams in ceiling required for strength. Skylights and windows of double glass. Display ledges hold renderings and fabric boards.

Conference room with display ledges doubles as private and business dining room. Glass table gives feeling of spaciousness. Hall storage cabinets seen through door; bar is at left.

three months he was in business. "Gutting" the suite of all that had made it a doctor's office, he proceeded to create a designer's office that could double as real living space. An executive and reception room serves as a living room, and a conference room serves as a dining room. A kitchen was relocated from the latter space to an adjacent maid's room. There's also a bedroom, a bath, a drafting room, and a small room for files (see plan). In a brilliant stroke, Mr. Baker enclosed an air shaft terrace to add a large display showroom. Its ceiling of steel beams had to be strong enough to "stop a falling office safe."

The beauty of Mr. Baker's suite is that it's his apartment when he stays in the city, and as a home as well as an office, it welcomes clients with special warmth. Business is discussed in living room comfort, even over dinner. What's more is that the whole suite itself is a testament to the high quality of the product Mr. Baker sells.

Bar, at end of conference–dining room, serves clients and friends. Cabinets here, as throughout suite, are of white oak and have piano hinges.

Reception room–living room has wall of mirrors that make room seem larger. Note vertical blinds in reflected windows. Business here is transacted in home comfort.

Suite kitchen is compact and efficient, with range, sink, dishwasher. Cabinets are of white oak, counter tops of polyester resin material. Fluorescent lighting in ceiling is dimmer controlled.

## Another City Remodeling Job

Top floor and attic of remodeled city row house served as office for architect William Leatherbee until his expanding business outgrew the space and he moved his office to downtown Philadelphia. This area was then made into a sophisticated suite for his oldest daughter. For remodeling story of this town house, see page 160.

## Studio Puts Attic to Use

Existing attic space, though not accessible to business clients, can nonetheless be utilized for business or creative work. An attic has the advantage of remoteness when privacy is desirable. Windows and skylights can be installed for natural light. The above sketch, from the American Plywood Corporation, shows how the floor can be kept clear for activities with the use of a storage panel suspended from the rafters.

## Business Office in Basement

A fine office can be had without adding to the size—or the tax-assessed value—of your house by remodeling in your basement. The drawing above, courtesy of the American Plywood Corporation, shows just such an office. It could be that of a realtor or a public relations consultant. Note the conference table, comfortable seating, and work space behind the counter at the right. The "window" at the far end of the room is an indirectly lit mural panel. The sheer drapes add to the illusion.

## You've Heard of the Telephone-Booth Office—Don't Overlook a Closet

With imagination—even with inspiration—space as small as that of a closet can be put to office use. Above, physician Todd Anderson has ingeniously created an efficient office in his home.

Wanting a place to work away from family activity, Dr. Anderson chose this closet in a guest sitting room. The "office" doors are simply closed (and can be locked) when there are guests.

His office, as can be seen, has shelf, drawer, and file cabinet space, as well as a lighted desk surface. Professionally, he uses his office to study journals and papers; there is even a view box for studying X-rays. Privately, he balances his checkbook there. A phone is located outside the closet space within easy reach.

*Small country colonial with two new wings retains charm, adds elegance.*

*Custom contemporary grows "organically" to suit changing family needs.*

*Via local redevelopment authority, historic city building becomes architect's home.*

*Town house receives careful restoration—and harmonious modern amenities.*

*"Sun Belt" adobe, rescued and enlarged, makes handsome "fortress."*

*Deserted fishing lodge rebuilt by "empty nesters" into lovely lakeside home.*

*Tired "speculation" house turned into gracious home for retirement—and a little business.*

*Row house in returning neighborhood reshaped by artist-engineer couple into nifty maisonette.*

*"Dream site" inspires exciting expansion of retirement community house.*

*Levittown tract house—just a few years ago—now a Cinderella showplace.*

*Cement cottage turned into "silk purse" by Frank Lloyd Wright school graduate architect.*

*Run-down bungalow on romantic canal enlarged up for chic creative home.*

# 14. Redesigning That Affects the Whole House

Certain home improvements involve more than a new room, even more than a new suite of rooms. Sometimes the problems in your present living arrangements are so great that a complete overhaul is called for. A house may be "turned around," reorienting it to the back, rather than the front, of the lot. Wings may be added, giving a house an entirely different shape. The interior may even be gutted and its space totally rearranged, or major living spaces may be redefined for a dramatically different floor plan.

In each case, the result is effectually a new house. Since this is true, you need to think big—as you would when building a house. All the principles of design, from orientation to sun and wind to zoning and circulation, need to be considered.

Improving the whole house is no small challenge, but as is shown in the following pages, the challenge can be met with marked success. Going ahead with such a major undertaking presupposes that a sound decision has been reached by the homeowner that it is indeed better for him to improve rather than move. This decision should be grounded in full confidence that the considerable remodeling investment will pay handsome dividends, whether in terms of dollars or an improved quality of living.

On the following pages, as listed on the facing page, are a dozen examples of redesign affecting the whole house. Long-lived-in homes were remodeled to meet changing lifestyles. In some cases, houses were bought expressly for remodeling (here, a sound decision to move is presupposed). A small colonial home expanded in two directions and saw rearrangement of existing space. An abandoned Arizona adobe structure was transformed into a stunning desert home. A retirement community house, on "an ideal site," grew to become an ideal home. In one case, a young couple bought and restored a New Jersey brownstone. In another, an older couple turned a deserted fishing lodge into a charming lakeside home. In all instances, imagination, determination—and careful planning—led to a better home for a better life.

A word about professional help. As a rule, redesign affecting the whole house calls for the services of the experts, from the architect or designer through the general contractor to the various subcontractors. (Their services are discussed in Part Two of this book.) But even with such large scale remodeling, this need not be so. The following pages contain noteworthy exceptions to the rule. The wife designed the remodeling of the fishing lodge and served as general contractor. Both husband and wife planned the restoration of the brownstone, and the husband taught himself to do the wide range of necessary jobs.

The case histories that follow combine to argue most persuasively our stand of "Don't move, improve." Each of the dozen homeowners involved not only elected to re-model but to do so on the grand scale. Their needs and desires were big, and their planning was big. With conviction, with determination, with courage and even daring—above all, with imagination and with intelligence—they brought it off. The message to be received, here even more loudly and clearly than in the previous chapters, is that you too can bring it off—on whatever scale.

Old chestnut beams in cathedral ceiling highlight new living room.

## Old House Grows to Meet New Needs

When book editor Theodore M. Purdy and his literary-agent wife bought a small 1790 farmhouse in the Connecticut hills, it suited them well. They lived in a comfortable apartment in New York City and wanted a small place in the country—a weekend retreat from the problems of the book business.

The house had room enough for the two of them with the necessary conveniences. That was in 1950. As the years passed, however, their needs changed. To begin with, more and more they found that they were entertaining their city friends in the country. Then, to their pleasant surprise, they found that they were making many new friends in the country and entertaining them as well. They needed more room, and since they liked the community they decided on a bold enlargement concept.

Their remodeling job was considerable. With architect Burton Ashford Bugbee, they planned to add to the existing structure in two directions, and to rearrange the existing rooms as well.

The original house was a two-storied, nearly square, saltbox. On opposite ends, they attached one-story wings, one at such an angle (to bypass a huge rock outcropping) that the effect was to enclose the garden at the rear—a chance result that delighted the Purdys.

The larger wing, in line with the house, included a spacious new living room, with a cathedral ceiling spanned by old chestnut beams, and a library, also high-ceilinged, separated from the living room by a wet bar. The angled wing contained a bathroom, a walk-in closet, and a large master bedroom.

The rearrangement of existing space turned the farm kitchen into a dining room, the dining room into a kitchen, and the living room—ingeniously—into an entrance and hallway, the latter with a storage closet and a powder room.

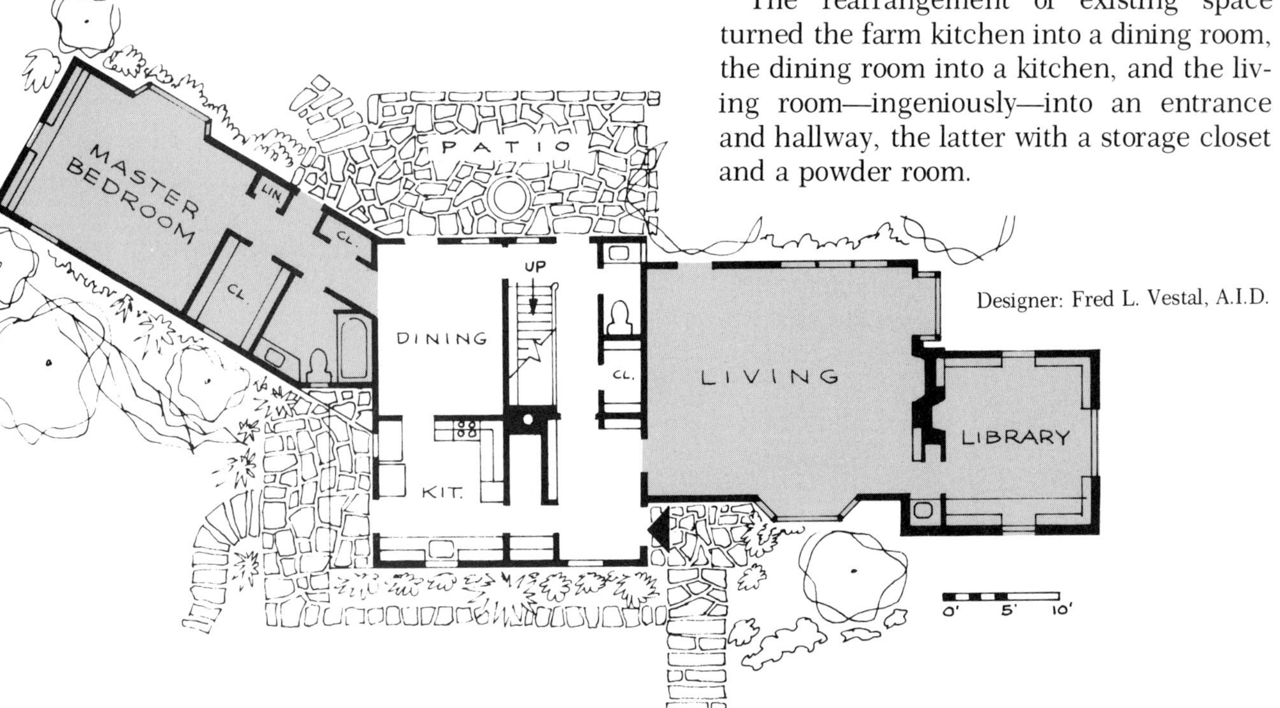


Designer: Fred L. Vestal, A.I.D.

New England farmhouse, as it appeared in 1950 when it met owners' needs for a small country place.

Same view of home as remodeled to meet their new needs and enriched lifestyle.

Shelves of books fill wall space both along and below new staircase. Books abound in the Purdy home.

Wet bar, with refrigerator, joins new library to new living room beyond and makes for convenient entertaining.

New Purdy living room as viewed from library, with book-lined entrance hall in background. Bay window with window seat is to left. Dutch door, background right, leads to patio at rear of house. Chestnut beams from old barn.

Fireplace, faced with Dutch tiles, adds warmth and charm to tray-ceilinged library off living room, in one of two new wings of Purdy home. Room, which serves Mr. Purdy as office, warmly reflects his personality and tastes.

New master bedroom is brightened by bay window which faces garden in rear of house. Chaise is favorite morning reading spot for Mrs. Purdy. Wing also includes walk-in closet and master bath, to left of camera.

"Sun shade roof" covers brick walk to house entrance.

Attractive gardens enhance walk.

## Home Reflects Well-Planned "Organic" Growth

The elegant Arizona home of architect Fred Guirey of Phoenix is the natural result of a family's changing living needs. It is the product of not one but two major home improvements over a period of more than twenty years.

The first addition to the basic 1942 house (see plan opposite, top) included a second bedroom, a family room, a patio, and a garage. That was in 1949. Another fifteen years brought the second addition (see plan opposite, bottom). With this second remodeling, new space was not only added, existing space was considerably altered.

New living room, formerly family room, houses collection of miniature liquor bottles (above windows), cupboards for games, and game table, at left. Sliding glass door opens to patio beyond. Former living room now new family room.

The second addition included a dining room, a master bedroom and bath, an extension of the kitchen with a laundry room, a guest bedroom with bath, and an entrance hall. In the addition process, the family room became the living room, the living room the family room, one existing bedroom the den-library, and another the dressing room and closets for the new master bedroom. Further, old closets were transformed into a glass-enclosed gallery leading to the new guest bedroom, formerly a garage.

Today, from both new bedrooms, sliding glass doors lead to fenced-in garden areas. Slat "sun shade roofs" cover much of the garden area around the house.

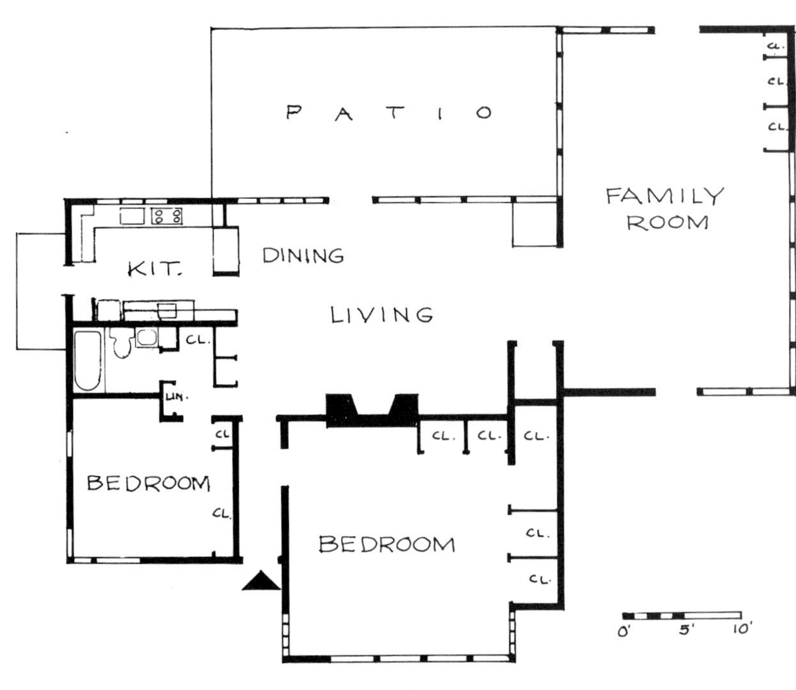


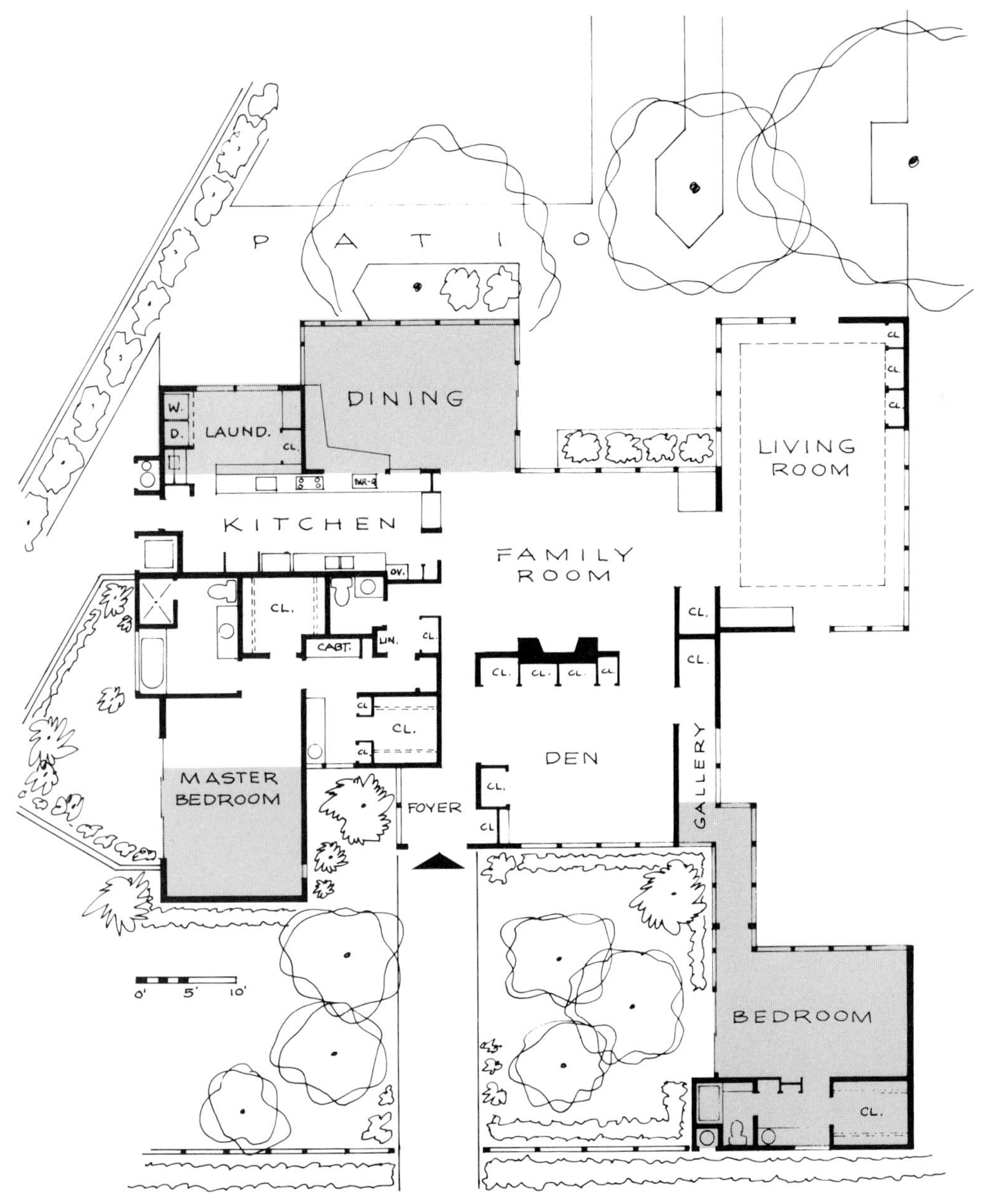

New kitchen is old kitchen extended to include laundry room, in background at right. Pass-through to dining room shows at right. Grill near pass-through doubles as warming table. Note kitchen access to out-of-doors.

The Guirey's remodeling speaks to the trend to an open flowing of space in the living area of the home. This trend is especially suitable to warm climates such as Arizona's. Architect Guirey is clearly sensitive to the freedom of movement the trend implies. Notice in the plan of the present home how the dining room, family room, and living room spaces blend, and how the family room and den blend as well. Notice the flow of space from the living area through the gallery to the bedroom.

The remodeling champions another trend, that to house-site relationship, the "marriage of indoor with outdoor living" discussed in Chapter 1 of this section. Notice in the plan how every major room, bedrooms included, opens to an outside living area. Not only does glass abound for viewing, but sliding glass doors for access.

New master bedroom, left, opens onto fenced-in garden area

Bath faces small garden, privacy assured by fence.

New dining room opens onto patio. Note wood-to-wood merging of indoors with outdoors for harmonious living.

Patio, below, offers spacious outdoor living, with both sunny and shady areas. Note luxuriousness of plantings.

"Before"—abandoned house in bottomed-out area.

## Certified Historic Building Comes to New Life

Remodeling a city "row house" (or brownstone or town house) presents some specific problems, but it also offers some very special rewards in living near theaters, shops, galleries, university facilities, and other city offerings.

In many cases, extraordinary bargains can be found in urban areas.

Philadelphia architect William Leatherbee wanted an individual city house for his young family. He found a badly neglected, three-story brick row house in a district that was earmarked for improvement by the City Planning Commission and offered for sale by the local Redevelopment Authority for $2,800. The building had been designated a historic building by the Philadelphia Historical Commission.

Mr. Leatherbee obtained a $12,000 Urban Renewal loan at 3% interest.

(If you're considering following his example, be sure to explore the possibilities of obtaining advice and financial help from your local planning commission or other community, city, state, and federal redevelopment authorities. Since such urban renewal groups are principally concerned with eliminating slums and renewing the housing supply, certain incentives are offered to qualified buyers.)

The building Mr. Leatherbee bought was little more than a shell. All the windows were beyond repair and had to be replaced. The same was true of the roof. The interior walls were in bad shape and enclosed spaces were too small.

One year and another loan later, this time a conventional bank loan of an additional $9,000, the Leatherbees moved into this very choice and exciting small town house. Over the next five years, they did most of the finishing work themselves.

City home of architect William Leatherbee after courageous and imaginative remodeling.

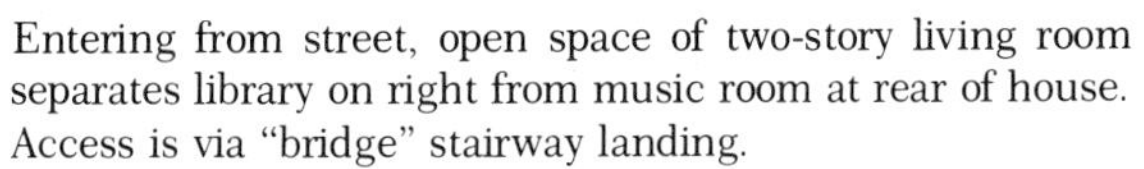

Entering from street, open space of two-story living room separates library on right from music room at rear of house. Access is via "bridge" stairway landing.

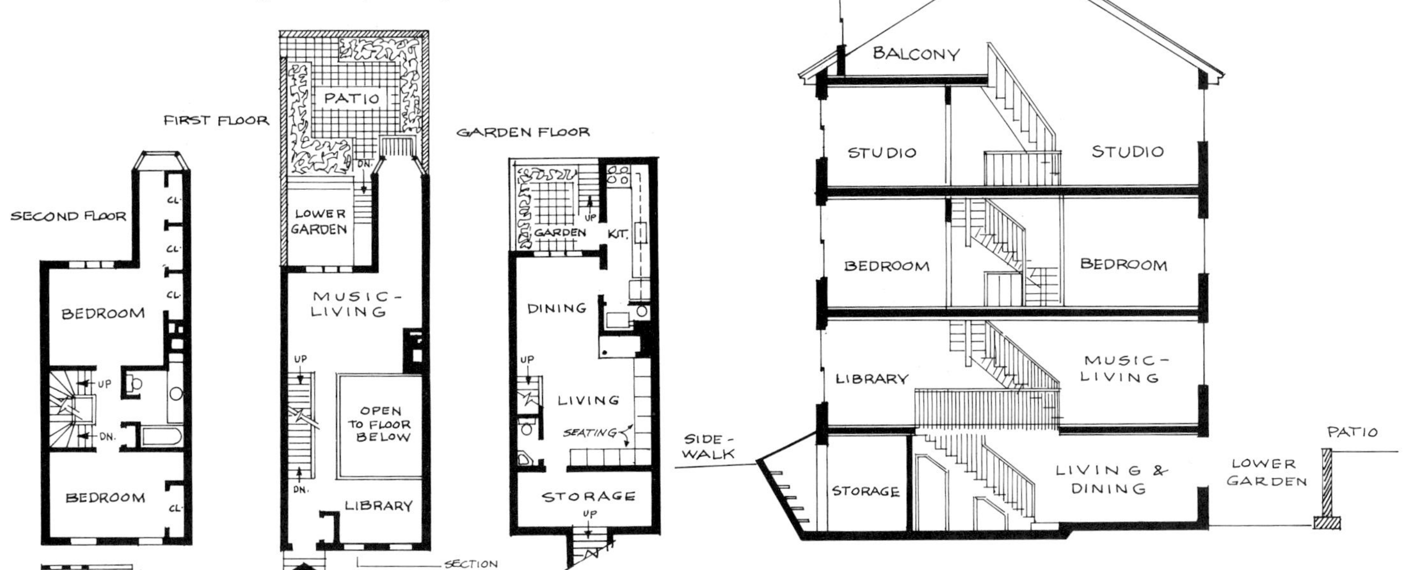

View from library of dining room below and dramatic stairs to bedrooms above captures open, spacious feeling of house.

Lower level living room or family room. Dining room, behind camera, is reflected in mirror on storage room wall.

Unique bay on back of house offers extra light and space.

## Opportunity and Challenge In the Inner City

The whole point of urban renewal is, as in the old song, to "accentuate the positive, eliminate the negative." Architect Leatherbee's talent was to see the positive in the "bottomed-out" row house in Philadelphia, then to effect the accentuating while, in the remodeling process, eliminating the negative. The positive he saw is worth noting. First, there was the building itself, as just a row house, with its possibilities. Second, there was the historic building designation by the historical commission, and, third, the fact that the building was in a district slated for improvement by the planning commission. Fourth were the redevelopment authority's price tag and the attractiveness of the urban renewal loan. It's no wonder that the architect, wanting a city home for his family, jumped at his opportunity. The added benefit involved, of course, was that in doing for himself, he was doing for his city.

In the case history that follows, a young journalist becomes involved in a similar urban renewal adventure, this time in New Jersey. Once again, the positive and the negative are present, but with a difference. Here the adventurer is bent, and bent with a passion, on remodeling as restoration—of a brownstone. Again, the positive includes definite financial incentive. The newspaperman's "doing for his city," though, is a unique doing, coincidentally in keeping with the Philadelphia Redevelopment Authority's own program providing for "cultural development" in urban renewal.

But urban renewal need not be so dependent on authorities and commissions. Any remodeling in the inner city that enhances the inner city is a positive accentuation and a negative elimination. The architect's remodeling and the journalist's restoration would have been city contributions without official blessing. Buildings crying out for new life abound, as do the challenges for their renovation. Consider the mass movement to city lofts and other industrial space.

Stairs in restored hall on main or second floor lead to rented apartments on third and fourth floors.

## Town House Restored with Faithfulness to the Past

"With a single-mindedness I'd never seen in myself before," young Tom Golodic, with his wife, Pat, has almost completed the restoration of their 1890 Queen Anne Romanesque brownstone in Jersey City, New Jersey.

Tom, a journalist, and Pat, a schoolteacher, bought the building in May, 1975, at a Federal Housing Administration foreclosure sale held through the Newark area FHA office. The house had been boarded up by the FHA when the two families living in its four floors failed to meet their mortgage obligations. Along with other properties, it was being auctioned off to meet the costs to the FHA of paying off the lending institution.

Tom read of the impending sale and, having long been interested in the house, arranged to see it with the local realtor handling the local FHA business. After learning the building's assessed valuation at the city hall ($14,300), he borrowed from his parents and bid a thousand dollars less. The house became his and Pat's.

The Golodics moved into their brownstone in August. By that time, working evenings and weekends with help from Tom's brother, the ground floor was "livable." The main floor was as livable in another five months. After a year, 75 per cent of all interior restoration work had been done, at a cost of $7–8,000, excluding the Golodics' labor. Yet to be completed is the exterior restoration work—to be done by a brownstoning contractor—which will cost from $4–6,000, depending on the authenticity of the restoration.

From the start, the Golodics were "lucky that former owners had been too poor to change things"—the house was practically in its original condition, though in need of major repairs. The most time-consuming work involved plumbing and electricity (Tom read books: "It's 90 per cent mechanical, 10 per cent knowledge"). This work was done first. Next, all woodwork was dismantled, labeled for reassembly, and sent out for stripping. Certain curved pieces which broke when dismantled were reproduced. Walls and ceilings were plastered and painted, and floors were sanded and varnished. Stained glass windows were repaired and cleaned. Finally, the stripped woodwork reinstalled, there was shopping to do for authentic furniture and lighting fixtures.

Today, Tom and Pat occupy the first two floors of the house and rent apartments on the other two floors. In their own apartment, they installed a modern kitchen and added a shower in the bathroom, but on the other floors even the bathrooms have been faithfully restored.

The Golodics' town house is in one of Jersey City's neighborhood preservation areas and is considered by the city to be an historic district. Accordingly, the Golodics' taxes, $1,400 their first year, are frozen for the five years following completion of their restoration. As landlords, they also have a tax write-off on their improvement expenses. When Tom's loan from his parents is paid off, he will be "living free."

Looking back on the whole venture—his point of view a Victorian stuffed chair—Tom notes that "you've got to love the idea of doing it," and adds that you've got to have patience.

Restoration of the brownstone involved shopping for furniture, fixtures, and stained glass of the period.

The Golodics "live" much of the time in modernized kitchen on ground or basement floor of brownstone. Kitchen nonetheless has authentic feeling. Fireplace was original cook stove recess. Door to garden to left of fireplace.

Talone house, left, in its abandoned condition and, below, as handsome desert home it became. Privacy wall in foreground.

## Modest Enlarging Makes Handsome Home of Old Adobe House

For Dr. and Mrs. Frank S. Talone of Paradise Valley, Arizona, a 1929 adobe house, long abandoned, became a charming desert home. With E. L. Nickels, AIA architect of Tempe, the Talones achieved their desired change by both adding to existing buildings and reworking present space.

Two additions to the house itself were made. A sun room, with six-foot sliding glass doors, now overlooks a dry wash and the desert and mountains beyond. A new entry leads into the living room, the former entry into the dining room having become a glass planter bay.

Within the original house, a large bath has replaced two closet-sized baths, at the same time allowing for larger clothes closets in the bedrooms on either side. The kitchen has been redesigned, and the old utility room now contains a recess for the refrigerator and a wet bar off the living room. The kitchen connects conveniently to the new sun room, which is used for informal dining as well as for sitting.

A further addition involved the old two-car garage, a separate building. The garage now houses a guest room with bath, an office, a shop, and a work or hobby room. The garage was extended eight feet to include storage areas, much needed when a house has neither an attic nor a basement.

Since the house is only forty feet from the road, to ensure privacy a final remodeling touch has been the erection of an eight-foot-high solid adobe wall. The driveway enters a gate in the wall, passes the entrance patio, and continues along the house for parking.

With new entry into living room, old entry into dining room has become lovely planting bay.

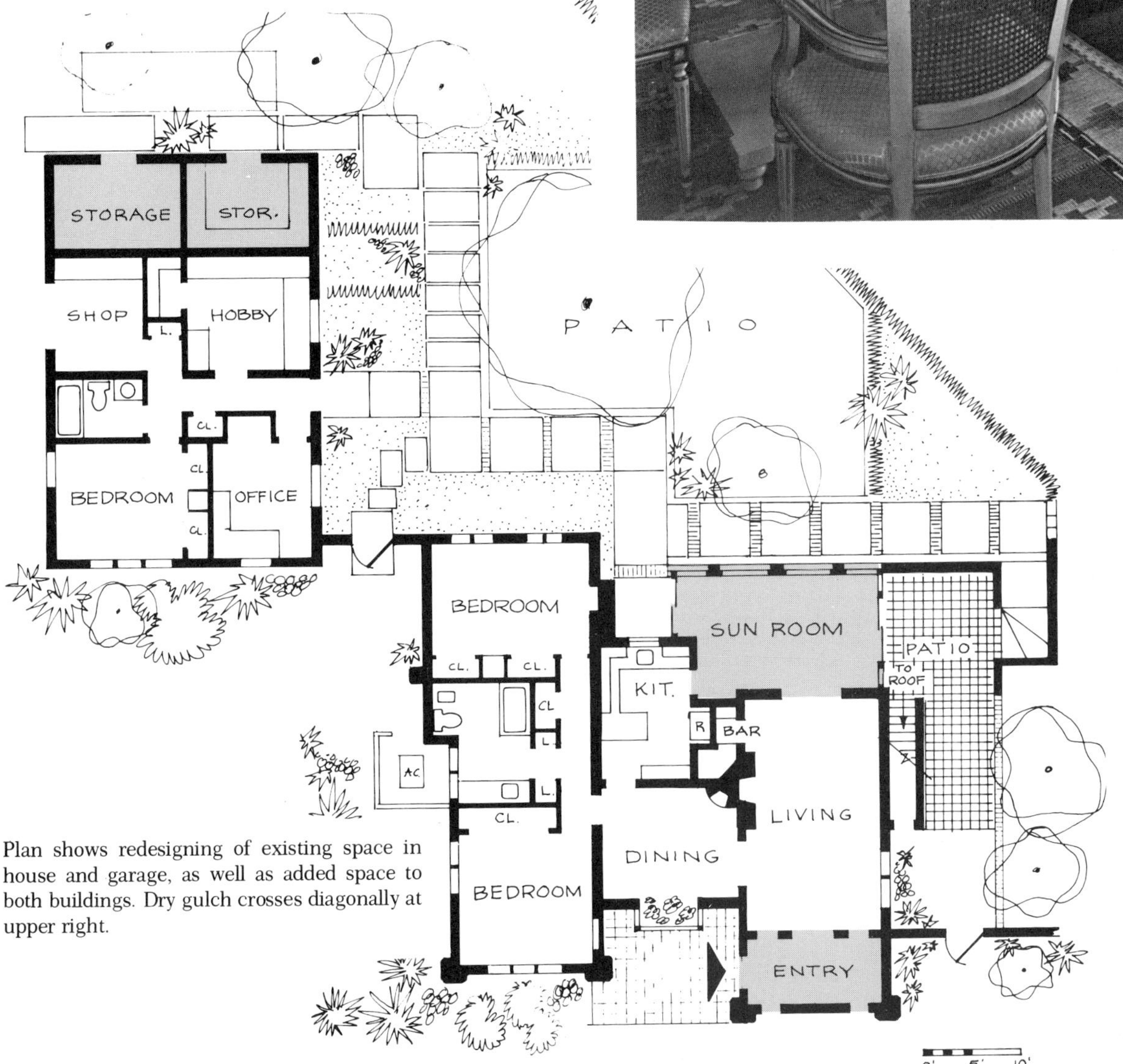


Plan shows redesigning of existing space in house and garage, as well as added space to both buildings. Dry gulch crosses diagonally at upper right.

New entrance leads into living room. Archway was former exterior door. Main entrance is at far right. Dining room entrance is just beyond fireplace.

Below bright sun room replaced rickety screened porch. Sliding glass doors open to patio beyond. Living room is through French doors, center.

Access is easy from redesigned kitchen to added sun room, used for informal dining. Note refrigerator, recessed into wall of former utility room. Note, too, hanging utensils.

Below, Dr. and Mrs. Talone relax on patio, one of many outdoor living areas of their home. Sliding glass door opens to sun room. Stairway leads to roof and chimney draft control.

Dormer and new roof are added as remodeling of abandoned fishing lodge gets underway.

## Deserted Vacation Lodge Becomes Snug Lakeside Home

With a little bit of luck and a great deal of imagination and determination, the Henry B. Andersons of Sherman, Connecticut, have turned a summer "fishing shack" into a charming, year-round lakeside home.

It all started when Mrs. Anderson, boating with her husband on western Connecticut's Lake Candlewood, sighted a hillside covered with mountain laurel. Later, by car, she made her way to the site and its building, a vacation fishing lodge that had been deserted for five years.

The lodge was dank and dark, with no windows for a view, "really unfinished inside—a hodgepodge." Downstairs were a living room, a bedroom, a small kitchen, and a hallway; upstairs, there was undivided attic space.

The property was purchased in the fall of 1973. The building was stripped to its usable bare frame, as the Andersons went to work. Mrs. Anderson herself designed the entire remodeling, and she acted as her own general contractor. A year later, with only minor hitches, their new home was ready.

The first-floor space was rearranged into a living room with a dining area, an enlarged kitchen, a study with closet, and a powder room. The old staircase, opposite the front door, was replaced with a wrought-iron staircase set in a living room corner. The attic, with an added shed dormer facing the lake view, was divided into a landing, two bedrooms, a full bath with shower, and an ingeniously conceived storage area under the roof opposite the lake. The basement was converted into living space amounting to a guest suite. Window spaces are large, and sliding glass doors open onto a deck.

Lodge's new look includes large window areas for brighter interior, and deck leading to gazebo.

Spiral staircase, tucked neatly in corner, leads from living room up to bedrooms and down to guest suite in basement. Note use of space behind staircase for book shelves. Living room furniture is informal, comfortable.

New sun-lit, modern kitchen, below, is separated from living room by eating counter. Access to new gazebo dining room is to right. Note antique bottles at window and plants, to right—giving room added personality.

New gazebo, for formal dining, extends from kitchen and has sliding glass door access. Shed dormer windows offer view of lake from both bedrooms.

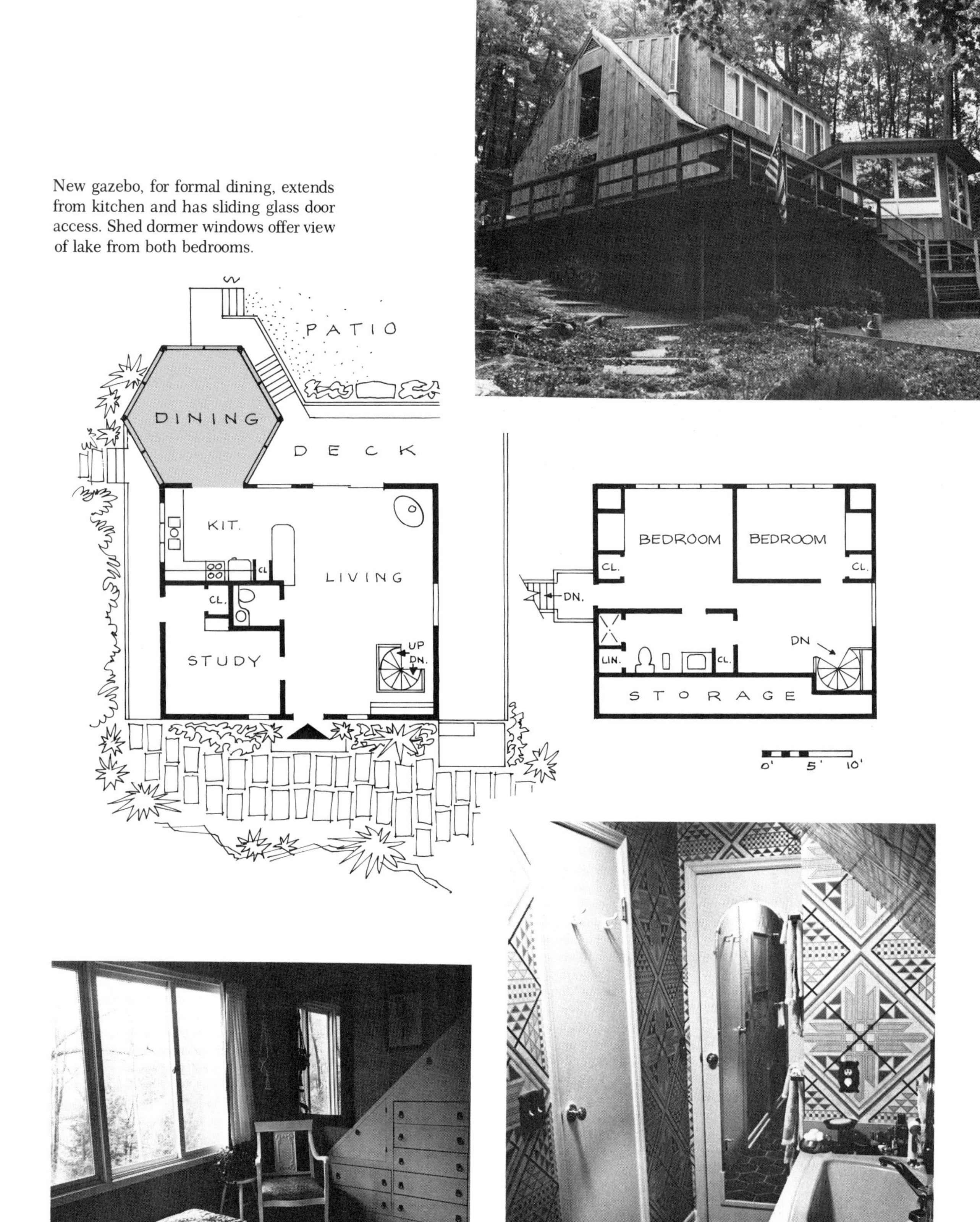


Ingeniously, space under roof beyond end of dormer serves as dresser. Note triangular cabinets for storage.

Full bath fits nicely under roof at front of house. Closet door mirror gives sense of greater space. Remaining space behind wall at right is used for storage.

Latest remodeling project, gazebo for formal dining, has spectacular view of lake and hills. Antique fan cools area in summer, and hopper windows open for ventilation. Table to fit new space was result of long search for "just the right one." New dining area supplements dining area in living room and eating counter in kitchen—a real plus!

Bay window for plants, made of stock casement windows, makes new dining room bright and spacious. Valence displays owner's antique china. Kitchen, dining room, and entrance hall floors are tiled in Spanish-motif terra-cotta, which harmonizes with cherry-stained kitchen cabinets and living room fireplace brick.

## Expanded living with Small Addition and Adroit Re-Arranging

When Sherman Stambaugh retired early from his New York job, he and his wife found themselves in need of a new home to meet a new lifestyle. Their daughter and his mother were no longer living with them. They wanted a smaller house in a more rural setting with a lower tax rate. He wanted workshop space for his retirement-framing business, and she wanted outdoor space for gardening. They found the house they were looking for and, with the help of an architect friend, set about remodeling it to meet their needs and wants.

Removing a wall between the living room and the dining room, and incorporating the dining room space, the living room was enlarged in an L shape. Sliding glass doors replaced the former dining room window for access to the deck.

A full bath, located for some strange reason behind the kitchen, was eliminated.

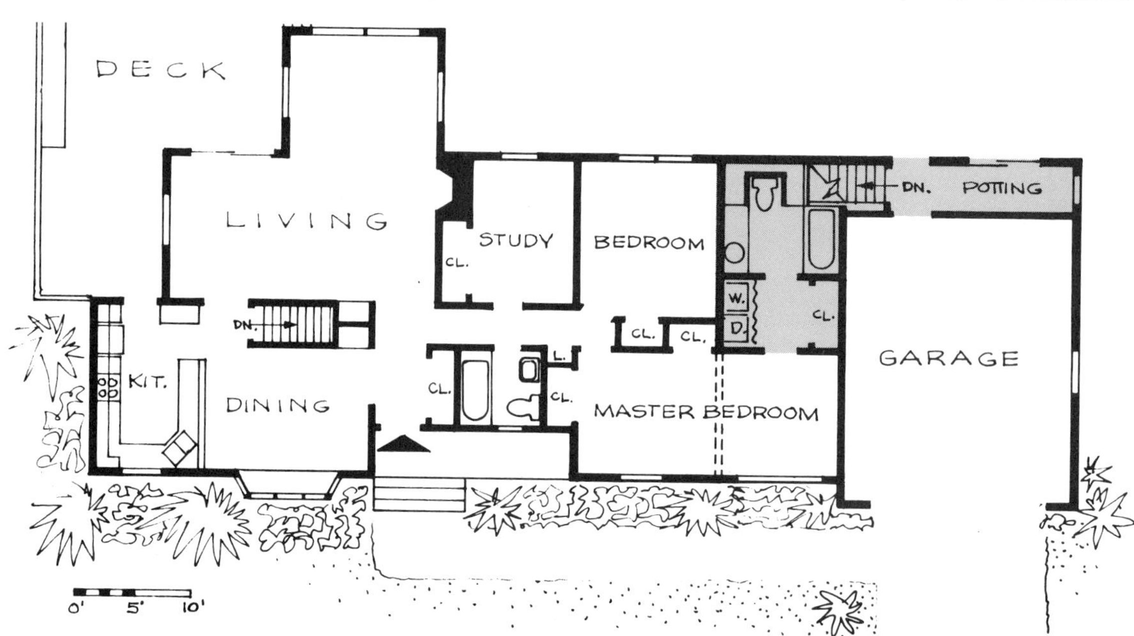

All-new kitchen has ample cabinet and counter space, including marble-topped counter section (foreground) for bread and pastry making. Capped splash rail hides view of kitchen working area from dining room.

Large bay window, to left of entrance, improves house appearance, opens up dining room, and provides plant area.

Former breezeway becomes section of new master bedroom. New master bath is through door at left rear.

That space, with the kitchen and breakfast area space, was reworked into a kitchen and dining room. Three small windows were replaced by a bay window for plants in the new dining room. A hutch and a broom closet in the former breakfast area were removed for greater space. A closet between the living room and the new dining room became a music cabinet and a liquor cabinet with lighted glass shelves.

A bedroom was extended to include the breezeway, and a master bath added between the house and the garage. A potting room was added to the back of the garage, providing new access to the basement of the house.

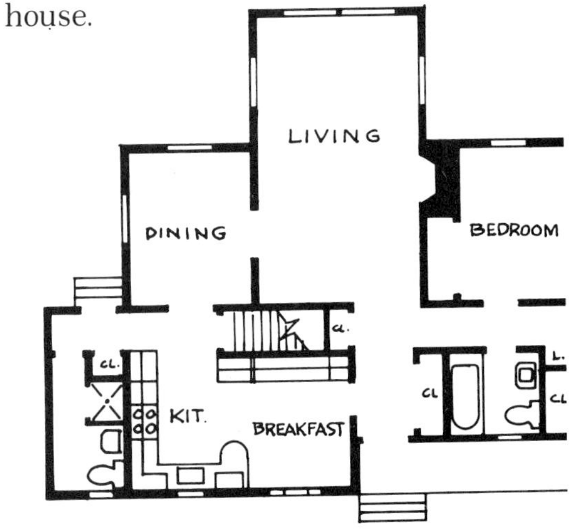


Kitchen and dining arrangement—before.

Section of master bath as seen from dressing room, which has large closet. Skylight provides sufficient natural light.

## . . . And a Basement-Based Business

For his retirement business, Mr. Stambaugh finished his basement to include a family room that doubles as a gallery display area for his frames and mats, a workshop, and a room for storing frames.

The basement also gained a half bath, a cold room, and another storage room.

Mr. Stambaugh in his workshop, framing. Bay to left houses power tools.

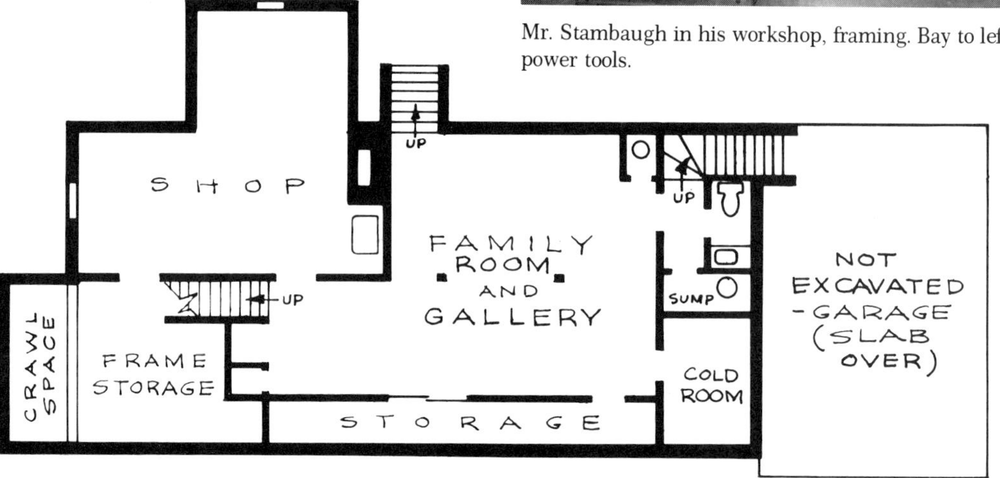

The Stambaughs, center, discuss sample of Mr. Stambaugh's work with a client in new combination family room–gallery in basement of their home. Gallery serves as a permanent display area for his frames and mats.

"Sunken" living room seen from dining-kitchen level. Note entrance hall. Open, carpeted stairway shows at right.

### A Chic Maisonette from a Small Row House

Not wanting to leave the convenience of city living but not happy about staying in an expensive little apartment, Renata Holod and Oleh Tretiak solved their dilemma by buying and totally renovating a small row house near the Philadelphia Museum of Art.

For Renata, an art historian teaching at the University of Pennsylvania, the location was ideal. Oleh, a biomedical engineer, could walk to his office. And the remodeling of this unprepossessing building was a creative challenge.

They started by tearing out all interior walls and stairs. The final result is an open, free-flowing use of space and elegant use of paintings, prints, plants, and accessories.

This row house is 15 feet wide, 34 feet deep, two and a half stories high, and has basement.

Dining area opens onto garden. Second level glass floods kitchen and dining area with light.

Compact, semi-open kitchen, under balcony, permits view of garden space across dining area.

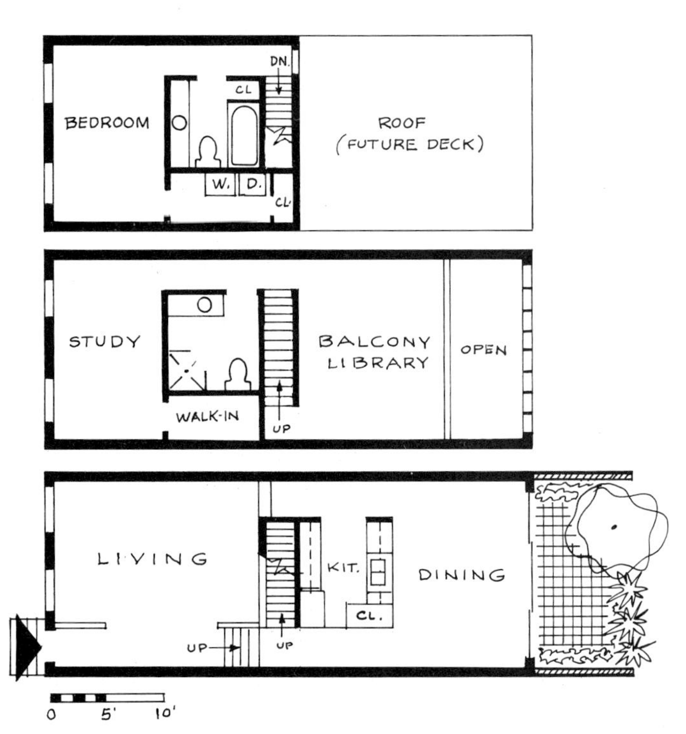


In the mid-eighteen hundreds, most city brick houses had a wooden lean-to kitchen, with a servants' sleeping loft above, attached to the back, a holdover from the detached "plantation" kitchen and the New England summer kitchen that kept heat and odors out of the house. The two-story-high dining area replaced the old tacked-on kitchen. The bi-level first floor was dictated by the bi-level basement. This house was built on a hill by builders who were not about to excavate any more than they had to. With the open stairway, this "sunken" living room effect adds greatly to the charm.

Balcony, library-study and music room for Oleh, enjoys natural light from two-story wall of glass. And from balcony, owners can look out across dining area into garden. Dining area was "tacked-on" kitchen. New kitchen is under balcony.

Central core contains stairway. Beyond stairway is kitchen and dining area facing garden.

Renata's study, on same level as balcony, is separated by bath and stairway.

Door in archway is main entrance, opening into garden room that was formerly open court space.

## Expanded Living on an Ideal Site

The fine, three-bedroom home of Mr. and Mrs. Cletus Reilly in Sun City, Arizona, overlooks the city's largest lake. The Reillys loved being where they were, but they wanted expanded living space. Rooms were just plain too small, especially the living room and the master bedroom. They decided to improve.

Enclosed court, now garden room, becomes entrance room for cheerful year-round living. "Clerestory" windows provide light with privac

Reilly house, as seen from lakeside, showing glassed-in addition to living room.

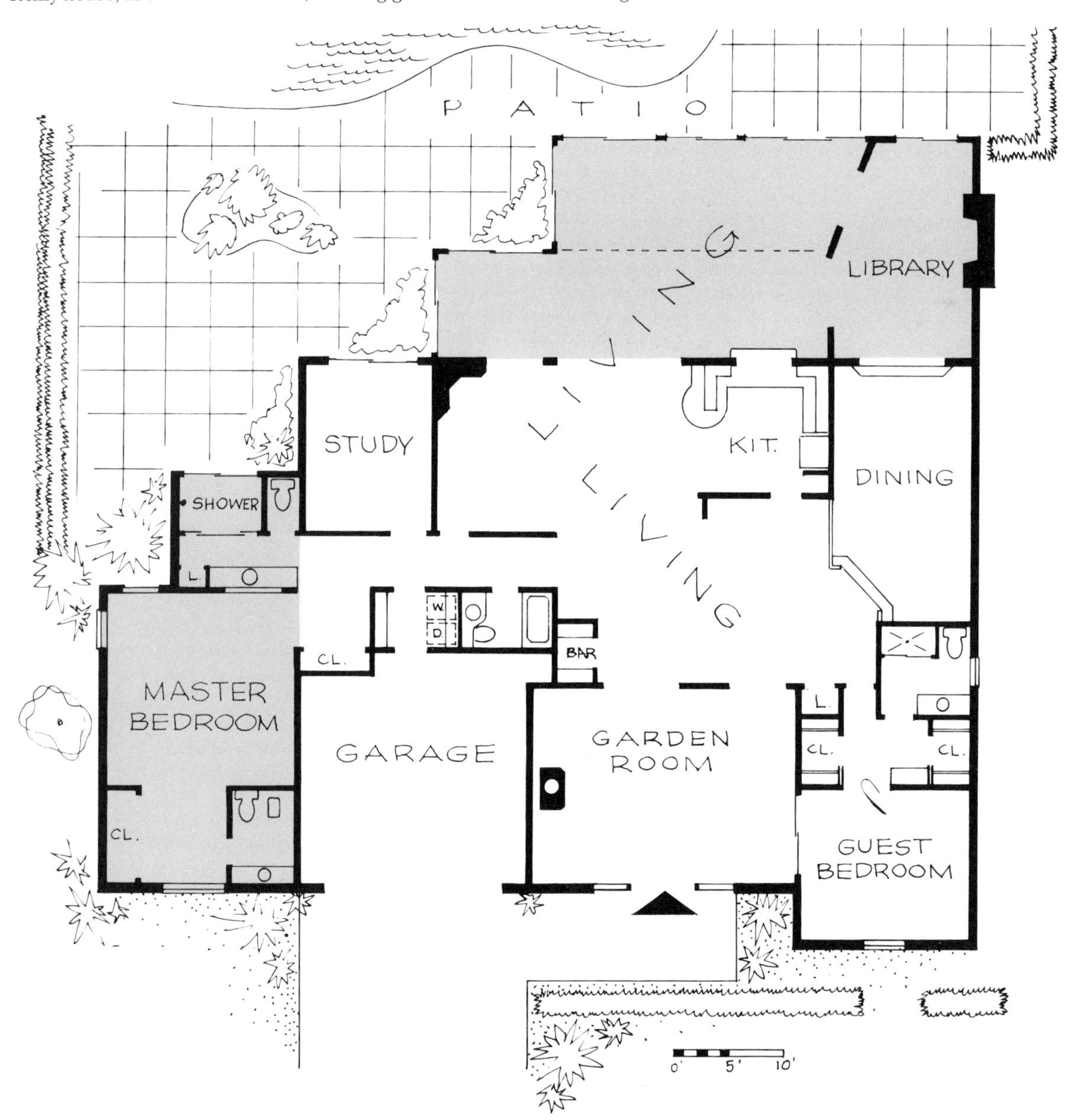

One end of new Reilly living room, which opens onto patio and pool. Glass-walled alcove in background serves as card room. See plan on previous page for interesting shape of greatly enlarged space.

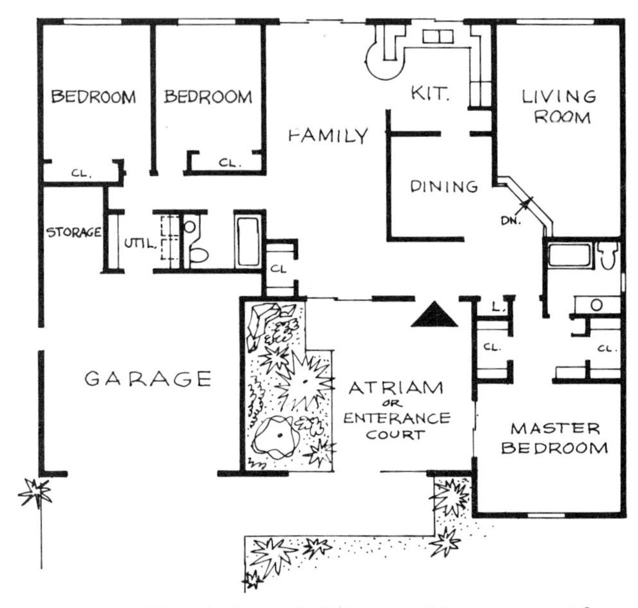


Original three-bedroom Reilly house, with open court at front entrance and two small bedrooms in rear.

The open entrance court seemed a waste of space and, as such, a good place to begin. Their plan was simple—put a roof over the court and enclose it. Clerestory lights of pebble glass in the wall extensions let in ample daylight, and tinted plastic sheets behind the iron grillwork in an entrance arch and door offer cool light with privacy for a "garden" room main entrance.

Both the addition and conversion of space resulted in a new living room, formerly the family room, that is nothing short of immense. With a new master bedroom, the Reillys added old bedroom space to the living room by removing an interior wall. They also appropriated the old dining room space by removing two of its walls when the new dining room moved into the old living room.

Other end of living room addition, opening through to library with fireplace.

To this greatly increased space they added even more in the form of an addition, which has a library with a fireplace at one end and a card room at the other.

Other interior changes saw the conversion of a former small bedroom into a study and the addition of a corner fireplace in the new living room.

The Reilly story is a convincing argument to improve rather than move. While they had a real need to better their lifestyle, they had as real a desire to continue to live in their home—they were able to have their cake and eat it.

An outstanding feature in their remodeling is the great imagination shown in reworking existing space and, notably in their living room, extending old space into new.

Intimate formal dining is enjoyed in former sunken living room. Beyond is guest bedroom, formerly master bedroom.

The new master bedroom suite, above, is located for utmost privacy at the end of a hall off the living room. Spacious and elegant, it includes a daylit woman's dressing area with ample closet space and a lady's vanity and toilet, as well as a master bath that is off the bedroom but has a communicate-through opening. Also off the bedroom is a man's dressing area and closet.

The master bath features a shower room with both interior and exterior sliding glass doors. The outside sliders open onto the patio and pool area. Of course, both sides of the shower are curtained.

In this home, the modern, informal open plan is carried even into the master bedroom suite. As the plan on page 181 shows, the main bathroom has a door on the toilet only, the rest of the bathroom being open to the dressing area. And there is as well the above-mentioned opening for communication.

Certainly adding to the open feeling in the suite are the exterior sliding glass shower room door in the main bathroom and the large expanse of glass in the woman's dressing area.

Master bath has large shower accessible not only from inside but from outside patio-pool area as well.

View across swimming pool of added new space which, with converted existing space, resulted in huge living room.

## Cinderella Story of a Levittown Ranch House

To meet the urgent demand for housing by returning servicemen at the end of World War II, William Levitt started mass-building 800-square-foot ranch houses on a 1,400-acre tract on Long Island, just 28 miles from New York City.

There were four exterior styles, designated only as Types 1, 2, 3, and 4. Each type had the same efficient floor plan, a carport, and an expansion attic, planned with enough head room that two small bedrooms could be finished by the owner. Even by 1946 standards, these plans were modest, but everyone who has worked with a Levitt house agrees that it's a sound design with great flexibility and potential for enlarging and modifying.

The basic house, which could be purchased at the time for $7,900 (actually, the earliest houses sold for $6,990), now sells for $30,000 and more without modification. However, there are few Levitt houses that haven't been enlarged, and the variety of improvements is as delightful as it is astonishing.

Many of the people who originally bought homes in Levittown—when it still looked like the potato field it had been—stayed on. Even though a much enhanced financial condition has made it possible for many to move to a "finer" area, a strong community feeling, good schools and libraries, convenience to New York City, and pride in their homes make Levittown for these residents too attractive to "move up."

The Alfred Lederkramer family of five expanded their Ranch #4 on a pleasant curved street into a rich, spacious home of great taste. Moreover, they've made maximum use of the outdoor space behind the house. Fenced-in and shrubbed, the outdoor living area includes a large deck/patio, a fountain/pool, garden sculptures, and many unusual and elegant shrubs and trees.

Like no doubt thousands of their Levittown neighbors (including the Worthingtons, whose remodeling story appears on page 78), the Lederkramers chose to stay where they were happy being to make their good house a great one. With conviction and imagination, they succeeded in turning their basic type ranch into a stunning home that is truly and uniquely theirs.

Former garage was converted into library/music room. Bay window is made from small sliding units.

As discussed in the Introduction, there are sound reasons not to move, but to improve, and as with the Lederkramers, being happy where you are is the best one of all.

In the best sense, they "moved up."

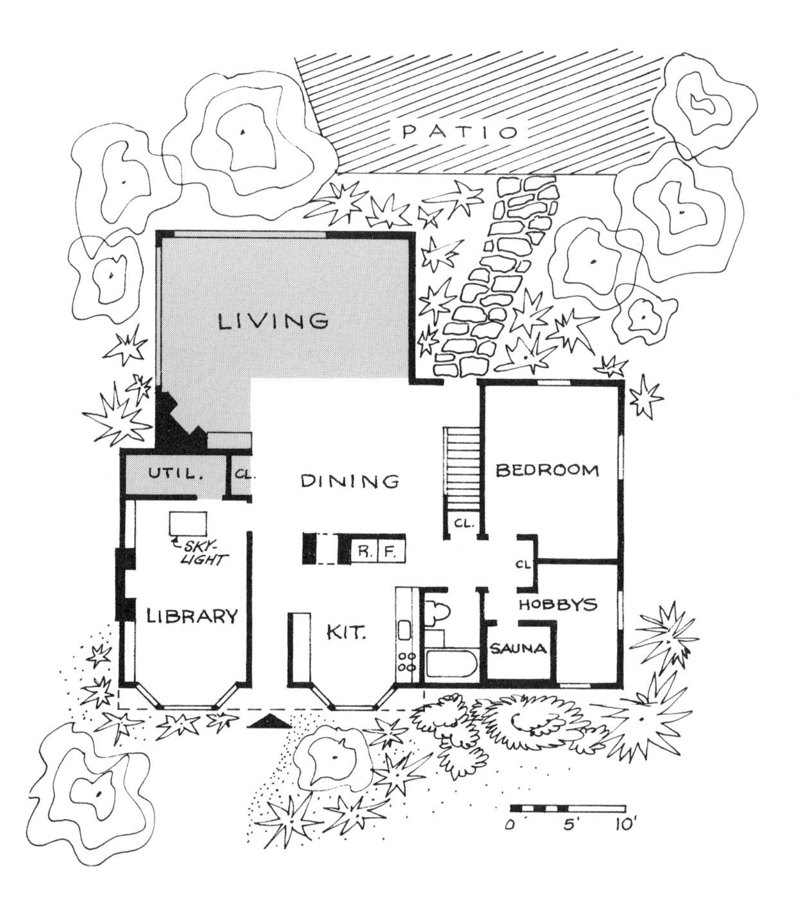

Generous living room with corner fireplace is mostly new space. Glass walls on two sides flood room with natural light.

Below, library/music room has own fireplace, floor-to-ceiling bookshelves, and large skylight.

The decision to enlarge the 12′ × 19′ living room and provide a dining room at the same time was ingenious but logical. The original house was extended in two directions (see plan) to make one large space but two room areas.

To achieve an even greater feeling of "big space," a cathedral ceiling was introduced in the new space and carried into the old space. The upstairs floor space sacrificed was regained by adding dormers on the back roof to create two good-sized bedrooms and a bath.

The gracious dining area, with its own fireplace (originally the living room fireplace) works beautifully for family and for entertaining. There's double direct access to the kitchen. For parties, traffic flows easily from area to area.

With the remodeling, one of the downstairs bedrooms became space for a sauna, assembled from a kit by the owners, and a sewing room. The garage, originally a carport, was converted into a library/music room.

Large plant bay, replacing small casement window, is only structural change in kitchen, above. Tasteful decorating makes for pleasant family dining.

Gracious dining area, below, was formerly small living room. Wide opening to new living room gives "big space" feeling to both areas. Kitchen is beyond fireplace in background.

## Gardener's Cottage Goes Contemporary

Architect Victor Stimac has designed many modern buildings as a graduate of Frank Lloyd Wright's Wisconsin school and later a staff member of his firm in Arizona. However, when Victor and his wife Christine returned to his native Pennsylvania, there was no time to build that "dramatic contemporary" for themselves. They were about to have their first child and needed a place to set up housekeeping.

They found a small, four-room gardener's cottage in a rural area of Newtown Square, close enough to Philadelphia for commuting.

Soon they fell in love with the location. Although the house was too close to the road, they discovered overgrown garden beds, stone walls, and walks at the rear. So they began to plan the reorientation of the house toward the rear, which happened to have a great view into an intimate valley.

Of course, Victor saw hundreds of possibilities for remodeling the cottage. He set himself the challenge of combining modern convenience and style with 1927 cottage and stucco.

By comparing the before and after plans at the right, you will note that with very slight structural changes, the whole original part of the house changed. And it worked beautifully. The bedrooms are clustered together in the desired private zone. The former porch became a wardrobe and dressing area for the new master bedroom, and the greenhouse a master bath (see page 136).

In contrast to the small rooms of the old house, the addition is one large, dramatic space that contains two sitting areas and a dining area. Even the new kitchen is part of this new space, separated from the living and dining areas only by a column and eight-foot-high storage walls.

Orientation of the entire house is now to the rear and to the view, with access to terrace and gardens, relating indoor living to outdoor living.

Starting with the two steps down from the

"Before" rear of the gardener's cottage.

In "before" picture of house front, door is behind tree trunk between outdoor lamps.

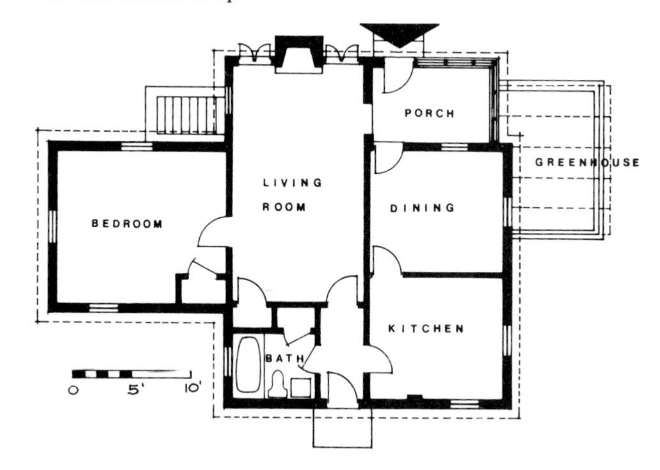

New front entrance, to left, is part of addition. Glass sliders to studio replaced small window of former bedroom.

Rear view after: Addition to right contains living-dining area plus kitchen. New bath and bedroom extension are at left.

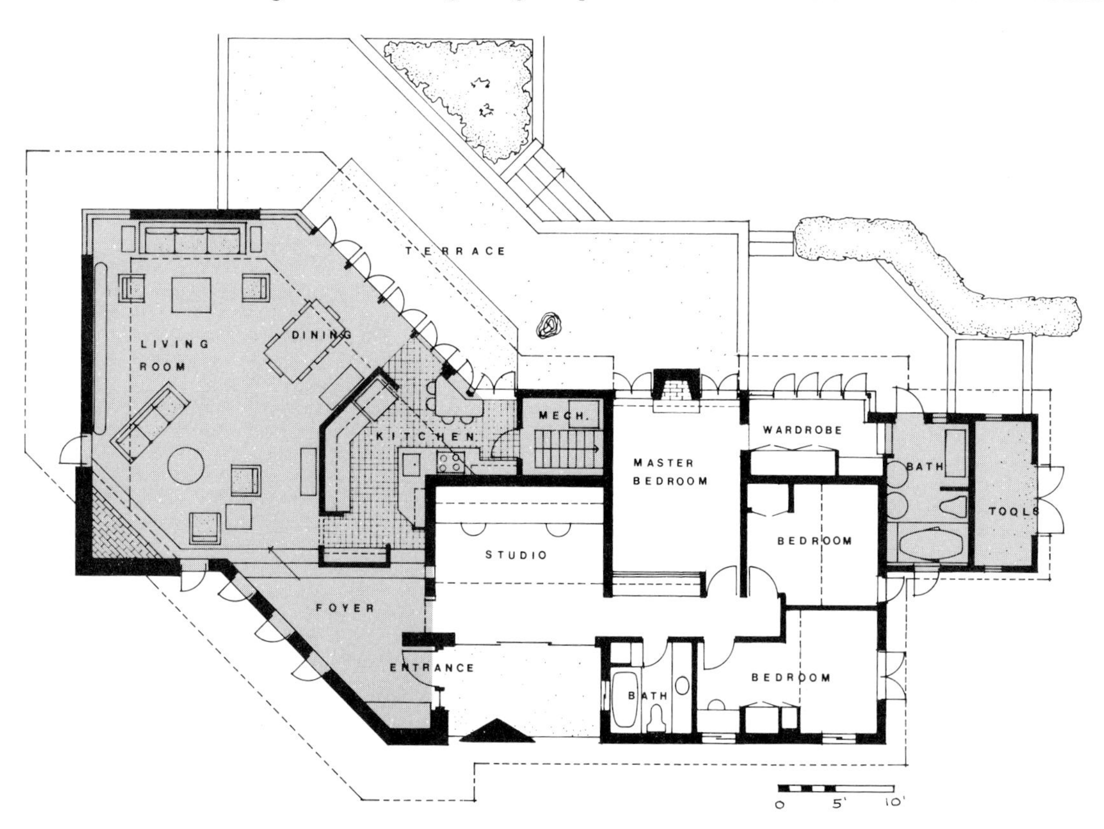

Living room from entrance hall. Spectacular ceiling of tongue and groove Douglas fir makes the whole wing elegant and unique.

Dining area. Glass doors lead to patio. Kitchen is entered via opening left of buffet as well as through arch at right.

entrance hall into the main living area, with its faceted ceiling of tongue and groove Douglas fir, each area is a fresh and exhilarating experience. Notice on the plan, on page 189, that, except for the bedrooms and baths, there is an open flow from one living space to another and a happy, easy access to the outdoors.

Another addition is planned for the near future, a master bedroom and bath wing beyond the living room.

Huge corner fireplace has piano-hinged bi-fold doors backed with asbestos, which keep house heat from escaping when fireplace is going out. Fumes go up chimney.

Other end of kitchen exits to dining area, behind refrigerator, and to patio. Breakfast counter is beyond sink to right. Note cork veneer on cabinets and ceramic tile on countertops.

Second floor was built on two thirds of this canal front bungalow by creative young homeowner.

Two organizations of creative homeowners are planning canal sidewall improvement projects.

## Work in L.A.—Live on a Canal in Venice!

This remodeling went up—from a humble four-room bungalow of the twenties to a lean, clean maisonette of today. Its unique location on the old canal system in Venice, California, now a suburb of Los Angeles, made it a prime prospect for improving.

Venice is now emerging from a long period of neglect. In 1904, it represented tobacco tycoon Abbott Kinney's vision of an American Renaissance—Italy's city in the United States, complete with gondoliers. His dream for a cultural center failed, largely due to faulty engineering. In 1912, the state board of health called the canal a menace to health. The project deteriorated into an amusement park for weekend pleasure-seekers. In 1925, Venice was incorporated into Los Angeles, and in the belief that land is worth more than water, much of the canal system was filled in. For a few years, the site was an oil field. Today, especially for young people, the area is a challenge to rebuild.

Designer-owner Monique Schlick began her rebuilding by removing all interior walls except those enclosing the bath. A bedroom, a bath, and a deck were added on top of the rear two thirds of the house. The front third remains one story. The attic floor was removed and the tie beams left in place so that the end of the living room has a cathedral ceiling with a skylight on each side. An eight-foot-square addition at the rear accommodates the stairway, a guest closet, and a laundry under the landing.

The second-floor bedroom and bath both have French doors leading to a sun deck.

Kitchen has old world charm.

Large living room runs full length of house. "L" at left, beyond bath wall, is study.

Doors taken from downstairs walls and dark trim give crisp accents to new bedroom. French doors lead to deck; bath door is at right.

Morning sun, through French doors, floods bath. Antique commode and Persian rug spell luxury.

View from patio shows deck and French doors to bedroom above kitchen door. Stairway tower has exterior access to tool room and laundry.

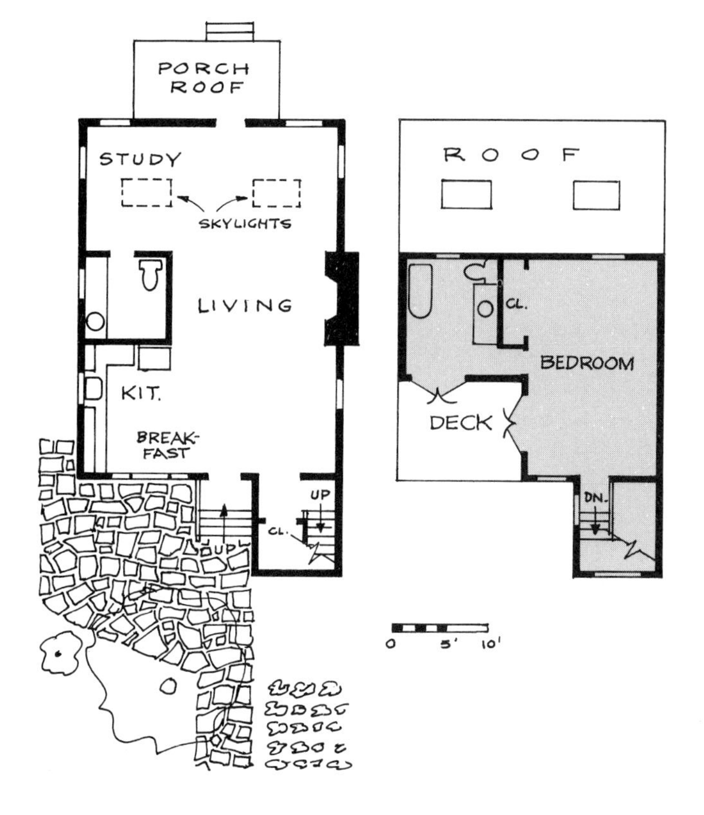

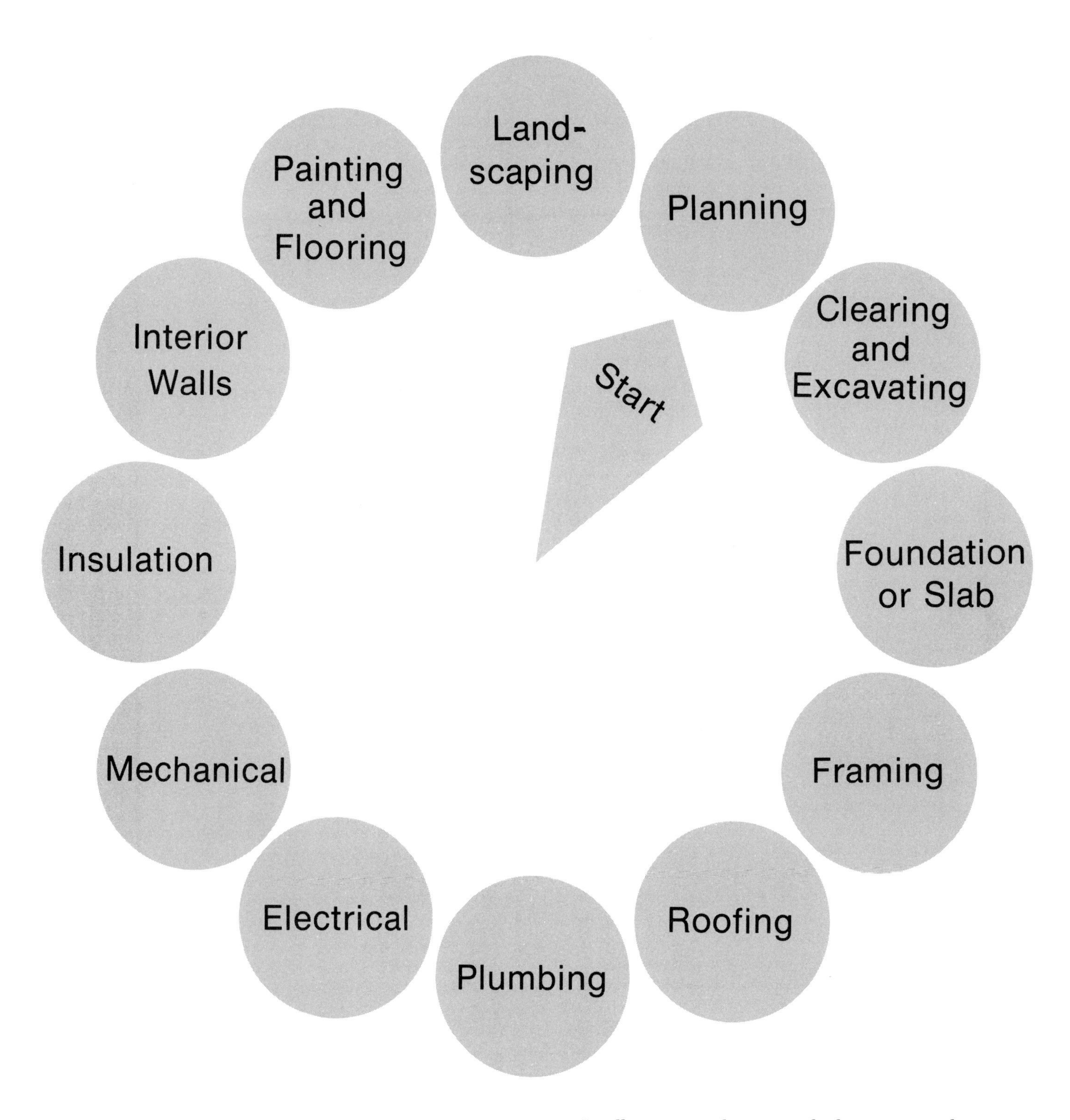


It all starts with you and planning, with or without the services of an architect or designer. The planning done, consider where you might well plug in your talent, energy, and time—and determination—not only to ensure the best job done but to save money!

PART TWO

# HOW TO BEGIN

Clients meet with architect in his office, above, to discuss features of remodeling plans. Close working relationship involves several such meetings. Top left: draftsman translates ideas into detailed working drawings and specifications for builder to follow during construction. Bottom left: clients, with architect, discuss plans with contractor in architect's office. Architect will oversee construction to make certain it is going according to plans. Often, unforeseen circumstances require construction changes, for which architect provides new drawings and specifications. Below: plans in hand, architect discusses work in progress with builder on site.

# 1.

# Planning and the Architect

Before you begin any remodeling job, you should know what you're letting yourself in for. Our intent in this section is to alert you to the various aspects of planning.

We'll assist you in evaluating your ability in the several areas where you could "do it yourself" and discuss the contributions of the professionals, from architect or designer to interior decorator. We believe that, once you're aware of the services offered by the professionals, you'll find that here and there you can contribute ideas and labor, resulting in both savings and a better job. In any case, we feel that the more informed and comfortable you are in each area of remodeling expertise, the more you will be able to become actively and confidently involved. The job, after all, is your job. You've counted your home headaches, assessed your home's assets and potential, and compared the cost of relocating to that of remodeling. You've decided not to move but to improve.

You've also determined your desires and needs and have a remodeling idea in mind. You've decided on more space—a larger living room. Or new space—a third bedroom. Or new and different space—a family room. Or rearranged space—a more efficient kitchen.

Where do you go from here?

The answer is research. If your home improvement is to be a better bathroom, for example, the thing to do is to learn all you can about bathrooms. You'll find abundant information to clip—in magazines, in brochures, in catalogues. Collect the literature, study it, and file it for reference. Study this book and other books on home improvement. Compare, contrast, and combine ideas. Incorporate what you learn into your own thinking. Borrow, too, from what you've seen and can arrange to see in the homes of relatives and friends. Share your thinking with others and be open to their suggestions. Then, sum up your thoughts and translate your thinking into a sketch.

## Making Your Sketch

Start rough; you can refine later. Make sketch after sketch and set them aside. Keep erasures on any drawing to a minimum, since you might remove a good idea. Experiment with general dimensions and with specific ones. Try doors, windows, and closets here, then try them there. Consider traffic flow, sunlight, and prevailing breezes.

Refining your drawing, work to scale. For single rooms, one-half inch to the foot is common, for entire floors one-quarter inch to the foot.

Keep furniture in mind. You'll want to be able to arrange the furniture as you'd like to have it. Is there enough space for the bed between the windows, and for the bureau between the closet and the corner? Using the same scale used in the sketch, make cut-out representations of the furniture to be placed in the room. Moving these about on your drawings gives you a surprisingly definite feeling of the space furniture will occupy and the space you'll use around it. As with furniture, include consideration of heating units, electrical outlets, telephone jacks, and light fixtures.

The actual addition of a room, as opposed to remodeling an existing room, involves exterior as well as interior planning. Here, you'll want to start with scale drawings of your present structure, so that you'll be able to attach same-scale drawings of your addition for an overall picture—from all relevant views. The ideal starting point would be the original elevation drawings of your present house. A sound alternative is to draw your house to scale (say, one-quarter inch to the foot) as it is now, then add your addition drawings. The essential measurements of your house should not be hard to take.

## Consider the Exterior

Exterior considerations abound. Aside from practical and aesthetic considerations, you have to keep in mind any legal restrictions. Before any extensive planning on paper is undertaken, you should inform yourself of zoning regulations and building code requirements in your area. What you want to do will be subject to what you are permitted to do.

Both aesthetically and practically, how your addition will suit your present house involves how your house with the addition will sit on your land. An added room that obscures from view a favorite tree, or detours entry into the house itself, could amount to a subtraction from good living.

Whether planning for the interior alone or for the exterior as well, once you've refined your sketch or sketches to most accurately reflect your thinking, you're ready to plan to build.

## The Architect

Planning to build might well involve the services of an architect. Do you need one? Do you want one? What does he do, and what will it cost?

An architect who does residential work is a professional trained, licensed, and experienced in designing homes and home improvements to meet people's living needs. His special talent is to see, to understand, to plan, and later, to oversee. Working for you, he works from you—that is, he designs around you and your family, your house and site, and your budget.

The value of an architect can be seen in three lights: that of his EXPERTISE, that of his PRODUCT, and that of his SERVICE.

The architect is *expert* as both designer and engineer. He plans a house or a remodeling for his client that is aesthetically pleasing, efficient, and structurally sound. He's as attuned to his client's desires and needs as he is informed on zoning regulations and building codes.

For both interiors and exteriors, he knows styles and what materials relate to them. He knows the relationships of shapes and sizes. He has a developed sense of space and of how it is best utilized—the size and shape of rooms, the location of rooms and their arrangement, the orientation of rooms to the sun and wind and to outside space. He understands traffic flow, from room to room and within rooms.

The architect knows houses and how they are built. His knowledge encompasses all phases of construction, from excavation to landscaping, from foundation to roof. He knows construction components, from doors and windows to heating systems.

It should be pointed out here that construction knowledge is the proper realm of the contractor. If your remodeling job is sufficiently simple, given your own sketches and instructions, any reputable builder can guide your selection of components. Still, though, you will want to be well enough informed to effectively communicate your wants and needs. Your local building materials supplier can help you become informed with manufacturers' catalogues and specification sheets, and advertisers in the home magazines usually have customer literature available on request.

The second half of this chapter discusses in depth the following construction components to be considered: doors and windows; ceilings, walls, and floors; heating and air conditioning; lighting; and, as it can pose a question, plumbing.

Once again, the architect shares the contractor's knowledge of these components. It is his expertise in his own right. It is a measure of his value.

## Working with the Architect

With a general construction knowledge under your belt, you can appreciate that the architect, with his vast store of specific knowledge, is an expert. His *product* is the translation of his expertise—in terms of you and your remodeling needs and desires—into detailed working drawings and specifications on which to build your home improvement. As will be seen, his product begins with rough sketches, continues through preliminary drawings, and ends with the working drawings and specifications themselves.

The architect's *service* can best be presented in a discussion of how one would work with you. A typical involvement with an architect follows.

At your first meeting with the architect, preferably in your home, you become acquainted and begin to establish a rapport (if you engage his services, you will be working together closely for some time).

You explain in general your needs or desires and present your home improvement plan. He discusses your plan with you and suggests alternative solutions to your problem. You decide on the extent of his services you'll require, and he informs you of his fees and their manner of payment. He should give you a rough estimate of the construction cost of your remodeling, and you should be candid with him about your budget. Too often, serious conflicts arise because a homeowner is not as candid as he should be about the amount of money he has to spend or otherwise misleads the architect.

At the end of the meeting, a verbal agreement is reached, which the architect will later verify in writing. In a more formal situation, the architect may leave a contract with the homeowner, probably the standard American Institute of Architects form, to be signed and returned, or he may request a letter of confirmation of the agreement.

Before the meeting is over, you should furnish the architect with any existing surveys, showing the present house and lot and any existing working drawings or blueprints of the present house.

Instead of first meeting the architect in your home, you might meet him in his of-

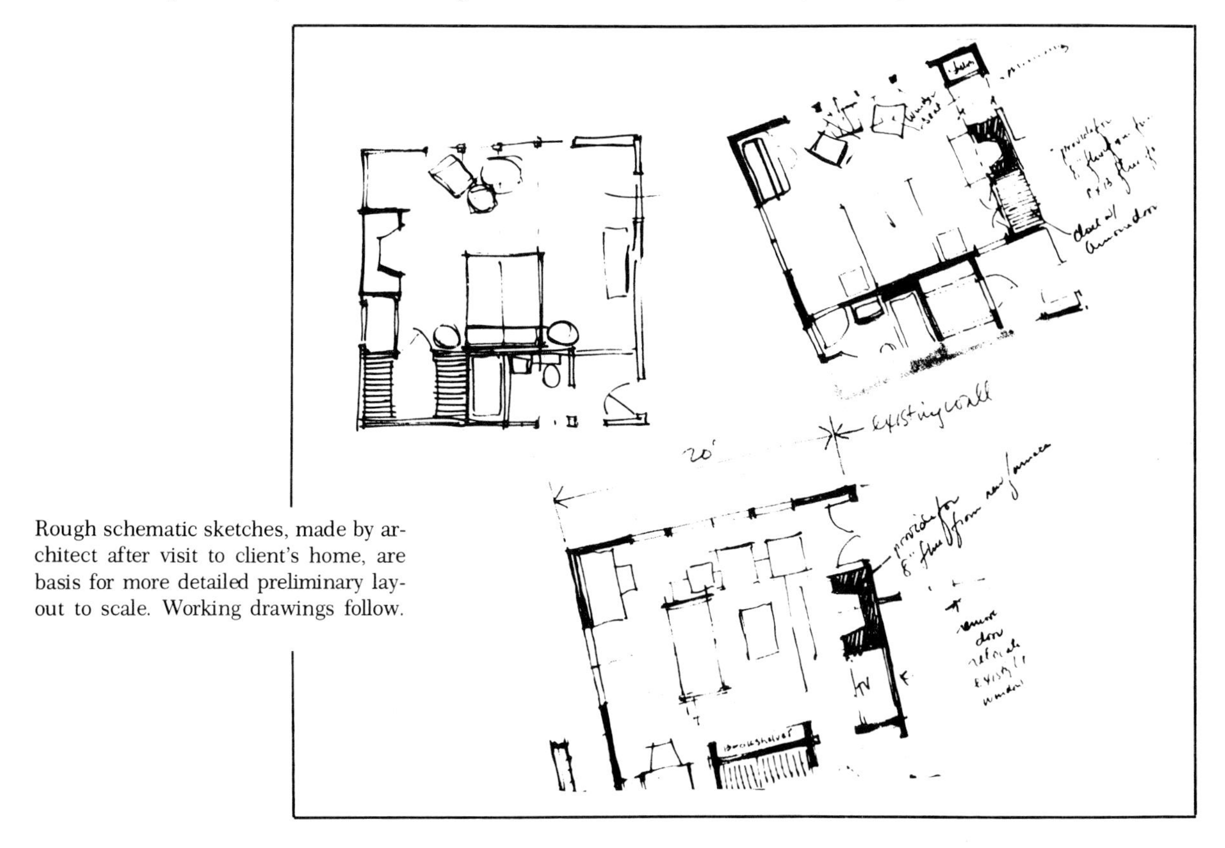


Rough schematic sketches, made by architect after visit to client's home, are basis for more detailed preliminary layout to scale. Working drawings follow.

fice. Such a visit gives the homeowner an opportunity to take a look at the architect's business operation and, through photographs, gain a feeling for the work he has done for others.

At a second session in your home (the first, if the initial meeting was in the architect's office), the architect will measure your house, particularly the area to be affected by your remodeling, for plans and elevation drawings. He may take photographs, and he'll probably at this time further assess your desires and needs.

## Schematic Plans

Back in his office, the architect then prepares rough but scaled schematic plans or studies of the remodeling to meet your requirements. He'll probably rough out alternatives as well. He'll further try to arrive at a more accurate estimate of construction costs, using rule-of-thumb figures. If the new estimate is appreciably higher than the first, this is a good time for you two to meet again.

When you approve of the architect's schematic drawings, he then makes a preliminary layout to scale, beginning to develop final details. At this time, he could well show these plans to one or two contractors to arrive at a more accurate construction cost estimate, even to learn if he or they would be interested in bidding on the job.

## Working Drawings and Bids

The architect next prepares working drawings of the remodeling with specifications of the materials to be used. Blueprint copies of these are sent out to contractors for bids. When the bids are returned, the architect and you sit down again to decide on your contractor. Both the amounts of the contractors' bids and their reputations, as known to either or both of you, will influence your decision.

It should be pointed out that throughout the planning stages with the architect, you're in contact with each other, in person, by phone, or by mail. Over and over again, there are occasions to discuss the progress of his work. It should be noted further that all of this takes time, as much as three months in some cases. A homeowner shouldn't push an architect for work overnight—not if he wants the work done as it should be done.

## The Architect's Services

Something else should be stated here, and stressed—if you deal with an architect, it's not an all-or-nothing proposition. What services an architect provides you with depend

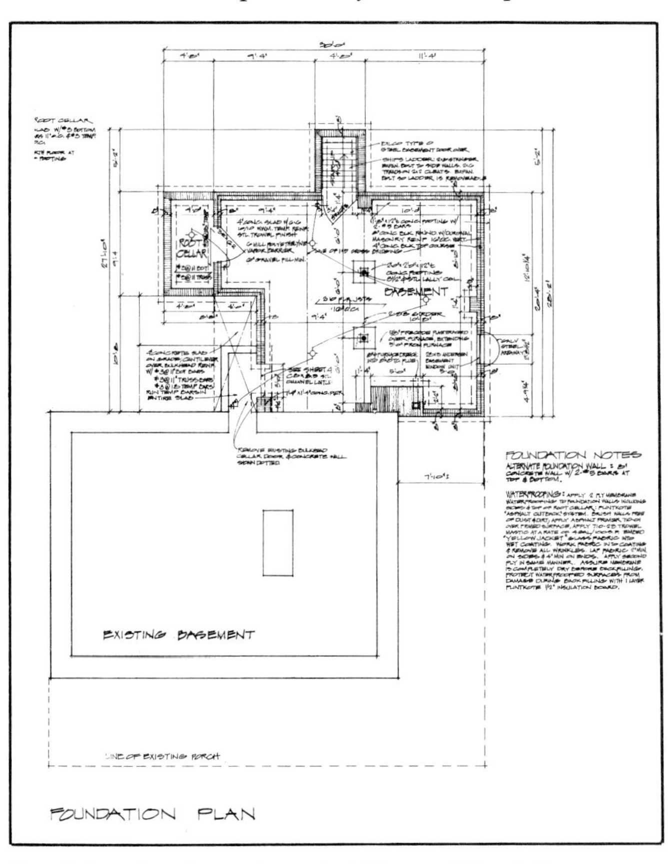


Foundation plan shows size and thickness of foundation walls and width of footings. Notes indicate type of floor, materials, construction specifications. (Site plan, not shown, locates buildings and new addition on plot.)

In floor plan drawings (top, opposite page), new walls (usually shaded) are shown in relation to old walls. Shown too are all dimensions, location of electrical and heating outlets, cutting and patching needed for fitting new construction to old. Included is written description of mechanicals—plumbing, electrical, heating—amplified by notes.

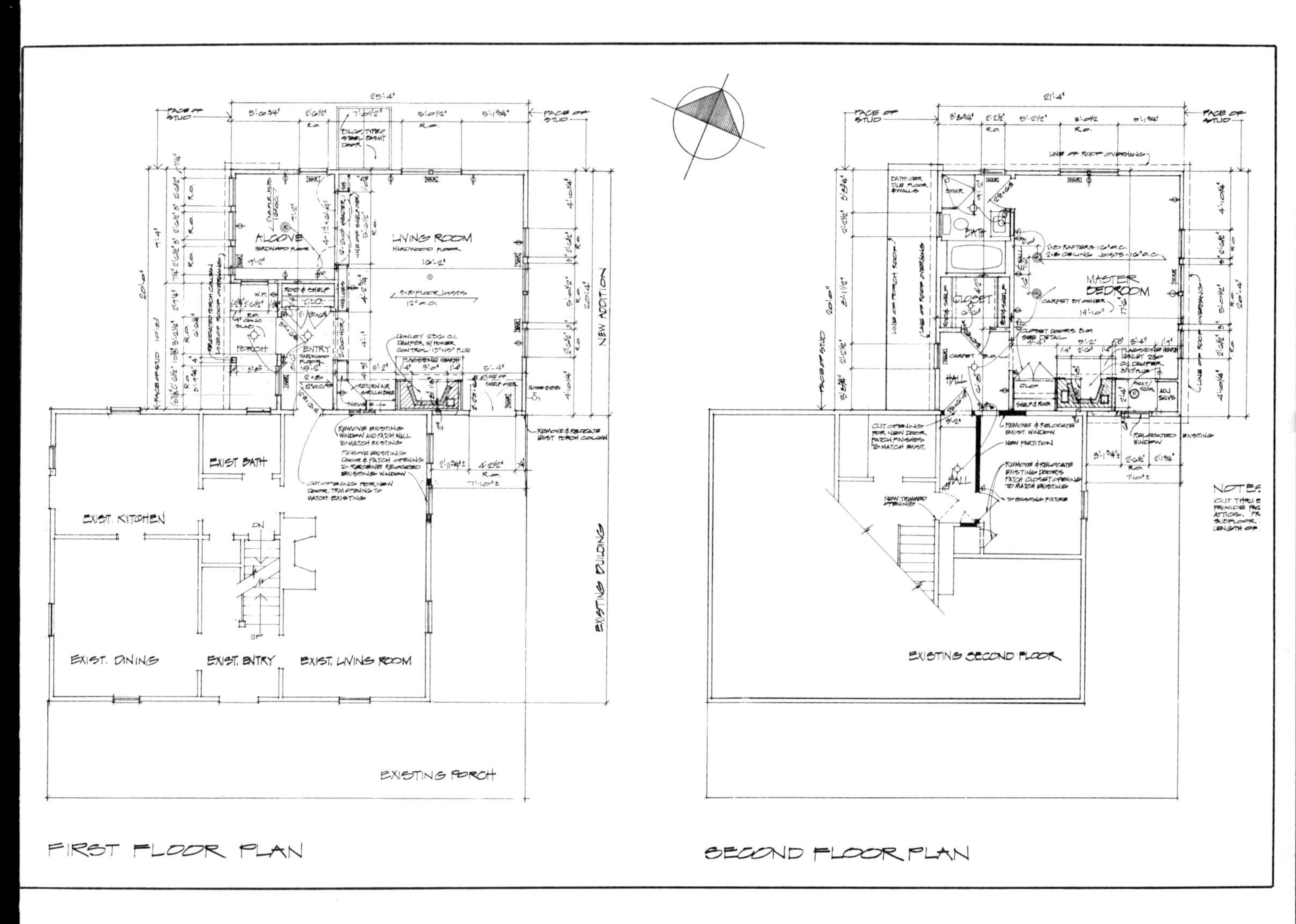


on what services you contract with him to provide. It could be that all you want is an hour or two of consultation with him. It might be that you only need schematic drawings, or preliminary ones. In any case, his services can be terminated at any point you decide on—and you pay for no more than what you've gotten.

If you've contracted for all the architect's services, these continue to the completion of construction and beyond.

Simply, the architect sees to it that your remodeling is done as you and he have planned it. He makes regular visits to the site to make certain the work is progressing according to the working drawings and specifications. He provides additional working drawings and specifications for changes that couldn't have been foreseen. He settles any controversies that might arise between you and your contractor. He approves your payments to the contractor. He retains a percentage, commonly ten per cent, of the contractor's price until the work is satisfactorily completed and the contractor assures your release from any liens against your property.

## Cost and Payment

The cost of an architect's services varies, as does the method of fee payment. Once again, you pay for what you get. A visit to an architect's office to discuss your home improvement won't cost you. If, however, he's made a visit to your home and has provided a service—whether a series of ideas or a thumbnail sketch or two—he'll charge you for that service, and rightly so.

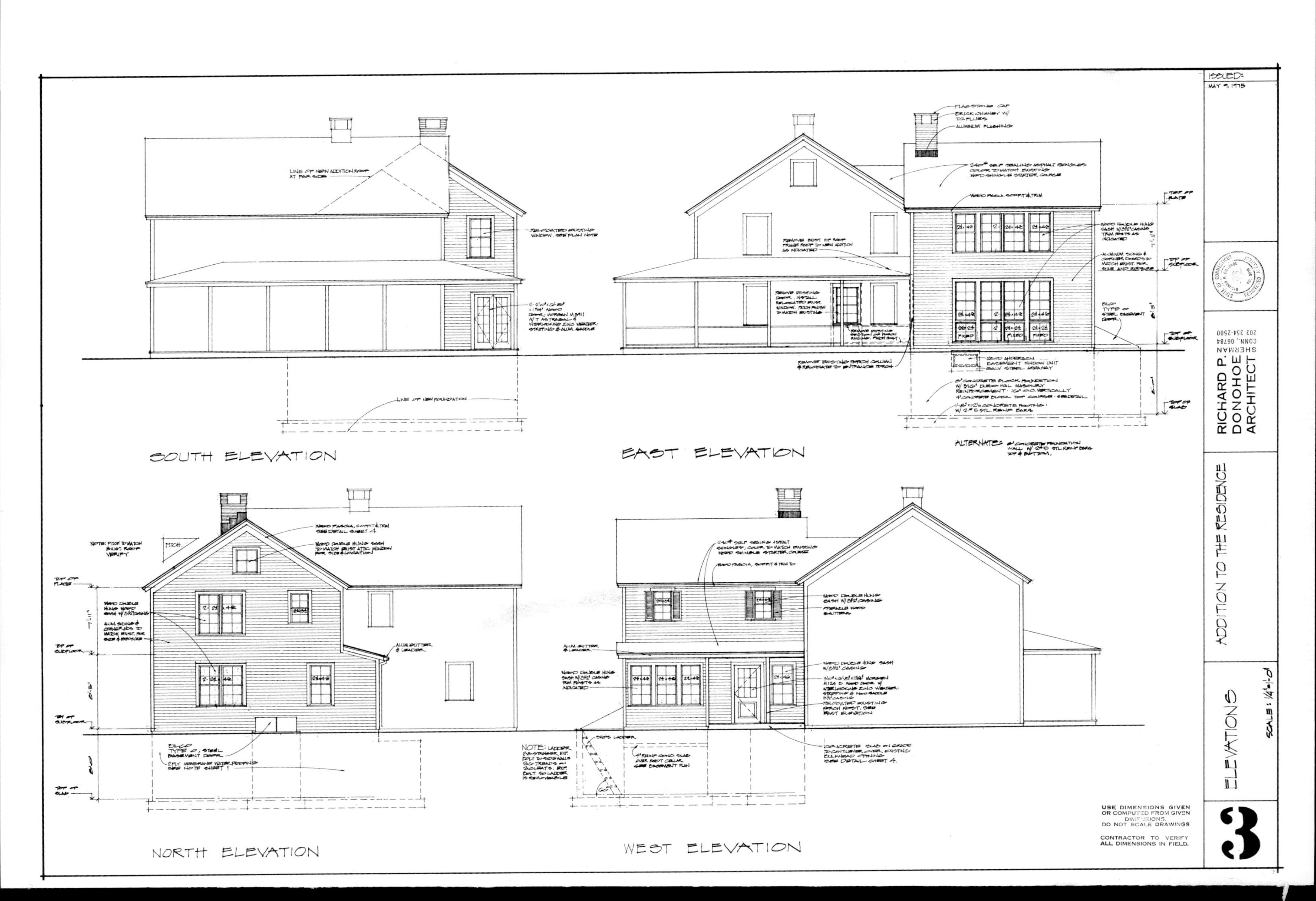
SOUTH ELEVATION
EAST ELEVATION
NORTH ELEVATION
WEST ELEVATION
ISSUED:
MAY 9, 1975
RICHARD P.
DONOHOE
ARCHITECT
SHERMAN
CONN. 06784
203 354-2500
ADDITION TO THE RESIDENCE
ELEVATIONS
SCALE: 1/4"=1'-0"
3
USE DIMENSIONS GIVEN
OR COMPUTED FROM GIVEN
DIMENSIONS.
DO NOT SCALE DRAWINGS
CONTRACTOR TO VERIFY
ALL DIMENSIONS IN FIELD.

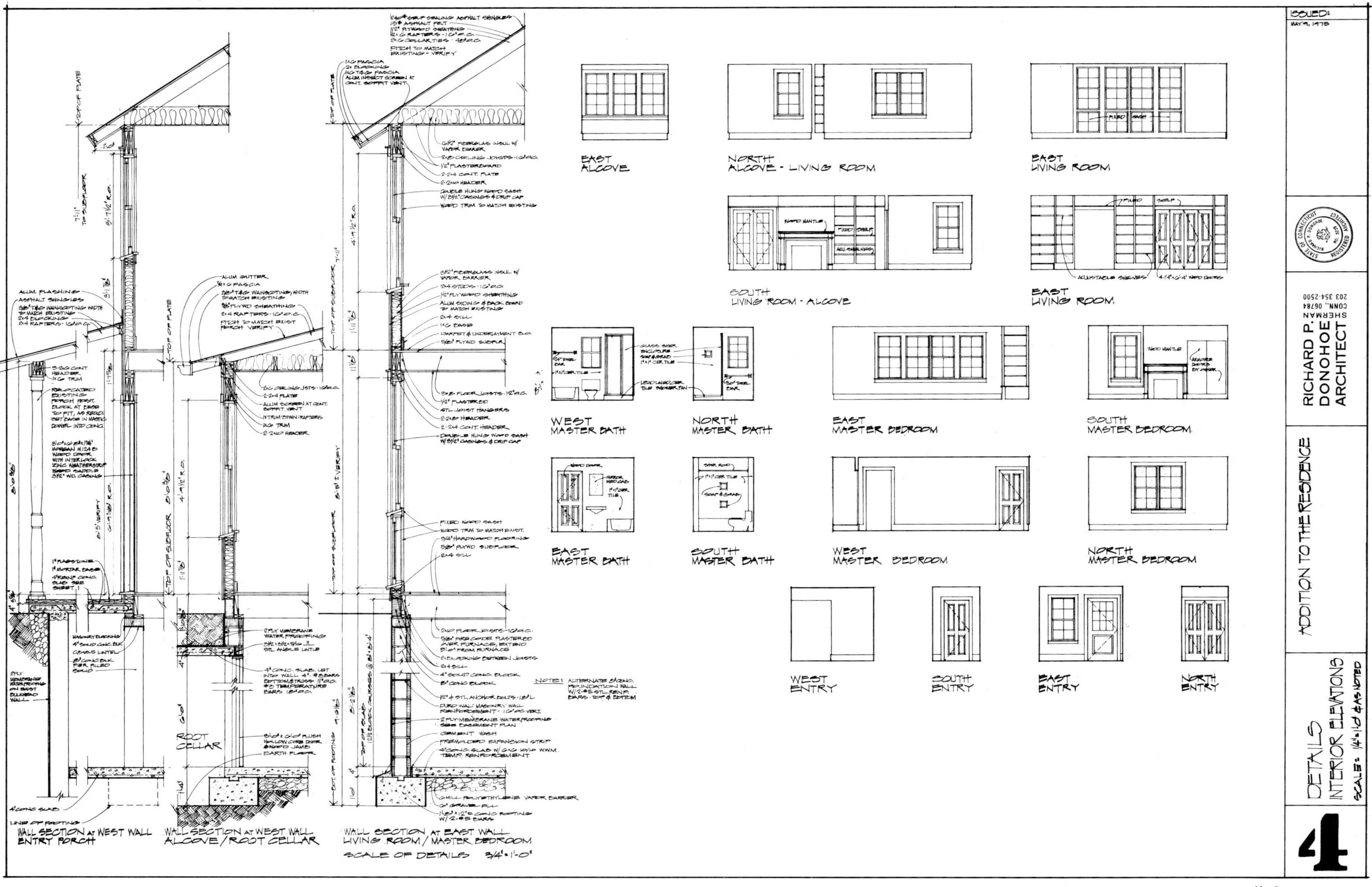


In elevation drawings (opposite page), new walls are indicated by delineation of siding. While drawings give representation of appearance, purpose is to establish heights (only vertical dimensions are given). Little detail is shown. Above, construction details with interior elevations serve as detailed guide to builder, showing construction materials and their relationships and describing construction of wall, floor, ceiling, and roof systems. Interior elevations show proportions of walls and location of windows, door, and other details.

More often than not, an architect providing complete services is paid a percentage of the remodeling cost, from ten to twenty per cent. A common method of payment is the following: five per cent of his fee as a retainer when you sign a contract with him; a total of fifteen per cent when he's completed his schematic drawings; a total of thirty-five per cent when he's completed his preliminary drawings; a total of eighty per cent when the contract has been let; and the remainder during or at the end of construction.

There are alternative methods of payment. These include a flat fee plus expenses; an hourly, daily, or weekly rate plus expenses; or a multiple (one and a half to two and a half times) of his direct expenses, for everything.

The method you use and the amount you pay an architect are matters to be decided at the outset.

Finding an architect isn't difficult. The classified pages of your phone book are a ready source. The nearest AIA office, which has a list of area residential architects, can be called. You could turn to contractors for their recommendations. Finally, you might have relatives or friends for whom architects have worked.

Selecting your architect involves finding more than one. If you've decided on having an architect, you'll want the right one. Meet and talk to several. Get a feeling about both the architects and their work. Ask them for names of former clients in the area and contact these people to learn about them—and try to see the results of their work. Take your time—it's your money and you want to invest it wisely.

In considering the architect, it must be made clear that membership in the AIA is by no means a prerequisite for competency. There are thousands of able architects who are unaffiliated with the AIA.

## Alternatives to the Architect

For that matter, there are alternatives to the architect for your remodeling. A draftsman can draw plans from your sketches and instructions. A building designer, who most likely belongs to the American Institute of Building Designers, can produce working drawings for you. A contractor, depending on the nature and scope of your remodeling and on his knowledge and experience, can often meet your needs and desires.

Finally, you could go it alone. It's been done successfully before. The intent of this chapter has been to inform you of the expertise, product, and service the architect brings to your job. The question is: can you do the same job yourself? Your answer to the question will depend on the demands of the remodeling itself, on your knowledge and experience in planning and building, on your time, and on your determination.

Discussed in the remaining pages of this chapter are the various construction components mentioned earlier. For you as a remodeler, a solid grasp of each is highly advisable if you're working with an architect and all but mandatory if you're going it alone as planner.

## Doors

Doors for your home come in many styles, types, and sizes. Each has its own best uses and its own advantages and disadvantages.

Styles range from panel to flush to louvered, French, or Dutch. Types include hinged, sliding, folding, and swinging.

Door sizes run from one and a half to three feet wide and six to seven feet high, with thicknesses of one and three-eighths inches for interior use to one and three-fourths inches for exterior use. These dimensions apply to both single and double doors.

The most common door in the home is the hinged door. Its advantages are that it opens and closes smoothly, it shuts tightly so that it can be made weathertight more easily than other doors, and its surface can accept a mirror or a hook. Its disadvantage is that it takes up floor and wall space. Panel doors suggest depth and solidity; flush doors are less expensive but serve well for openings meant to be unobtrusive; louvered doors are attractive and provide ventilation; French doors have that old world charm and admit light; and Dutch doors are quaint, and useful in keeping pets or toddlers where you want them.

Sliding doors slide over each other, along a wall or into a wall recess or pocket. Usually, they are of glass and are used as exterior doors to open onto a patio or deck. These should be insulated against cold in winter and heat in summer. For architectural harmony, when appropriate the large expanse of glass can be separated into smaller areas with snap-in mullions that can be removed for window cleaning. A disadvantage shared by all sliding doors is that they move in tracks that must be kept free of dirt to prevent jamming. Also, if the doors aren't correctly aligned in the tracks, they can malfunction. The advantage of sliding doors is that they take up so little space. When used on closets, sliding doors have the drawback of permitting access to only half of the closet at a time. Doors that slide into a wall recess are convenient for closing off one area of the house from another, for example, a bedroom hallway from a living room.

For closets, the bi-fold type of door is useful, for it allows complete access to the closet. Furthermore, louvered bi-folds allow air circulation. Bi-fold doors, too, can jam if improperly installed.

Swinging doors are used almost exclusively as kitchen doors opening into a dining room. Their obvious disadvantage is that they require floor space on both sides. Swinging doors should be hinged with a stop device to hold them open in either direction for serving and clearing.

Usually, doors in the home should have a continuity of style and should have similar hardware.

## Windows

No architect worthy of the name would underestimate the role played by the window in your home. From the exterior, windows more than any other feature both state and reaffirm the style of your house. For the interior, they define the rooms. With doorways, they determine the placement of furniture, and—most importantly—they bring light and air into the house. At the same time, windows open the home to the out-of-doors.

In traditional and other styles, windows come in a wide variety of sizes and types. In remodeling, as well as in building, the choice and placement of windows is critical. The style of your house will dictate window style and type, and its scale will determine window size.

Your placement decision will be influenced most by your desires and needs for light and ventilation. Here again, though, the character of a house has its say.

The basic window types are fixed glass, double-hung, single-hung, casement, sliding, hopper, awning, jalousie, and pivoted. A window type can be used alone or in groups, and types can be combined.

Fixed glass can be used in combination with another window type for additional light and view. It also works well in small wall spaces for more light.

The double-hung window is the traditional American colonial type. It's among the most economical. Able to be opened at both top and bottom, it provides excellent ventilation control, although only half the window space is open at a time. As currently designed, it's easily operated, although, since leverage is required to open it, it shouldn't be positioned high in a wall or over a counter. New models come out of the frame, or pivot in the frame, for cleaning. Some models have window, screen, and storm sash in a single sash.

The single-hung window is like the double-hung except that the upper sash is fixed. Its drawbacks are that ventilation is poor and cleaning difficult.

Casement windows have one or more sashes that usually swing out. (So-called "French" casements can be hinged to swing in, but such units require special fabrication because they are not standard manufactured products.) The whole window space opens so that ventilation can be easily controlled. Casement windows are operated with cranks or levers. Screens and storm sashes are variously installed (with insulated glass, storm windows are unnecessary). Some casement windows are designed so that both sides of the glass can be reached from inside for cleaning.

Sliding windows, like double-hung windows, allow only half of the window space to be open at a time, but they lack the ventilation control. They slide in tracks in the frame, as do their storm sashes and screens. The tracks must be kept clean for operational ease.

Hopper windows, usually used in basements, are horizontal sashes that open inward and downward. They can be screened and stormwindowed. At times, they are used above or below windows of fixed glass.

Awning windows, used singly or in a series, open out and up, operated by a crank or lever. They can be opened to let air in while keeping rain out and generally provide good ventilation.

Jalousie windows are like awning windows, but the panes are narrower and more numerous. Jalousies are best suited to tropical climates, where there is a need for constant ventilation, while at the same time protection from frequent rains. A particular disadvantage of the jalousie is that the panes cannot be made air-tight.

A pivoted window is a single sash that pivots at its center, either vertically or horizontally, in the frame. As it can't be screened easily, its use is highly limited.

A discussion of windows would be less than complete if it didn't include references to both window sash materials and screening.

New window sashes are either metal (usually aluminum but often steel) or wood. Aluminum windows may be subject to corrosion if not painted. By definition, those with permanent finishes need no upkeep. Steel windows require painting, and even painted they can rust. Wood windows, inexpensive and easily fitted to present frames, must be painted or otherwise protected and maintained.

Screens come in fiberglass, copper, aluminum, and plastic. Fiberglass, considered by many to be the best screening material, is light, strong, and long-lasting. It needs no painting. Both copper and aluminum weather unfavorably. Copper discolors the window sill, and aluminum corrodes, especially in salt air. Copper bends easily. Plastic screening, while it needs no painting, sags easily.

## Window Styles

Windows come in styles as well as types: bay, bow, projected, and clerestory.

Bay windows consist of three window surfaces, a flat front and angled sides, extending out from the house. They can carry down to the foundation or be cantilevered above the foundation. In either case, they bring abundant additional light into a room. They also add space to the room if the floor continues into them.

Similar to the bay window is the bow window, so named because it is shaped in a graceful, unbroken curve. Bow windows are, by far, the more expensive of the two.

Projected windows are bays with the sides at right angles to the front.

Clerestory windows are placed high on a wall, well above head level, and are usually found only in rooms with high ceilings. They can be useful in admitting sunlight and in exhausting room air.

## Skylights

Skylights successfully and dramatically admit overhead light and air. They are most effective in areas of the home that aren't otherwise exposed to natural light, such as interior hallways and bathrooms. In rooms that have windows, they can be a pleasant additional light source.

The common skylight today is a raised rectangle or dome of durable plastic. It comes in different shapes and sizes ready for installation. The plastic can be clear, diffuse, or tinted. Some skylights are designed for ventilation as well as illumination.

## Ceilings, Walls, Floors

When remodeling, consideration should be given in the early planning stages to what kind of ceilings, walls, and floors your new rooms will have. There's a wide range of possibilities in each area.

## Ceilings

Dry-wall construction—called gypsum wallboard, plasterboard, and "sheetrock"—has long since replaced plaster for ceilings, as well as for walls. It's inexpensive and not difficult to install. When skillfully taped (not so easy a job), and when the joists are even, a smooth, flat surface results. Plasterboard ceilings are often sand-painted for a textured effect.

Ceiling tiles, of wood or cane fiber or mineral fiber, are commonly used. The tiles are stapled or nailed to furring strips nailed to the joists. Tiles do not require painting, are available in several textures, and offer noise-absorbing characteristics. A new method of installation involves vinyl-coated tiles that interlock in a metal grid nailed to an existing ceiling. Also available are ceiling blocks of glazed, prefinished hardboard that are applied with adhesive to smooth surfaces.

Suspended ceilings are popular. These consist of metal grids, fastened to the joists with wire or metal clips, into which panels are dropped. Panels can be of various materials, from hardboard to fiberglass, and come in a variety of colors, textures, and patterns. The panels are easily removed for replacement and for access to ducts, pipes, and wiring. Suspended ceilings lend themselves readily to recessed lighting. Luminous ceilings use light-diffusing panels of plastic or glass set in a dropped framework of wood or metal.

It bears repeating here that skylights can add visual excitement to your ceilings.

## Walls

While most walls today are of sheet-rock, painted or wallpapered, the homeowner has a broad selection of alternate materials.

Walls paneled with solid wood, especially hardwoods, bring richness and warmth to a room, all the more so when used in contrast with other materials, textures, patterns, and colors. Old barn-siding, for example, works wonderfully with deep shag carpeting. Solid wood is, however, expensive.

Paneling also comes in plywood with various hardwood and softwood veneers. Unlike solid wood panels, which are no more than a foot in width, these come as much as four feet wide. Some are prefinished, and some are grooved. Usually a quarter-inch thick (solid wood paneling is usually three quarters of an inch in thickness), they are applied with contact cement, nailed, or nailed with a clip method (that hides the nail heads) to furring strips, studs, or the existing wall surface.

Prefinished hardboard paneling is available in numerous colors and patterns, including simulated woods. The finish is frequently vinyl. It usually comes in four-foot widths but can be had in sixteen-inch widths. Perforated hardboard, long used for hanging tools or utensils, can be used attractively on walls.

On the market as well are rigid plastic laminates, like those used on kitchen counter tops. These, too, are available in many colors, designs, and wood grains. Widths run from two to five feet. Only a sixteenth of an inch thick, these panels require a backing of sheetrock, plywood, hardboard, or particle board.

Particle board, of compressed and bonded wood flakes and chips, is sometimes used for walls, as is insulating wallboard.

With imagination, exterior materials like cedar shakes can be used for the interior.

Other wall coverings range from cork to brick and stone veneers.

## Floors

Flooring runs the gamut from hardwood and softwood through resilient materials such as vinyl and linoleum to wall-to-wall carpeting.

Like solid wood paneling, wood flooring is warm and rich. Parquet floors are nothing less than elegant. Wood, especially hardwood, is as durable as it is handsome. Softwoods wear less well and are less attractive. Wood flooring comes prefinished or unfinished, in strips, in blocks, or in parquet squares.

Resilient flooring materials include solid vinyl, vinyl-asbestos, and asphalt tiles, vinyl and linoleum sheets, and cork and wood tiles. Solid vinyl is the best resilient surface, vinyl-asbestos the next best and most often used, and asphalt the cheapest.

Cork is high in quality. Linoleum is an old standard kitchen flooring. Neither cork nor linoleum is suitable for a basement, where moisture problems may exist.

Also used for flooring is wood tile, consisting of a wood veneer with a protective coating and a backing of resilient material.

Resilient tiles are commonly made to be self-adhering for ease of installation.

Wall-to-wall carpeting can be laid on hardwood or softwood flooring, on plywood subflooring, on concrete, or on a resilient material surface. Carpeting comes in a variety of materials, from cotton and wool to nylon and acrylic. Indoor-outdoor carpeting is recommended for moist surfaces. It should be pointed out that wall-to-wall carpeting on subflooring is wise only if the area is always to be so covered. Also, a hardwood floor as a base, while more expensive, is an asset rather than a debit when selling the house to new owners who don't share your preference for wall-to-wall carpeting.

Other floor coverings are flagstone and slate, ideal for foyers, and ceramic tile, usually but certainly not exclusively used in bathrooms.

## Heating

Planning a new addition to your home involves planning for the added heat your home will require. Construction can progress only so far if a heating decision has yet to be reached.

One solution to the problem is to extend your present system into the new space. The big question is whether or not your furnace or boiler can meet the increased demand. The answer lies in the extent of the increase. The capacity and efficiency of your present system should be established. It could be that it could do the job if your present house were better insulated. A reliable heating contractor or your fuel dealer could tell you. It should be able to heat a new room. If, however, the addition is considerable, an auxiliary system will probably be needed.

Should you have to install a new heating plant, a knowledge of the basic kinds and their merits is of value.

Most common in homes today are forced warm-air, hot-water, electric, and radiant heat. Steam heat is rarely installed nowadays.

A warm-air heating system consists of a furnace, a blower, and ducts that direct the heat to registers. A big advantage of this system is that it can readily be converted to a central air conditioning system using the same ducts. Other important assets are that it costs less to install than hot-water heat, that it filters the air, and that it can be used for humidifying. Drawbacks are that the registers, usually placed along outside walls and under windows, can hinder furniture placement and that they can occasionally be noisy.

Hot-water heat originates in a boiler. The heated water is pumped by a circulator through pipes into radiators. Hot-water heat is more even than warm-air, and the boiler and pipes take up less space than a furnace and ducts. If used for floor radiant heating, the pipes are hidden. Hot-water heating, though, is more expensive than warm-air to install. It cannot be converted for air conditioning. It has no air filtration or adaptability for humidifying. And the system needs to be drained in winter if the house is closed up.

The advantages of electric heat are many. To begin with, the system runs on electricity, requiring no furnace or boiler. (It does, however, require larger electric service than normal.) It is clean and silent. It allows for individual heat control in separate rooms. It is trouble-free. While installation cost itself may be less than for warm-air and hot-water, insulation requirements for the electrically heated home are stiff. It is wise to check electric rates in your area to compare electricity with other fuel costs.

Electric heat comes in different forms: baseboard heaters, recessed wall heaters with fans, and glass wall and ceiling panels that radiate heat. Also, a warm-air system can be powered by electricity.

Radiant heat is of two types, hot-water and electric. In the hot-water type, a boiler furnishes hot water to pipes embedded in a concrete floor slab or in a plaster ceiling. Here, advantages include even heat, warm surfaces, and the fact that the heat source is unseen. Disadvantages are that the system is expensive to install and to repair—if a pipe leaks, the floor or ceiling has to be torn up. Further, the heat is slow in response and thus hard to control. The electric radiant heat consists of wiring in glass panels in the ceiling or in walls. A superior type of radiant electric heat consists of wiring embedded in plasterboard ceilings. This system provides even heat with quicker response than piped systems.

It should be pointed out that there is an alternative to either extending your present heating system or installing a separate system when remodeling. If your addition isn't large but cannot be heated by your present system, consider using an independent unit.

Electric heat is easily installed in the forms already discussed. Gas and oil heaters that can be recessed in the wall are available; these require venting to the outside. Or you could install gas or kerosene heaters that stand out in a room (they also should have venting). For single rooms, vented gas baseboard heaters are available. A heat pump, run on electricity, is in effect an air conditioner that heats in the cold weather and cools in the warm weather. Since it draws heat from the outside air, it's more efficient in warmer climates.

Whatever your source of heat for your addition, your new room or rooms should be thoroughly insulated against heat loss. As noted, electric heat has such a requirement. Good insulation makes good sense.

A few words about heat control. Thermostats are designed to sense the heat in the room. To do so, they should be placed on interior walls, away from areas of heat or cold. Keep them away from heating outlets, the fireplace or chimney wall, television sets or radios or any other heat-producing appliance, and from particularly sunny areas. Above all, don't place them on exterior walls, since they will sense the cold outside and will call for excessive heat inside. Keep thermostats out of drafts and off walls behind doors where air doesn't circulate.

## Fireplaces

The fireplace today, at least in the northern climate, has practically become a necessity. The problem is that it's a highly inefficient home heater. The problem is made worse by the skyrocketing price of cord wood. Simply put, when the fire is going, most of its heat goes straight up the chimney, and when it's out, with the damper open (as it would be if you went to bed with the logs still burning), out goes your house's heat—unless your hearth has glass doors to close.

Much in vogue these days are not only dozens of types and styles of free-standing stoves—from reproduction Franklins to modern Scandinavian models—but also stove units that make use of the fireplace and increase its efficiency considerably. Costs vary widely, but even the most expensive stoves and stove units can pay for themselves in a few seasons of fuel savings. Available, too, are ingenious fireplace heating devices, including a grate made of tubing through which heated air is forced out into the room.

In planning your remodeling, you'd be wise to consider the fireplace and stove as auxiliary heaters, if not as the sole heating source for the new room or rooms.

## Solar Heat

Today, any discussion of remodeling—or building, for that matter—should at least touch on the subject of solar heat. Solar heating is simply—if profoundly—the harnessing of the sun's energy for heating in the home, whether limited to supplying heat for the hot-water heater or extended to providing heat for the entire house. However long the tunnel to general use of solar heat might be, light is being seen at the tunnel's end—it works, and new developments and refinements appear regularly. Experts, from conservationists to architects, believe in its great promise as the alternative energy source of the future, and the not-all-that-distant future at that. Noting the advances already made in solar heat, one architect commented, "Ten years from now, we'll look back on solar heating today as today we look back on the first automobiles."

The world fuel crisis and the very crying need for an alternative energy source points to the sun. It's been calculated that the heat potential of all the earth's fossil fuel reserves is the equivalent of a mere three weeks of sunshine.

There are two kinds of solar heat, passive and active.

Passive solar heating refers to designing and orienting a house so that it admits maximum sunlight during the day and retains the sun's heat at maximum efficiency at night. The house itself is both collector and storage facility. For passive heating, window and sliding glass door space should abound and ideally face due south; interior sun-lit surfaces would be heat-absorbant, and walls, floors, and ceilings fully insulated. Concrete slab floors are excellent heat retainers during the day and serve as heat radiators during the night. Glass should be insulated glass, and glass areas should be covered with insulated drapes or otherwise insulated when the sun sets. Skylights serve as efficient entrances for the sun's heat. As with active solar heating, the south side of the house should have deciduous trees for summer shade and winter sun, and the north side of the house should have reduced window area. Passive solar heat constitutes auxiliary heat to assist the regular heating system of the house.

Active solar heating consists of special solar collectors, using either water or air, that are placed in the south roof of the house, a pump or a fan for circulation, and a storage facility for the heat collected.

Flat plate collectors are usually composed of a glass or plastic cover and a metal absorber painted flat black, with metal tubing built into it for water to circulate or with space for air to flow over it. Water flowing through the collector usually contains glycol to prevent freezing.

The usual storage facilities are an insulated tank for water and a bin of rocks for air.

In northern climates, a conventional heating system is necessary to support either kind of solar system. Nonetheless, a solar system of high efficiency can reduce heating bills by as much as 75 per cent.

Solar heat is not inexpensive to install. A system can cost $10,000 and more, and it will take twenty years or more to pay for itself, but from then on, the "fuel" is free. Solar hot-water heat has the shorter payoff period.

Solar heating systems are widely available today and should be carefully studied and compared before being purchased. The least expensive systems are likely to be the least efficient ones as well.

Homeowners interested in solar heat can contact the National Solar Heating and Cooling Information Center by writing to Solar Heating, Box 1607, Rockville, Maryland 20850. Homeowners would also do well to investigate governmental incentives for installing solar systems.

## Air Conditioning

Air conditioning in hot climates is the counterpart of heating in cold ones. Even in temperate areas today, air conditioning in the home is no longer considered a luxury.

While the main benefit of air conditioning is cooling of the air, there are others. With air conditioning, the air is also humidified, cleaned, and distributed. The process is a healthful one.

Central air conditioning is of two main types, single-package and split system. In the single package, all components—evaporator, compressor, condenser, and fans—are enclosed together inside the house. In the split system, the compressor and condenser are placed together outside the house, on a concrete slab. The compressor-condenser unit is noisy.

Air conditioning is most easily and inexpensively adaptable to a warm-air heating system, since it can utilize the same ducts. In a home heated by hot water or by electricity, the ducting will have to be installed.

An alternative central air conditioning unit is the heat pump, which heats in the winter and cools in the summer.

If you wish to install air conditioning, you should consult an air conditioning engineer or contractor. Your home must be surveyed to determine your cooling needs—in terms of your home's "heat gain"—to establish in turn the system capacity required. As with any other major home expense, it's wise to obtain at least two estimates of equipment and installation costs.

For the homeowner who wants air conditioning for a single room or small area of rooms, there are room air conditioners that run on electricity. These units are designed for placement in window areas or in walls, and there are even free-standing and portable units. Again, your cooling and equipment capacity needs must be determined. Room units can require new wiring for increased electric service.

The home remodeler adding to his house can extend a present central air conditioning system, install a system for the whole "new" house, or employ air conditioning units.

In remodeling, as in building, the orientation of the structure, together with design and landscape features, can supply natural home cooling. (This could be thought of as passive solar heating in reverse.) Gabor Lorant, AIA architect of Phoenix, Arizona, is expert in this area. He has written to us as follows:

Orientation in Arizona has always been very important because of the extreme weather conditions. Centuries ago, the Indians situated their cliff-dwellings so that they would be in shade in the hot seasons and in full sun in the winter.

Orientation of a dwelling is usually done by knowing the solar calendar and by knowing the effects of the sun. In June the sun rises here in Arizona in the northeast and sets in the northwest. In December it rises in the southeast and sets in the southwest. The angle of the sun's rays varies between those two extreme points on the horizon. By knowing where the sun is every hour of the day, one can design a house so that in the winter, when the sun's rays are low, they warm the walls of the house and penetrate through the windows; in the summer, when the sun's rays are high, the walls of the house and the windows are in shade. The shading of the house can be achieved by using overhangs, trellis work, louvers, the planting of trees or shrubs, and the combination of all of these. The shading of windows in the hot seasons is extremely important to reduce the "cooling load" to manageable proportions. (An unprotected sliding glass door facing west can add $100 a month to the electric bill.)

The Lorant living room is flooded with light without glare. Direct sunlight is kept out by slat overhangs, shown below. Mr. Lorant, AIA architect, is expert on "natural home cooling."

Orienting windows (and glass sliding doors) properly, protecting glass areas with overhangs, and shading walls against hot-weather sun are the basic design criteria to save energy and to make the house more livable.

Our house is flooded with sunlight (inside too) when the sun rises in the months of November through March for a couple of hours in the morning. That makes breakfast time rather cheerful. Later, when the sun gets hot (even in the winter), the sun is kept outside by slatted overhangs. In the summer, when the sun rises very early and is very hot, deciduous trees keep everything in shade, including the yard and roof. The summer heat is tempered by the moist air provided by trees, hedges, plants, and grass, and by the sprinkling system.

## Lighting

Lighting in the home is a matter both of natural and artificial light. In either case, lighting does more than enable us to see with comfort. How our rooms are lighted, whether by sun or electricity or candle or fireplace, has a major impact on how we live in the spaces of our home.

Natural light enters a house through its windows, sliding glass doors, and skylights. How a home is naturally lighted depends on its orientation to the sun and the placement and size of its glass areas. The sunlight entering a house is further controlled by trees and other plantings, roof overhangs, louvers and blinds, and drapes and curtains. In a room, natural light influences furnishing and decoration and even traffic flow. A room—a whole house—has feelings of spaciousness or intimacy, depending on natural light. Sunlight can serve to lead the indoors out-of-doors.

Practically, artificial light imitates natural light. But artificial lighting is more than a substitute. Electricity offers us a light source that can be controlled as the sun could never be. With artificial lighting, we can not only see but we can also be directed to look for the pleasure of seeing. The aesthetic joins the practical.

Candlelight illustrates this point. We don't dine by candlelight to see the food and drink on the table. We do so to see the candlelight and its reflection in crystal, china, and silver, and the faces of those with whom we're dining. Atmosphere is the word we use when we talk about candlelight. Similarly, we can and do put artificial light to such use.

Illumination in the home is of two kinds, general and specific; artificial lighting comes in many forms to meet both needs.

General illumination can be achieved in several ways. A chandelier can light a large area. Walls can be washed with light from fixtures in valences and cornices or recessed in or suspended from the ceiling. Such lighting can be directed from the floor. Track lighting, exposed or enclosed, offers considerable flexibility.

For the lighting of specific areas, there are table and floor lamps. The pin spot highlights a painting or other art object. Downlights, recessed in the ceiling or mounted, provide specific area illumination.

With both general and specific lighting, dimmers offer control of intensity.

In remodeling, lighting decisions should be made before construction is underway. Know how you want your room illuminated generally, where and how specifically. Investigate the range of systems and fixtures available. You'll want to visualize your room as it will be furnished and decorated, as it will be lived in. Lighting decisions are construction decisions.

Outdoor lighting, whether for safe house approach or for the pleasing sight of a stand of trees, too, should be planned in advance.

## Plumbing

New or remodeled kitchens, bathrooms, and laundry rooms involve pipes and plumbing for incoming water and wastes going out.

The placement of new pipes or the relocation of existing plumbing poses a problem for the homeowner.

Should the new bathroom be placed near—next to, above, or below—existing plumbing for convenient tie-in with the system? Should the new kitchen sink be exactly where the old one was? The answer in each case is yes, but only if you'll be fully satisfied with the result. The answer is no if, to so economize, the bathroom won't be where you want it or the kitchen arrangement won't be as you need it. To sacrifice the best plan for the relatively small dollar savings entailed would be foolish.

A plumbing job of major proportions had best be done by a professional, unless your amateur ranking is very high.

A word about insulation. Both hot and cold water pipes should be insulated, the hot for efficiency of the hot-water heater, and the cold to prevent condensation and dripping. Such investment pays off.

The intent of the discussion of construction components has been not only to inform as such but also—even more so—to stress the knowledge essential to sound home improvement planning. The architect, as professional planner, has this knowledge. It is the nuts-and-bolts part of his overall expertise, which is inseparable from his product and his service.

Planning your home improvement, assessing the contribution you can make as planner, by all means consider the architect.

Orchestrating men, materials, and machinery is the basic skill of the general contractor. He must know the techniques of each phase of home construction and be able to coordinate the work of each subcontractor for a smooth and efficient job.

Top: Loader excavates for new wing. Left: "Transitmix" cement is poured into foundation for basement floor, while at same time (bottom) construction lumber is delivered. Young homeowner shown will do his own general contracting and, in spare time, be carpenter's helper and general supervisor.

# 2. On Being Your Own General Contractor

With or without the services of an architect, you've planned your home improvement. You're ready to build on your plans. As was the question with the architect, do you need or want the services of a general contractor? Once again, the services should be understood fully before a decision is reached.

The "general" of the title could be misleading. A general contractor isn't a tradesman who generalizes in the sense of "dabbling." On the contrary, he's a specialist in the whole business of building or remodeling a house.

## The General Contractor's Job

Briefly, the general contractor has your remodeling done for you. When you hire him, he in turn hires the various other contractors, called subcontractors, required to do the varied aspects of the job. He organizes the work, schedules its stages, orders materials and has them at the site when needed, and supervises the work. From obtaining the building permit to securing the certificate of occupancy, he's in charge—and he's the one ultimately responsible for the job done.

The general contractor's worth, like the architect's, can be viewed in terms of his expertise, his product, and his service.

His expertise is his first-hand, working knowledge of, and experience in, the building business. He understands working drawings and specifications. He knows construction materials and methods. He has an understanding of electricity and wiring, of plumbing, of heating. He knows wells and septic systems. He's aware of zoning regulations and building code requirements. He's a businessman, managing the work of others.

The general contractor's product is your remodeling as completed. His service is the implementation of your plans for your home improvement.

The extent of the general contractor's service must be appreciated. A major remodeling job can be filled with headaches.

## Time and Scheduling

The biggest problem is one of time—a construction completion date has to be met. With this deadline in mind, the general contractor has to schedule the particular jobs to be done by his subcontractors, and he has to make sure the materials for the jobs are on the site in time.

In scheduling, he's got to make allowance for lost time. Inclement weather wastes time. A subcontractor held up on another job, or in bed with the flu, wastes it and delays other construction. So do delays in delivery of materials, or those resulting when defective materials have to be replaced. Equipment can break down. Jobs can take longer than expected or can require redoing because they've been badly done.

It's the general contractor whose head aches.

Another problem area is that of working relations. The very supervision by the general contractor of his subcontractors can make for headaches. Just as the general contractor is expert in his job, so are the subcontractors in theirs. Philosophies can clash, and so can egos, followed by tempers. Workmanship standards, too, differ. Workmen have walked off jobs.

The remodeling itself can be a problem source. Situations arise that necessitate design and thus construction changes. Excavating, a ledge can be discovered where it has no right to be. Adding on, existing construction can be found to be in need of repair. Again, it's the general contractor's head.

All of the above isn't to cry pity. Problems and headaches are part and parcel of the general contractor's job—they come with the territory.

## Choosing a General Contractor

The selection of a general contractor is as important as that of an architect. Good plans have to be well implemented.

The names of general contractors are to be found in the yellow pages of the phone book, under various headings. Local building suppliers and hardware store owners can often make recommendations. You might even consult local subcontractors who have worked with general contractors. The best sources for names would be friends, neighbors, and relatives who have remodeled with them.

Start with a list of many names and learn all you can about each man's reputation. Seeing examples of his work would be a great help. Narrow your list to the two or three most promising names. Call each of these to arrange a meeting to discuss your remodeling plans so that he can bid on the job.

At each meeting, make an effort to get to know the man and his business. Ask questions. How long has he been in business in the area? Does he have his own crew and does he work regularly with the same subcontractors? What is his building experience with your kind of remodeling job? Does he carry complete insurance—public liability, property damage, workmen's compensation? What clients has he had recently in the area?

## Bids, Contract, and Payment

When you discuss your remodeling job, be sure to present identical requirements to each general contractor, in whatever form you can, preferably as working drawings and specifications. If you can, give each a copy of your requirements to study. Try to get an indication of when he could do the job, and how long it would take. Then, ask him to put his bid in writing.

Waiting for the bids to be returned, you might ask your bank to investigate each bidder's financial situation, and you might even contact the local Better Business Bureau to see if any complaints have been filed against any bidder. If, at your meetings, you learned clients' names, you'd do well to call them for their assessment of the man and his work.

When the bids come in, consider the prices in terms of the men, as you've come to know them and about them. If the prices and reputations are all about the same, select the man you like the most—you'll be seeing a lot of him.

Before accepting a bid, take a good last look at your budget. The prices bid are the best estimates you have of your remodeling's cost.

Your contract with the general contractor should be in writing, preferably prepared by a lawyer. The standard "short form" AIA owner-contractor agreement can be used. In any case, your contract should specify the following: the contractor's duties and responsibilities; the materials and their quality (brand names and model numbers for such items as doors, windows, plumbing fixtures); the amount and method of payment of the contractor's fee; the dates construction will begin and end; the contractor's responsibility for liens against the property or construction; and the contractor's insurability.

A word about payment of a general contractor's fee. Payment, by you or by your bank, is usually made in stages corresponding to stages of completed construction: so much of the fee, say, when the foundation is poured, so much more when the roof is on, the rest when the whole job is finished. Often, a percentage is withheld for a period of time against defective materials or workmanship.

### You As General Contractor

When you become your own general contractor, his job—headaches included—becomes yours. The question is, as it was with the architect: are you both willing and able to take on the task? If the answer is long in coming, you probably should decide against doing so. Enough can be at stake that you should be sure of yourself.

Assuming such self-confidence, there are good reasons for being your own general contractor.

First, much money can be saved. As much as twenty-five per cent of the labor cost goes to the general contractor. You could be the earner—the saver—of the same money. Add to this savings the savings on materials. While you might not be able to buy materials at the general contractor's discount, which may vary anywhere from ten to thirty even forty, per cent, you can buy them at a discount by buying in quantity.

Another reason for being your own agent is the control you'd have over the hiring of subcontractors. You might well have your own choice of plumber or electrician, neither of whom may be your general contractor's choice. With the right knowledge and enough energy and time to implement your plans, the experience can be rewarding.

### Case History

A friend of ours took on such a challenge when he added on to his revolutionary period Connecticut home. The family needed a bedroom; three upstairs bedrooms had worked well enough for the five family members until his two daughters grew too old to share the same room. He and his wife decided to add a master bedroom and bath to the existing ground floor, and turn their room over to one of the daughters.

The couple engaged the help of a friend and neighbor who designs homes as an avocation. They wanted the addition not only to fit their living needs but to fit the fine old house itself (it dates back to 1775 and even appears on one of Washington's survey maps). The designer's plans were entirely satisfactory.

It was fall, and their completion target date was the following spring. As they had been fortunate to have the designer friend, they were equally fortunate to know, on their own or through him, the several subcontractors who would be needed to get the job done, from excavator to painter. The excavator knew a man who could match the original stone foundation.

With the designer, our friend lined up the contractors and scheduled the work. The site was excavated, the foundation laid, the structure framed, closed in, and roofed—all by the cold weather. During the winter months, the inside carpentry work went on along with the plumbing and electrical work. The walls were insulated, sheetrocked, and taped, the bathroom fixtures installed, and the walls tiled. The interior trim work was done, the interior was painted, and the subflooring was carpeted—all by spring. The siding and outside trim went up and was painted, and the gutters were hung, leaving only the landscaping to be completed.

Admittedly, our friend was blessed in that the "right" subcontractors were close at hand, and that they had an established working relationship. Also, he was able to be comfortable with informal, verbal agreements with them. He did, though, have to assume the general contractor's responsibilities for zoning and building code compliance and for insurability. He had to obtain a building permit and a certificate of occupancy. And while he saved money by dealing directly with subcontractors, he economized neither by buying materials himself nor by working on the remodeling himself—which a homeowner can do to be ahead.

The point is that he did it—he succeeded as his own general contractor.

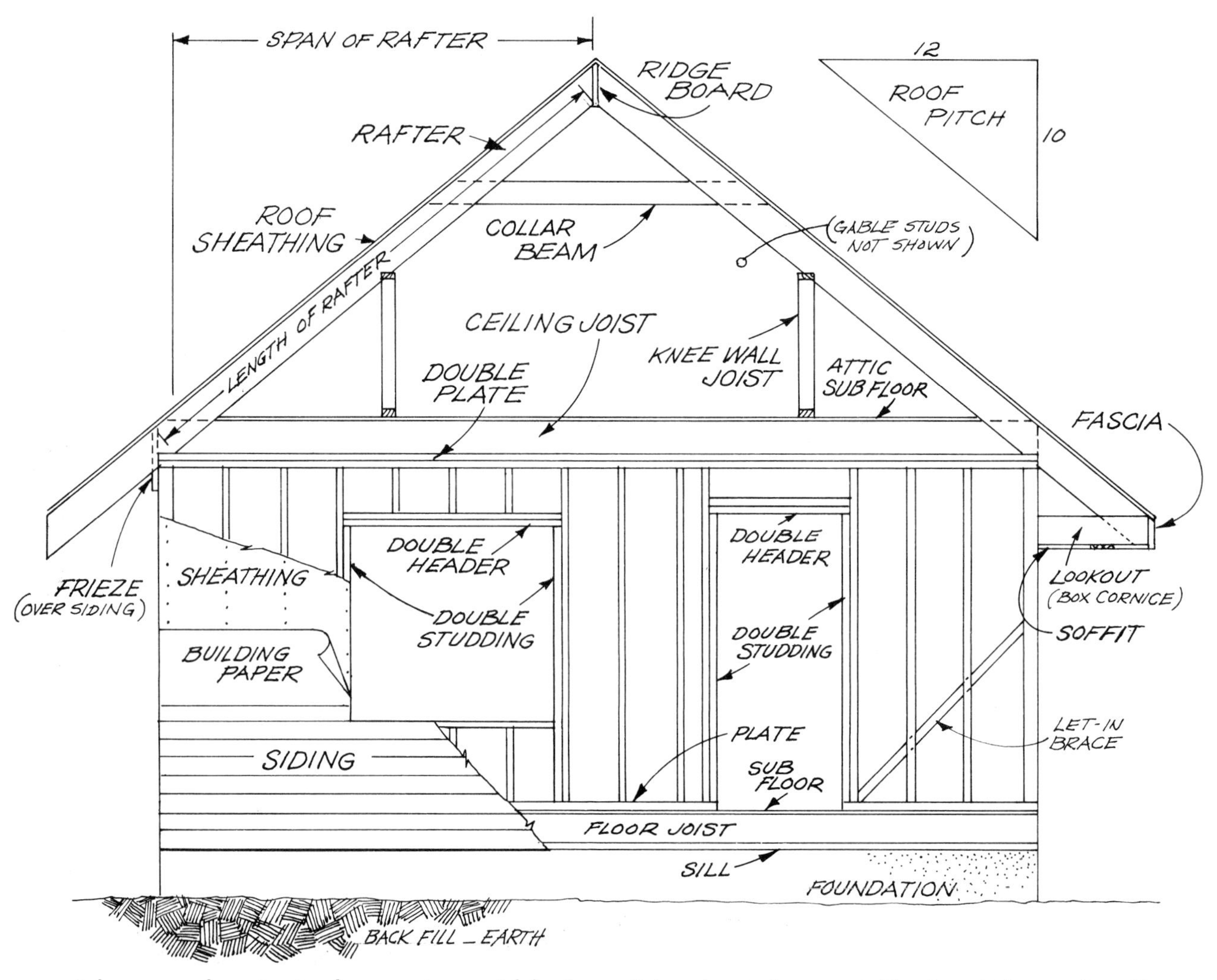


A firm grasp of construction language is essential for the homeowner who elects to be his own builder. As can be seen in the drawing above, the trade has a vocabulary of its own. Even if the homeowner works through a general contractor, he will want to be able to communicate intelligently.

Below: Area to be excavated has been laid out and outside foundation lines marked by erecting batter boards and stringing lines; these lines also serve as guide for building footings and foundations. Outside edges of foundation, poured or laid up in blocks, will be directly under the cords.

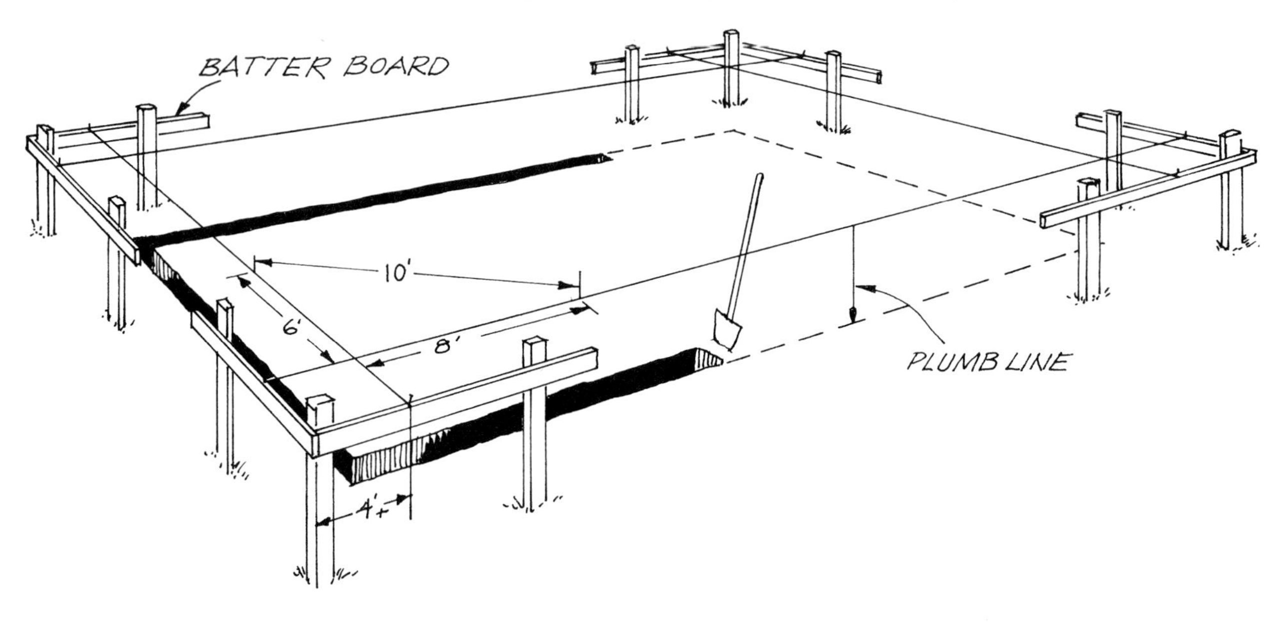

# 3.
# On Being Your Own Builder

There is an alternative to remodeling through a general contractor or as your own general contractor—you can be your own builder. The question is, *can* you? The point is that the option is there, but is your ability there as well? If it is, do you have the desire to do so?

Let's assume a major construction job—a garage, say, as opposed to a bay window. Building a garage involves much of the full range of construction stages involved in building a house, or a house addition. The site must be excavated; footings must be poured, the foundation poured or laid, and the slab poured; drainage provisions might have to be made; the structure would have to be framed and closed in; siding would probably be put up; doors, both for automobiles and people, must be hung, and windows installed; trim work must be done; the roof must be shingled or otherwise covered, and the exterior painted or treated in some other way; gutters might be required; wiring would most likely be necessary; insulation and plasterboard could well be involved; and landscaping would have to be done.

Clearly, building a garage encompasses many areas of knowledge and skill, many kinds of materials, much expenditure of effort and time, and more than a little organizational talent.

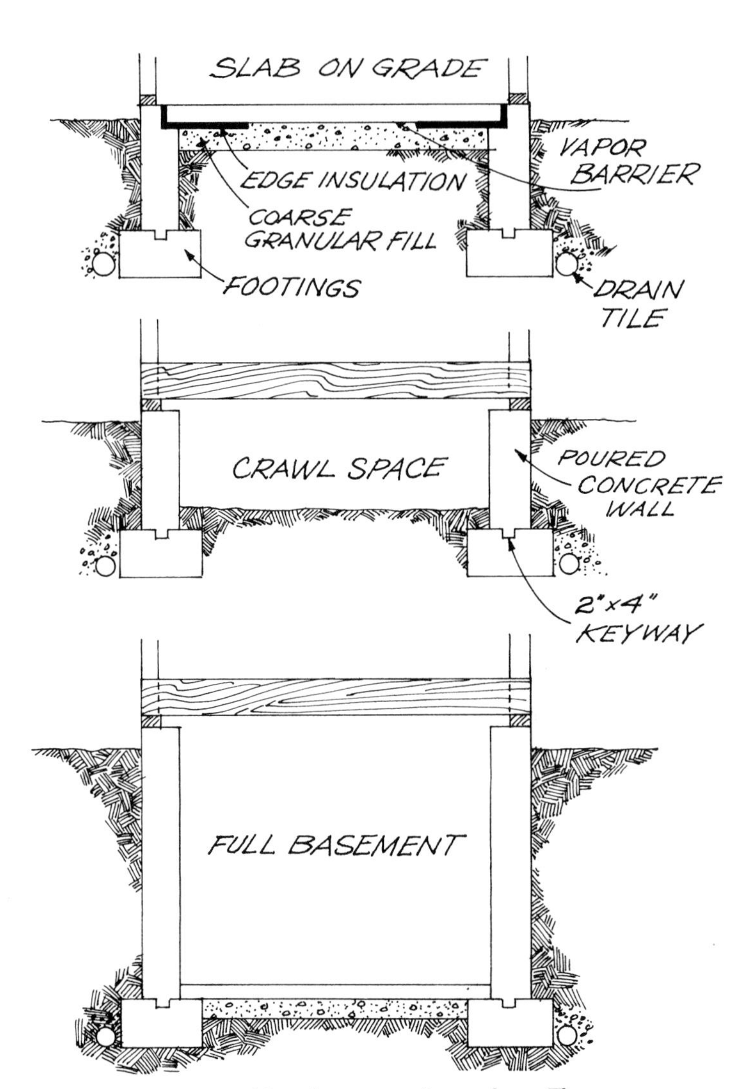


The three basic types of foundations are shown above. The slab on grade foundation, top, involves no framing for the first floor and so is the most economical. The crawl space foundation, middle, requires minimal excavation but offers minimal access. The full basement foundation, bottom, provides additional living space at low cost.

## Your Ability

A decision to build a garage yourself must be based on a solid confidence that you are in fact able to build one. An "Oh, what the heck, let's give it a whirl!" approach would be more appropriate for the bay window.

What about your ability? It could consist of nothing more than a good head, a good hand, and a good "how-to" construction manual, of which there are several available. In other words, if you can follow text and illustration directions and handle tools, you can probably do the job. Certainly, whatever building experience you have had stands you in better stead, since basic principles and techniques apply to small and big jobs alike.

Add to your good head and your good hand a good heart—determination. For whatever reason or reasons, you need to be driven to do the job. In deciding to be your own builder, you signed a contract with yourself and are committed to get the job done. Remember that you're it—general contractor, subcontractor, and more. If you don't have the drive to see all of the job through, who will? A half-completed garage or any other unfinished remodeling project is a sorry sight.

## Time Demands

The question of time is a vital one. Do you have enough? And do you have it soon enough? With a remodeling as big as a garage, not only weather but seasons come into foul play. Almost as sad a picture as a job left undone is one of a job left hanging, say over a winter. Do you have time in the right amounts? Two weeks of Saturdays and Sundays isn't the same thing as a two-week vacation. There are problems in building that demand large chunks of time for solv-

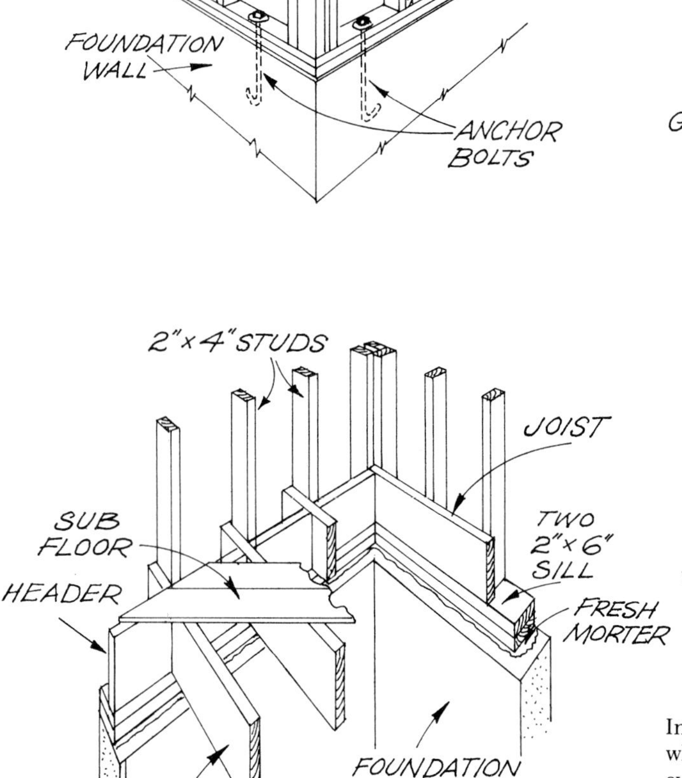


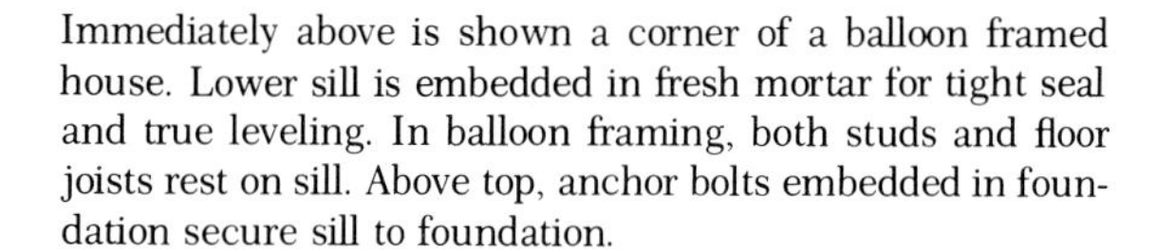
Immediately above is shown a corner of a balloon framed house. Lower sill is embedded in fresh mortar for tight seal and true leveling. In balloon framing, both studs and floor joists rest on sill. Above top, anchor bolts embedded in foundation secure sill to foundation.

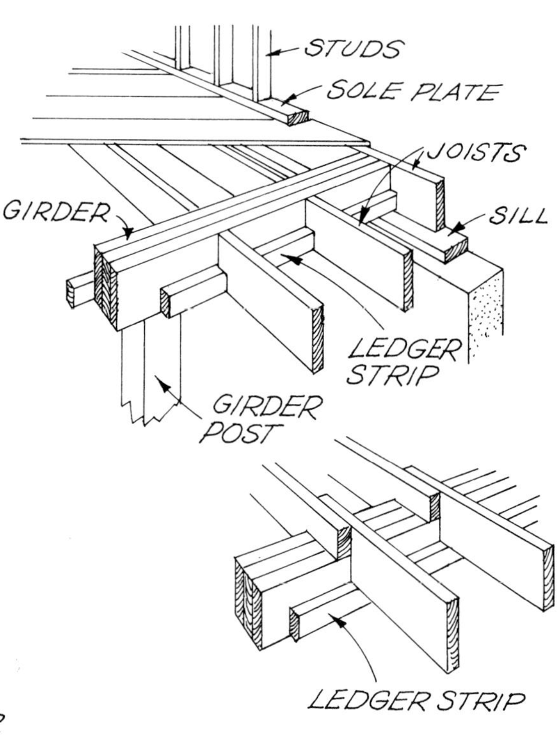


In platform frame construction, top, floor joists rest on sill, while studs rest on sole plate over subflooring, which extends over joists to outside edge of building. Load-bearing girders rest on foundation walls and supporting posts. Bottom, in balloon framing, joists are set on ledger strips to equalize shrinking of joists with that of sills.

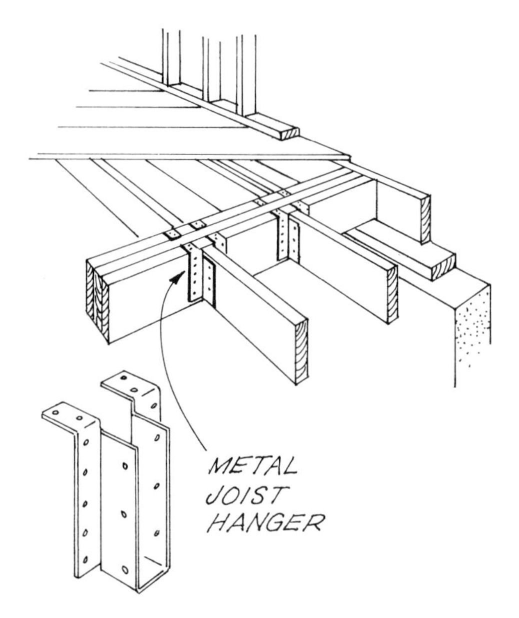


Metal joist hangers frame joists level with top of girders. Other helpful hardware, in various metal gauges and sizes, include header hangers, skewed hangers, blocking hangers, framing anchors, rafter ties, cross bridging, deck brackets, tie-down straps, column caps, and post anchors.

ing—you just cannot mix concrete today and pour it tomorrow. Nothing saps drive more than seeing a job dragging to completion.

## Options

Of course, at any problem point, the professional can be called in to step up the pace, but this isn't what you had planned on—and it costs.

Mention of the professional suggests a variation on being your own builder. You can be selective in what aspects of the remodeling you'll do. If carpentry is your strength, you might limit your involvement to just that phase of the project. Or you

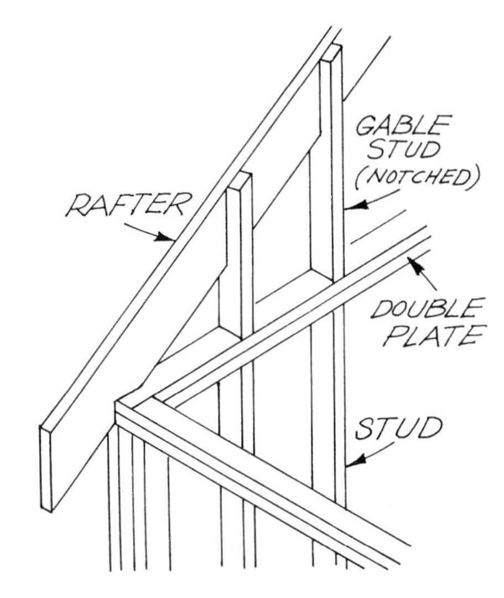


In outside wall framing, gable studs can be notched to fit rafter, as shown, or framed under rafter with bevel cut.

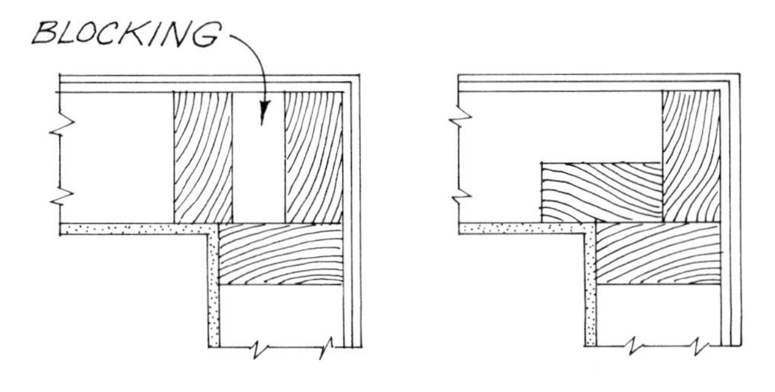


Shown above are two methods for assembling outside wall studs at corners. Note blocking required at left.

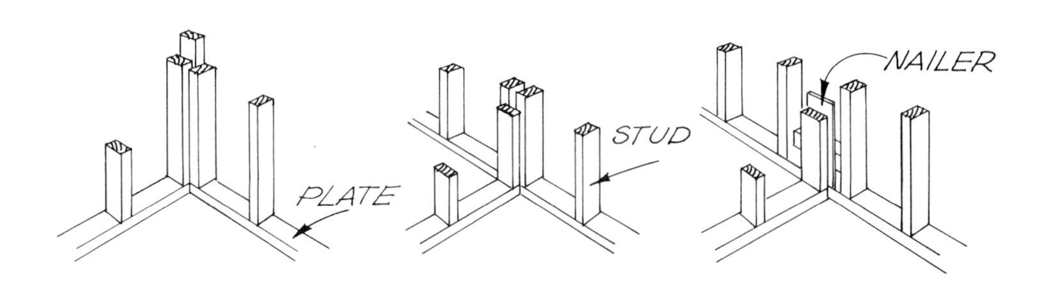


Shown, from left to right, are methods of (1) joining exterior wall framing at corner, (2) joining interior partition to studs of exterior wall framing, and (3) joining interior partition to blocking between studs of exterior wall framing.

might work alongside professionals in other phases.

Worth considering is nonprofessional help at any stage in the form of inexpensive local labor, namely the high school boy down the block or a comparable pair of hands. In any construction job, there is time-consuming work that requires little expertise. Often, you can't afford to do it yourself because your time is worth more elsewhere. You wouldn't want to pay a carpenter his hourly rate to move a pile of lumber from one spot to another, so why do it yourself when a strapping teenager could do it for you?

As an aside, a friend of ours once framed a stable in a single day by inviting a dozen or so friends to an old-fashioned barn-raising, to be followed by a new-fashioned party. The only drawback was that he received a similar invitation a few months later.

## Cost

A few words about the economics of being your own builder. The savings in dollars can be considerable, if the job is well planned and well executed. If badly handled, the job can cost more than it would have through a general contractor or with subcontractors. What you have to keep in mind as your own builder is that you are investing yourself—your talent and time and energy—for the remodeling returns. How much of you, as money, are you putting in? Or is the whole venture adventure, with its own nonmonetary returns, like satisfaction, pleasure, even excitement—the just plain good feeling of doing a job yourself? If this is the case, and if you do it right, you're doubly ahead.

Making that home improvement with your own hands, head, and heart is one fine thing.

# 4.
# On Being Your Own Decorator

As with all home planning, interior decoration begins with you. What counts is what's pleasing, comfortable, and functional to you. The only difficulty here is to know what means lead to this end.

An inviting room consists of a harmonious combination of colors, patterns, textures, scale, and style. To arrive at this combination, a basic understanding of the principles of interior decorating is required.

## The Interior Decorator

As there are architects and contractors, so there are professionals in this area. Like the other professionals, interior decorators have the talent to analyze your needs and wants to help provide them for you. They know about colors, patterns, and textures, about paints, wallpapers, and floor coverings, about fabrics, and about furniture and styles; and they know how all of the above work together for total effect.

If you choose to use a decorator, be sure of what services you want him to provide. Some give only advice; others advise and actually shop with or for you. You'll have to budget carefully.

Two cautions. First, remember that the decorating project is your project and that you've engaged the decorator's services to meet your requirements—stick to your guns. Second, if you're working with an architect who has his own decorating ideas, avoid bringing these and those of the decorator into conflict—don't turn your new living room into a battleground.

## You As Decorator

There are reasons not to work with an interior decorator. One, as suggested above, is that you're working with an architect who can provide the same services to your full satisfaction. Another is that you can provide them yourself. You might be certain enough of what it is you want and need, and confident enough of your ability to achieve it, that you'll do it all yourself.

If you decide to be your own decorator, inform yourself about decorating before you spend a dollar, unless that dollar (or few dollars) is spent for a good text on the subject.

## Color

The area of color is a study in itself. There's a vocabulary of color. To select colors, you'll want to be able to talk of hues (the names of colors), of values (their lightness or darkness), of tints and shades (colors nearer white in value, and those nearer black), and intensities or tones (the brightness or dullness of colors). Further, you'll want to be familiar with the color wheel, a circular representation of the hues obtained when sunlight is passed through a prism. In decorating, color schemes are based on relationships of hues of the color wheel. Your selection of a color scheme will involve as well the quality of the natural light that enters your room and an understanding of the effect of sunlight on colors.

## Pattern, Texture, Scale, and Style

The use of pattern in a room is critical, whether of wallpaper or of upholstery. There are rules to know. One says a room should be one-fourth patterned, another one-third; the classic Greek proportion—two parts emphasis to three parts rest—is championed. All of these weights can be used successfully.

Textures—stone, wood, cloth, metal, plastic—should make their positive contributions.

Scale is a major factor for consideration. Furniture size relates to both the size of the room and the size of other furniture in the room. The sum of relationships should be pleasing.

Then there's the matter of style. Furnishings can be traditional or modern, or a blending of both, called "eclecticism." The mixing of styles must be a careful mixing, with some other aspect or aspects of the room serving as a catalyst. The hue of a wall, the pattern of the drapes—something has to wed the American Traditional table, say, to the Swedish Modern sofa.

Interior decorating aims at a successful whole that's more than the sum of its successful parts. Being your own decorator calls for short views and the long view, and to be able to see you have to first know.

## Inform Yourself

For decorating ideas, turn to the widely available literature on the subject, in magazines, in newspapers, in books, in building suppliers' brochures and catalogues. Visit stores to window-shop for furniture, fixtures, carpeting, wallpaper, and paint. Learn about new materials for room surfaces. Study things that please you in the homes of friends and relations.

Keep in mind that you're planning for your family, so plan with your family. Each of you has needs and wants that involve the decoration of your home. Rooms of a house are lived in together.

# 5.
# If You Need Financial Help

Under ideal conditions, a homeowner won't need financial help for his home improvement. He'll have wisely anticipated his remodeling job far enough in advance to have methodically set aside the necessary funds in a high-interest-yielding bank account. He'll have only to withdraw money as needed. If the job is a modest one, the money could come from his savings account, possibly even his checking account.

Realistically, though, you won't be so prepared and will be looking for financing, especially if your remodeling job is considerable.

## Shopping for Money and Loan Types

Looking for financing means shopping around. Just as you compared professionals and their fees, and shopped around for materials, compare money costs.

There are various types of loans, and within these types, varying terms and interest rates. They vary from community to community and from one lending institution to another in the same area. They vary as well from month to month and from year to year. You'll want the best terms at the lowest interest rate, and for this you'll need to shop.

One common type of loan is the home improvement loan, available at most lending institutions. The money isn't restricted in its home improvement use. If your credit isn't satisfactory, or if the amount of the loan is unusually large, collateral may be required as security. Interest rates are not among the lowest.

The FHA (Federal Housing Administration) Title I loan, while one of the lowest-cost loans to be had, isn't available at all banks. This loan is restricted to essential home improvements and excludes such luxuries as a swimming pool.

The FHA 203 (K) loan, also not obtainable at all banks, is restricted to houses at least ten years old and to major structural improvements. The cost is low, but considerable paperwork is involved.

If your present mortgage has an "open-end" clause, you can borrow as much money as you've paid out to date. Your present mortgage is usually extended, often at its present rate.

Or you can refinance your present mortgage, obtaining a new mortgage that pays off your old one as it finances your home improvement. Refinancing does involve new closing costs, and the new interest rate is likely to be higher than the old one.

Two other methods of financing are borrowing from your credit union, which involves low interest rates and easy terms, or borrowing against your savings account, at an interest charge that becomes less because your savings continue to earn interest.

However you finance your home improvement, you'll want to be assured that you've gotten the best terms possible. Plan sufficiently ahead of your need to be able to do just that.

Still another type of loan is the so-called "home equity" loan, which is another name for a second mortgage. Such lending is being advertised by banks in certain parts of the country as an attractive package. Here, you borrow against the equity you have in your home, the amount of principal you've paid off on your present mortgage in terms of the increased value of your home as determined by the bank. The advantages of such borrowing are low interest rates and long terms. Also, depending on the lending institution, the amount that can be borrowed can be as much as $25,000. The maximum amount for a home improvement loan is usually $5,000, and for FHA Title I and 203 (K) loans is currently $15,000 and $12,000 respectively. A disadvantage of "home equity" borrowing, as compared to "open-end" borrowing and refinancing, is that you now have two debts to pay off at once, two payments to make on two due dates. This is the case, of course, with other types of loans.

Finally, if your need is for a little money for a short time, you could simply take out a personal loan. But the interest rate is high.

A comment on interest and interest rates. Since the Truth in Lending Law of 1969, a lending institution has to inform a borrower of the total amount of interest he is paying and of the annual interest rate that amount reflects. Before this legislation, banking practices were deceiving. In one practice, as a borrower gradually paid off the principal of his loan in regular installments, he continued paying interest on the original amount of the loan. In another practice, the interest was deducted from the principal initially, the borrower in fact receiving a smaller amount by paying the interest on the original amount. With either practice, the true interest was in effect double the stated rate. The Truth in Lending Law spells out the cost of borrowing for the homeowner.

However you finance your home improvement, you'll want to be assured that you've gotten the best deal possible. One, plan sufficiently ahead of your need to be able to do just that. Two, when you talk with the man at the bank, be sure to get all the information you want about what he has to offer. Banks, like dentist offices, have a way of intimidating, if only because of banking vocabulary. Ask all questions you want answered, so as to fully understand—as elsewhere in home improvement, it's your money that's involved.

# 6. And the Living Is Good

This book is about creativity, about the homeowner as the creator. Certainly, not everyone can be a novelist, poet, or playwright, a painter or sculptor, or a composer. But everyone—every homeowner—does have it in him to make his home a better place to live. You can improve your home, as the people in this book, people just like you, have improved theirs—with modest know-how, with time, energy, and determination—and, above all, with imagination. Imagination is what it's all about—seeing what can be done. Creating, after all, is no more and no less than making something that wasn't there to start with, whether what's created is a novel or a new bedroom wing.

The fine thing about creating is the satisfaction that comes from the awareness that what's created is uniquely yours as the creator. The novelist's characters are his people, the composer's melodies his music. For you as the homeowner, whether you're planner, general contractor, builder, or decorator—even if you're only the initiator, calling on the professionals from the start—the job is yours because you envisioned it and made it happen. You have full right to be proud of what you've brought about.

It's our hope that this book has served, and will continue to serve, to stimulate your thinking about you and the way you live, and about your home. Generally, and specifically through the various and varied "case histories" presented, we've given you what we believe to be exciting home improvement ideas to consider. We've encouraged you to analyze your home in terms of your lifestyle, identifying those "headache" areas along with your home's assets and potential. As a basis for analysis, we've discussed the principles of zoning, circulation, orientation, and house-site relationship, and the plot plan. We've dealt with the professionals and their services, suggesting the roles you might assume. And we've talked about how to get your home improvement underway.

We hope that we've challenged you to do what so many others have done, and done so successfully. Don't move, improve . . . and live well!

## Acknowledgments

Plan drawings and designs courtesy of House Plan Headquarters, 48 W. 48th Street, New York, N.Y., page 10.
Drawings and designs of wood fences courtesy of California Redwood Association, page 20.
All photographs of fences and patios courtesy of California Redwood Association, page 21.
Photographs showing "before" and "during" construction, courtesy of Cleve Feussinich, page 34.
All photographs courtesy of Art Detrich, page 43.
Exterior "before" photograph courtesy of Mrs. Jerry Worthington, page 78.
Exterior "before" photograph, courtesy of Frank Dailey, architect, page 79.
Exterior "before" photograph, courtesy of David Jalbert, page 88.
Photographs courtesy of Armstrong Cork Company, pages 89, 90, 91, 93.
Drawings courtesy of American Plywood Association, page 93.
Photographs courtesy of Armstrong Cork Company, page 95.
Drawings and design for multi-purpose basement, courtesy of Georgia Pacific Company, page 96.
Photograph courtesy of Armstrong Cork Company, page 97.
Photograph of deck patio courtesy of California Redwood Association, page 99.
All "before" and "after" deck photographs courtesy of California Redwood Association, page 100.
Photographs courtesy of California Redwood Association, oceanside deck architect Richard Stowers, page 101.
Upper right photograph courtesy of Great Western Remodelers, Phoenix, Ariz., page 102.
Lower left photograph courtesy of California Redwood Association, page 102.
Photograph of finished "hot tub" courtesy of Peter Schneider, architect, page 113.
Photograph of "before" exterior courtesy of Allen Heimlick, page 115.
Photograph of "before" exterior courtesy of Frank Dailey, architect, p. 118.
Drawings and design courtesy of Georgia Pacific Corporation, page 119.
Photograph of "before" exterior courtesy of Dr. Walter Vogt, page 124.
All photographs by Joshua Freiwald, pages 128, 129.
Elevation and plan drawings by William B. Remick, architect, page 129.
Photograph at right of architect's office courtesy of William Leatherbee, architect, page 148.
Drawings and design courtesy of American Plywood Association, page 149.
Photograph of "before" exterior courtesy of Theodore M. Purdy, page 154.
Photograph of "before" exterior courtesy City of Philadelphia, page 160.
Photograph of "after" exterior courtesy of William Leatherbee, architect, page 160.
All photographs courtesy of William Leatherbee, architect, pages 161, 162, 163.
Photograph of "before" exterior courtesy of Dr. Frank Talone, page 166.
Photograph of "before" exterior courtesy of Mrs. Henry B. Anderson, page 170.
Photograph of "before" exterior and plan drawing courtesy of Victor Stimac, architect, page 188.
Plan drawing courtesy of Victor Stimac, architect, page 189.
Sketch drawings by Richard P. Donohoe, Architects, page 199.
Architectural drawings courtesy of Richard P. Donohoe, Architects, Sherman, Ct., pages 200, 201, 202, 203.
We gratefully acknowledge the help of Dale Hartford in providing some of the Litchfield, Ct., area photographs.
All drawings and photographs, except as noted above, are by the authors.

# Index